'Based on a wealth of experience, this is an excellent and lively contribution to the art therapy literature. Theoretically informed and clinically focussed, a compelling portrait emerges of the very sensitive work of psychoanalytically informed practice with very young children and their families. Illustrated with pictures and deeply moving case examples, an international group of specialists reveals the intense involvement of the therapists and their clients. This accessible book will be indispensable reading for art therapists, counsellors, and psychotherapists, especially those working with children and their parents.'

—**Professor Joy Schaverien PhD**, Jungian analyst,
art psychotherapist and author of *Boarding School Syndrome:
The Psychological Trauma of the Privileged Child*

'This is a landmark text for art therapy practitioners, clinicians, researchers and students engaged in working with the very young. The increasing significance and relevance of art psychotherapy to address mental health needs of infants, toddlers and their families is beautifully demonstrated in this new text. I am pleased to read chapters by several fellow Australians, therapists whose work locates art therapy in the mainstream of child and family services in this country. This is evidence of the advance of the profession world-wide into the suite of clinical options and practices which lend flexibility and adaptability to the needs of our small people and their families.'

—**Patricia Fenner PhD**, Department of Public Health,
La Trobe University, Melbourne, Australia

'This groundbreaking collection of papers will touch everyone who reads it, through the therapists' tender description and thoughtful analysis of their work with some of the most basic and most powerful of human emotions: love, loss, rivalry and the struggle with the inexpressible. One of the many valuable aspects of this collection is its continuous focus on the art as well as the therapy, the materials, the art works, and the interactions which produce them. This collection will be found relevant and enjoyable by a wide readership of teachers, early years practitioners, health visitors, family support workers, psychologists and everyone who is concerned with the emotional wellbeing and resilience of very young children and their families.'

—**Dr Julian Grenier**, Headteacher of Sheringham Nursery School and Children's Centre, National Teaching School, Newham, East London, National Leader of Education and former National Chair of Early Education

'This book is a welcome and important exploration of art psychotherapy with very young children. Art therapy has its roots in the creative interpersonal relationship between the infant and their primary carer, and this book productively opens up this "in between" space, extending theory and practice in the process. It offers a wealth of insights not only for clinicians working in the sector but for all art therapists engaged with the infantile within their clients. No doubt it will be a rich resource for professionals and students alike.'

—**Jonathan Isserow**, Convener, MA Art Psychotherapy Programme, University of Roehampton, London

'This book provides insights and narratives for those who work with young children and their families offering research, theory and practice, illustrating how young children make meaning of their world through thoughtful art experiences. The book invites readers to better understand how therapeutic interventions may be restorative and healing when young children are invited to engage with art materials, within a supportive setting, attending to their individual developmental needs. A book early childhood educators will no doubt come to value and refer to as it may shape and inform their own personal approach and practice.'

—**Cathy Milwidsky**, Director of Early Learning, Moriah College

ART THERAPY IN THE EARLY YEARS

Art therapy with infants, toddlers and their families is an exciting and developing area of practice. With contributions from Australia, the United Kingdom and Spain, *Art Therapy in the Early Years* has an international flavour. The authors describe clinical art psychotherapy practice with children under five and their families in settings that include children in care, mental health clinics, paediatric wards, preschools and early intervention programmes.

Divided into three sections, *Art Therapy in the Early Years* presents different clinical environments in which art psychotherapy with this client group is found:

- individual art therapy;
- parent–child dyad and family art therapy;
- group art therapy.

The book proposes that within these different contexts, the adaptive possibilities inherent in art psychotherapy provide opportunities for therapeutic growth for young children and their families.

Art Therapy in the Early Years will be of interest to art therapists working with children; students and practitioners from creative arts therapies; psychologists and psychotherapists; social workers; preschool teachers; and child psychiatrists, clinical supervisors and other professionals working in the early years settings.

Julia Meyerowitz–Katz is a Jungian Analyst and Art Psychotherapist in private practice in Sydney.

Dean Reddick is an Art Psychotherapist with fifteen years' experience working with children and families in a variety of settings. He currently works in a nursery school and a primary school.

ART THERAPY IN THE EARLY YEARS

Therapeutic Interventions With Infants, Toddlers and Their Families

Edited by Julia Meyerowitz-Katz and Dean Reddick

Routledge
Taylor & Francis Group

LONDON AND NEW YORK

First published 2017
by Routledge
2 Park Square, Milton Park, Abingdon, Oxon OX14 4RN

and by Routledge
711 Third Avenue, New York, NY 10017

Routledge is an imprint of the Taylor & Francis Group, an informa business

British Library Cataloguing in Publication Data
A catalogue record for this book is available from the British Library

Library of Congress Cataloging-in-Publication Data
Names: Meyerowitz-Katz, Julia, editor. | Reddick, Dean, editor.
Title: Art therapy in the early years : therapeutic interventions with infants, toddlers and their families / edited by Julia Meyerowitz-Katz and Dean Reddick.
Description: Abingdon, Oxon; New York, NY: Routledge, 2017. | Includes bibliographical references and index. Identifiers: LCCN 2016005958 | ISBN 9781138814752 (hardback) | ISBN 9781138814776 (pbk.) | ISBN 9781315742748 (ebook)
Subjects: | MESH: Art Therapy – methods | Family Therapy | Infant | Child, Preschool | Case Reports
Classification: LCC RJ505.A7 | NLM WM 450.5.A8 | DDC 615.8/5156083 – dc23
LC record available at http://lccn.loc.gov/2016005958

ISBN: 978-1-138-81475-2 (hbk)
ISBN: 978-1-138-81477-6 (pbk)
ISBN: 978-1-315-74274-8 (ebk)

Typeset in Bembo
by Apex CoVantage, LLC
Printed and bound by CPI Group (UK) Ltd, Croydon, CR0 4YY

For Martin and his family

CONTENTS

FOREWORD

It is a great pleasure to write the foreword to this exciting and innovative book on art therapy in the early years: art therapy as a therapeutic intervention with infants, toddlers, young children and their families and carers. I feel tremendously proud of my colleagues, a professional pride, in that they have been pioneering a new territory. This book will put art psychotherapy on the map with other professions that more traditionally work with this age group and demographic. It is unique as a collection of reflections on working with this age group. The reader is captivated by the thoughtful and generous understanding of the therapists engaged in this life-affecting struggle to aid unimpeded development for these families of young children. Art psychotherapy has developed and progressed from the first years of work with an adult population to being alongside every stage of human development, from mother and baby interventions to treatment in old age.

The book brings together new ways of working with the early years from around the world in a variety of formats and contexts and will be a handbook for practitioners working with this age group, as well as complementing and overlapping with previous books on art therapy with children. While reading the book I was impressed by the solid and strong theoretical underpinning to the chapters, which reflects the varied backgrounds and training of the different contributors. In the chapters, current work and new research are presented, showcasing different approaches, an invaluable resource for all who are working with families, infants and carers, toddlers and children.

The neurobiological research findings of the last twenty-five years or so have highlighted the need for early intervention programmes. We are now increasingly aware of the long-term impact on brain development of adverse early years' circumstances, such as neglect and trauma. Neglect causes actual damage to the developing brain, and neural pathways atrophy due to lack of stimulus at the right time. Trauma initiates primitive flight/fight responses where action to survive takes precedence over the development of reflective processes over time. The mother or carer of the infant and young child is that child's environment, so that supporting this relationship in these early years is essential to give the infant/child the best start in life and to optimise the parent/carer's skills and abilities in understanding his or her child and promoting the child's development.

Early intervention programmes, like Sure Start in the UK, Head Start in the United States, and Communities for Children in Australia, were designed to promote relationship building between parent and child, particularly in deprived areas, where many other social circumstances mitigated against a good start in life. They were also designed to promote positive interactions and set clear expectations for behaviour but in a non-aversive way. These programmes were designed to support parental figures while they supported their child, and some of the chapters explore art therapy work taking place in similar programmes.

This book is extremely moving to read. It contains some deceptively simple and powerful writing. The nuances of therapeutic work are beautifully articulated. One aspect of this is the trauma through which very young infants have already lived when still small. This might be through life-saving early medical intervention at birth, which may involve painful intrusive procedures, as well as necessary separation from mother and family in intensive care. Alternatively some infants have had a better birth experience but are born into situations where a mother is traumatised by past history or vulnerable to abusive relationships or social poverty or has suffered herself from neglect and abuse, and these all impact on the mother's capacity to give her infant a good start in life despite her best intentions. In this kind of case we are thinking of 'ghosts in the nursery' – the impact of either parent's past on their relationship with their child. Some young children are living with chronic conditions, a matter of life and death, in situations that we would more normally conceive to be a factor in older age. It is upsetting to read of the life-changing conditions that some young children are facing and yet uplifting to read the account of the emotional support that the art therapist is able to give, often to the child and family members in hospitals.

Early preventive work eases development where it has become stuck. What could be more natural for young children than to work together with their parents/carers in dyadic work in an art therapy setting, using materials together? This area of work is valuable for child and mother in a birth family, but there is also a crucial area of work with fostering, pre-adoption and post-adoption support of new attachments. This important area of work can help form a child's attachments for life. In the context of group work the support that can be offered by other adults in group settings shows the efficacy of social cohesiveness – that the group around the pair can heal and contain fragile relationships between a particular mother and toddler.

The moving and empathic accounts of work with young vulnerable children in groups and their support of each other in institutional care took me back to my first post as an art therapist in a residential and school context. Then and now, the amount of support that they can offer each other in a community is fascinating to experience; they can see and respond to each other's degree of hurt and trauma despite their own adverse circumstances. The art therapy group can be a containing and transformative space for children who are in transition as well as a creative arena for emotional learning. The art psychotherapist contributors write about their work with passion and commitment. A strength of the book is the emotionally close experience that is described and the way in which working in art therapy can give a voice and a sense of identity to a young child struggling in a traumatic context.

The range of centres offering art therapy as an intervention for this age group is wide: children's centres, which may be multidisciplinary – that is education, health and social services; preschool and nursery schools; hospital child and adolescent mental health service (CAMHS) clinics; and residential settings. The kind of client intervention and treatment offered is excellent in its breadth, from family work to individual treatment, dyad work, group work and parallel work with child and parent groups. This will be a stimulating book for all who work with this age group as well as practising art therapists and trainees. The challenges that the contributors have taken on and the way that they have pioneered new methods and found solutions are inspirational.

Several chapters focus on the strong countertransference experience for the therapists with this age group and the need for good supervision. There are some honest accounts of the highs and lows of therapeutic work. The therapist has to struggle with painful material, sometimes anguished at the suffering of their clients, and this material can be difficult to process. Unless the therapist's response is worked through in supervision and personal therapy, the therapist can be traumatised by the material that he or she hears. There are some very good chapters on the assimilation and understanding of the infant/child experience and the need for varied supervision processes, including the reflection on countertransference that can come through the art therapist's own artwork. This aspect of the book will be particularly helpful for trainees; sometimes trainees find it difficult both to realise their impact on the person with whom they are working and to understand the strong emotional charge that is inherent in the work that may be affecting them and needs to be thoroughly worked through in supervision. The book provides solid accounts of therapy and the support and space that the therapist needs to work most effectively.

Another aspect of this book is thinking about sibling relationships, whether they be a twin or other brothers and sisters or therapy siblings in a group work. These relationships and attachments have profound importance throughout the human life cycle, and several art therapists have focused on this aspect of work, whether they are children with their birth parents or children waiting for adoption.

This book is international in flavour in that there are contributors from the UK, Australia and Spain, and it is interesting and helpful to the development of art therapy to be able to compare and contrast what is offered in differing contexts. It becomes possible to cite best practice and hopefully raise the standard of interventions with this age group worldwide. In different countries some racial groups are struggling for equal opportunities and recognition impacting on a child's fragile sense of identity, and this is described and reflected upon in several chapters. Consideration is also given to the therapist's awareness of race and cultural difference and the issues that this raises in therapy. Lastly there are art therapists working with new immigrants to a country, which is a topic of pressing concern worldwide.

The editors, Julia Meyerowitz-Katz and Dean Reddick, have produced a brilliant and timely addition to art psychotherapy literature that confidently presents a wide variety of interventions in an area of art therapy work that has come to maturity and has much to offer to young children and their families worldwide. Throughout the book the reader is aware of the development of the child through stages of stuckness and delay, and the way in which this can be eased and development supported through intervention that is appropriate and ordinary for the child through the use of play and art materials within a context of containment by the art psychotherapist. The joys and discoveries that are made about the self and each other are beautifully written about and brought to life in the accounts of image making, mess making and sensory and tactile experiences. Art making particularly can be an agent for change where there is psychosomatically held material affecting growth and relationships. We can see and reflect on what is out there on the picture surface or in the model, recognise that it has to do with me, relate and understand it within a relationship with the therapist and, with necessary working through together, move on to the next stage. The centrality of the art materials within the relationship with the therapist, which is the strength of the art psychotherapy process, is fully described, reflected upon and developed in this new and exciting book.

Caroline Case

ACKNOWLEDGEMENTS

Editing this book has been a remarkable journey that we have navigated across the distance of continents, cultures and time. We wrote in our introduction that we were motivated by our conviction that a book that focused attention on art therapy for infants, toddlers and their families was long overdue, and so we are pleased to have finally arrived at this point: we have a book which we feel to be rich in its scope and depth. We are grateful to the many people who have contributed to the evolution of this book and whose identity must remain confidential.

A book like this could not be written without access to authentic clinical experience, and so we are grateful to those families who generously gave their permission for material from their therapy to be made available for the thinking that is represented in this book. If you come across it, we hope you feel that the book honours your experiences in art therapy.

In trying to realise our vision for the book we know that we have been rather demanding on ourselves and on our contributors as editors. However, we have found the process of creating the book to be a deeply creative and ultimately satisfying one. We have learned a lot through the editing process and we hope that our contributors share this experience. We thank you all for your dedication and commitment to developing your thinking and supporting the creation of what we consider to be a valuable offering that hopefully will support art therapists and other colleagues to enable children and families in the future.

The profession of art therapy is supported in a myriad of ways. We would like to thank our colleagues and the institutions where we all work for ongoing interest in and support of art therapy. Amongst the people who must remain anonymous are our own therapists, analysts and supervisors. We thank you all for consistently providing cradles for thinking.

We would like to thank Tessa Dalley, who was instrumental in bringing us together. We would like to express our appreciation to Joanne Forshaw and her team at Routledge for their support of us and faith in the book, and for their patience.

Acknowledgements from Dean Reddick

This was our first time editing a book and to my co-editor, Julia, a huge thank-you for the clarity of your thinking, writing and editing, your determination and knowledge, and for bringing a playfulness to the process that made editing the book enjoyable even when things got messy or tough.

Thanks also to my ex-colleagues at Goldsmiths College for their belief and for the 'debates', and to my colleagues at the nursery and school where I work.

Thanks to Ellie Roberts for fuelling my interest in infant mental health all those years ago.

A big thank-you to Alban and the artists at CollectConnect, to Dan on banjo, Maurice on guitar, Ginny on violin and to Judith. Thanks to Sue and the Sunday art therapy group.

Finally thank you to my friends and family for your love, patience and support.

Acknowledgements from Julia Meyerowitz-Katz

Embarking on any creative process means embarking on an unpredictable journey and developing this book has been no exception. I am fortunate to have had in Dean Reddick a companion with whom the sharing of the journey, the highs and lows, has been extraordinarily smooth and rich. Thank you, Dean, for inviting me to join you in this endeavour and for being utterly committed, thoughtful, facilitating and reliable, and for sharing the load.

Creative processes have to do with bringing threads together. Over too many years to count much has had to happen in order for me to have been able to see this project through. There are so many people, in South Africa, the UK, Australia and New Zealand whom I would like to thank. The list is long and includes members of ANZSJA, CAFPAA, the SAP, the editorial board of *ATOL: Art Therapy OnLine*, and ANZATA. I would like to thank the many talented ceramic artists whom I have worked alongside over the years. These include the Thursday Morning Group at HGSI in London and the community of ceramic artists at ARC at UNSW and subsequently at Claypool in Sydney; thank you all for being there.

But of course none of this would have happened without the support of the crucible of my family and friends. I am particularly grateful to you all; the value of your support is unquantifiable.

INTRODUCTION

Julia Meyerowitz-Katz and Dean Reddick

Our original conversations about developing a book on art therapy with infants, toddlers and their families began early in 2013, in London, at an International Conference on Art Therapy.[1] The book is the result of a collaboration between ourselves and contributors from Australia, the United Kingdom and Spain. To the best of our knowledge this is the first book to focus specifically on a range of practice in art therapy with this population. We are pleased to be offering a book that has an international perspective and that presents such a wide range of clinical practice in a variety of settings.

The idea that art making has a role to play in the treatment of adults and children suffering emotional disturbance and trauma emerged during the early and mid-twentieth century (Waller, 1991/2013, Case and Dalley, 2014). Jung understood that art making in the context of psychotherapy with adults had a 'living effect upon the patient himself' in which 'the patient struggles to give form, however crude and childish, to the inexpressible' (Jung, [1931], 1966/1982, para. 104). Adrian Hill's work with adults suffering from tuberculosis in the UK led to the publication of *Art versus Mental Illness* (Hill, 1945), in which he described the therapeutic value of art making for adults and coined the term 'art therapy' (Waller, 1991). Edith Kramer took a Freudian approach to her work with children, initially with Jewish children who were refugees from the Nazis in Prague in the late 1930s, and subsequently in the United States (Kramer, 1971, 1977, 1979), where she and Margaret Naumberg are credited with being the forerunners of art therapy (Waller, 1991). Judith Rubin (1978/1984) and Tessa Dalley (1984) published pioneering books on art therapy with children. There are edited books on art therapy with children (Case and Dalley, 1990, 2008), art therapy with children is referred to in handbooks (Case and Dalley, 2014), and there are books addressing art therapy research (Gilroy and Lee, 1995, Gilroy, 2006, 2011).

Ideas for this book were conceived out of our shared experience. We had both worked over a long period of time as art psychotherapists, as university tutors, and as supervisors of art therapists who work with infants, toddlers and their families. We were aware that art therapy with infants, toddlers and their families had been developing unobtrusively in parallel with more widely known developments in infant observation and attachment theory, biological sciences, child psychotherapy, psychology and education. We knew of a small, dedicated body of art therapy literature (Dubowski, 1984, Deco, 1990, Milavic and Fenton, 1995, Reddick, 1999, Ambridge, 2001, Willemsen and Anscombe, 2001, Davies, 2003, Meyerowitz-Katz, 2003, Proulx, 2003, Hosea, 2006, 2011, Hall, 2008, Westwood, Keyzer and Evans, 2010, Bat Or, 2012, Choi and Goo, 2012, Arroyo and Fowler, 2013, Prokofiev, 2013, Chong, 2015, Metzl, 2015).

Our understanding was that because art therapy with this age group had not been well represented in the literature, it had barely reached an audience. This meant that it was not widely considered to be a resource for this age group and was therefore underused. We were also aware that in an ordinary way, professionals from other disciplines, such as psychologists and preschool teachers, routinely offer art materials to this age group and that a deeper understanding of what art making offers the developing infant and toddler might be useful for non-art therapists.

Historically there has always been a relationship between art therapy theory and practice and developments within psychoanalysis. However, resonating with Fraiberg, Adelson and Shapiro, who write, 'The babies themselves . . . have been the last to be the beneficiaries of the great discoveries of psychoanalysis and developmental psychology' (1975, p. 389), the population that is the subject of this book, and which has been the focus of so much recent research in the field of neuroscience and psychoanalysis, seems to have been the last to have had attention focused on them by art therapy.

This book is an attempt to redress this situation and to bring some of the varied, innovative and very good clinical work and thinking that are being carried out by art psychotherapists in this area to a wider readership. By appealing to art therapists and those interested in becoming art therapists, we hope that this book will make a significant and lasting contribution to the profession, and that it will enrich art therapy theory and practice internationally. We hope to stimulate further developments in art therapy theory, research and practice for infants, toddlers and their families. We feel that the book has a lot to offer professionals from other disciplines who work with this population. This includes child psychotherapists, paediatricians and paediatric nurses, play therapists, psychologists, preschool teachers, nursery nurses, community workers and anyone who has an interest in using art with very young children and their families.

Theoretical orientation

Psychoanalytic underpinnings

Our approach to the book is underpinned by psychoanalytic thinking. By 'psychoanalytic' we are referring to the experience of understanding and thinking about the impact of unconscious experience, the lived experience of our internal world of which we are not conscious, in order to aid understanding and development. We were both trained within a psychoanalytic model of art therapy that included British object relations and Jungian thinking. At that time models of theoretical approaches to art therapy were in their infancy. Psychoanalytic ideas and practices were prominent, as were thoughts and discussions about the 'art' in art therapy: 'open studios' still existed in big psychiatric hospitals. The passage of time, the plethora of journals, books and online platforms devoted to art therapy and the emergence of theoretical approaches that are unique to art therapy have not undermined the value we place on psychoanalytic understandings of art therapy.

We believe that theory develops out of clinical practice that has been deeply felt and thought about. When planning the book we wanted it to represent sensitive clinical work that was underpinned by solid psychodynamically orientated understanding and thinking, and how this is interpreted and used by art therapists with this population group. Consequently, this book consists of a collection of case studies.

Working with infants and toddlers and their primary carers

Drawing on Freud's 'psychical system' of mother and baby, and anticipating recent research, Winnicott presciently wrote, '"There is no such thing as a baby" . . . if you set me to describe a baby, you will find you are describing a *baby and someone*. A baby cannot exist alone, but is essentially part of a relationship' (Winnicott, 1957/1964, p. 88, italics original). This is a central idea in our approach to the book: the belief that infants and toddlers are inherently relational. Winnicott's 'someone' can take a range of forms. Although the primary carers referred to in this book are usually mothers, we are aware that the role of primary carer can be fulfilled by a whole range of people, including fathers, older siblings and other members of families and communities who take on the responsibility for looking after babies and toddlers.

Much has been written about the importance and complexity of the relationship between children and their carers. Winnicott (1960) conceived of the idea of a holding environment created by a good enough mother. Bion (1962) placed the infant–mother relationship at the centre of his theory of container-contained, which leads to the development of thinking.

Initiating research into attachment dynamics and building on the observational work of James and Joyce Robertson (1953), Bowlby (1969, 1973, 1980) described how the relationship between the infant or toddler and attachment figures provides a secure base for the developing child and how the emotional quality of the attachment relationship is dynamically determined to be the best fit for the emotional environment in which it was formed. Stern (1985) describes 'attunement', and Brazelton (Brazelton, Koslowski and Maine, 1974) 'reciprocity': the ability of the primary carer to tune in to the infant's communications, rhythms and needs and to respond in a sensitive way, leading to the development of a sense of self in the infant and the ability to regulate emotion. Trevarthen and his collaborators

(Malloch and Trevarthen, 2009) have discovered the musical, rhythmic quality of infant-mother communication; babies can literally compose musical conversations with their mothers, and infant-mother conversations have been successfully turned into musical scores. Furthermore the musical language of infant-mother communication has a high degree of commonality in different cultures and is consistent with certain deep rhythms within evolutionary primitive parts of the brain (Malloch and Trevarthen, 2009).

Research from the biological sciences

In recent years advances in technology have led to a burgeoning of research in the biological sciences. Some of this research has focused on the mother-infant relationship (Schore, 1994, Gerhardt, 2004, Siegel, 2012) and some has focused on the neuroscience of aesthetic experience (Kandel, 2012, Shimamura and Palmer, 2014).

Evidence from research has confirmed many of the basic tenets of psychoanalysis – that the development of children in infancy and in relationship with their primary carers is crucial to the healthy development of an individual. According to this research, the mother-infant relationship is the crucible in which an infant's brain (and, therefore, mind) is nurtured (Schore, 1994, Gerhardt, 2004, Siegel, 2012)/This is because crucial neural pathways are laid down and reinforced when an infant's experience is received by an emotionally attuned external environment. This is usually, but not always, the infant's mother. When the infant's need for emotional regulation is not met in attuned ways by the external environment/mother, through neglect or trauma, then emotional integration and development are hampered.

Research shows that the developing human infant is hugely responsive to its environment and especially to the relational environment with its primary carers. The plasticity of the human brain allows it to form connections based on the quality of the baby's relationships with its carers (Gerhardt, 2004, Siegel, 2012). Different aspects of this process have been described by different writers. Images and data from neuroscience and experimental data from developmental psychology provide different types of evidence for the fundamental importance of the loving relationship between an infant and its mother, father and other significant figures.

The plasticity of the brain also means that therapeutic interventions where the therapist is attuned to his or her patient, much in the way that a good enough mother might be to her infant, can effect changes in the patient's brain. This can therefore support emotional repair and integration. When working therapeutically with infants and their carers, the relationship between the two is considered to be the patient; therapeutic interventions support their interactions, support their relationship and ultimately support them as individuals.

In addition, research into the nature of aesthetic experience emerging from neuroscience suggests that art making can aid neural integration, and some of this research has found its way into art therapy practice and theory (Hass-Cohen and Carr, 2008, O'Brien, 2004, 2008, Chong, 2015). We were curious to discover how art therapists working with this population were navigating their way through, engaging with and integrating this research, and how it was impacting on practice.

Intergenerational transmission

Thinking about infants, toddlers and their carers raises questions around culture and intergenerational transmission that are both conscious and unconscious. Parenting includes the transmission of cultural traits across generations (De Mause, 1976, Zornado, 2006, Frosh, 2013).

> Because psychic structure must always be passed from generation to generation through the narrow funnel of childhood, a society's child-rearing practices are not just one item in a list of cultural traits. They are the very condition for the transmission and development of all other cultural elements.
>
> *(De Mause, 1976, p. 3)*

The interpersonal mechanisms whereby cultural traits are passed from generation to generation therefore rely on the central importance of the mother-infant bond.

Frosh considers that intergenerational transmission is personal, relational and sociohistorical, so that cultures 're-enact the founding violence that lies at their source' (Frosh, 2013, p. 124). He writes that 'each generation lives its life not just in the light and shadow of its predecessors, but also as a function of its own hidden past.' He refers to Laplanche's (1999) idea of an overwhelming enigmatic message that is passed down from parent to child as well as encrypted and inaccessible trauma, so that 'what is too terrible to symbolise becomes encrypted, hidden away in a place where it is inaccessible, but from where it continues manifesting itself, leaking out and perhaps eventually taking the subject over' (Frosh, 2013, p. 124).

The structure of the book

The art therapy described in this book occurs through different interventions in a range of contexts. Each of the three parts in the book represents three different clinical environments in which art psychotherapy with this population is found: individual art therapy, parent-child dyad and family art therapy, and group art therapy. Settings include mental health clinics, paediatric wards, community interventions, preschools, early intervention programmes and a children's home. Contributors draw on a range of theoretical approaches, including psychodynamic theory and attachment theory. Within these different contexts, the adaptive possibilities inherent in art psychotherapy offer opportunities to this client group for therapeutic growth to occur.

The parts

In Part 1, Individual Art Therapy with Infants and Toddlers, the chapters are focused on individual art therapy with infants and toddlers – mimicking the 'two-body' relationship of infant and mother (Winnicott, 1957/1964). In Part 2, Family and Dyad Art Therapy with Infants, Toddlers and Their Parents, the focus shifts to art therapy where parents and families of the children are present during the work with the children. There are settings where children are offered group art therapy in situations where connection with their parents is not possible. This kind of work is presented in Part 3, Group Art Therapy with Infants and Toddlers, which describes group therapy in preschools, a community setting and an orphanage.

Part 1: Individual art therapy with infants and toddlers

Part 1 begins with 'An Odd Mirror'. This is Dean Reddick's account of art therapy with a three-year-old boy. In this chapter, Reddick explores changes in the complex relationship between prematurity, traumatic birth, hospital experiences and being a twin through play, art and the developing therapeutic relationship. He describes the complexities of twinning in the transference and an intensely felt countertransference consisting of panic, loss of relating, grief and mourning. Reddick draws on Tustin's ideas about autistic defences and Ogden's proposal of the autistic contiguous position in order to understand the boy's withdrawal from relating and meaning in the face of perceived threats to 'going on being', as well as his response to his traumatic and precarious start to life. This was in a special intensive-care baby unit and included repeated life-saving, invasive and traumatic medical interventions. The loss of being with his twin in utero, the catastrophic loss of his bodily connection to his mother's body, and his struggle to emerge from machinelike forms of relating are described. Reddick explores the idea of the child's attachment to the hard technology of the incubator and his struggle to let go of his umbilical-like relationship to his gastronomy feeding tube.

In Chapter 2, 'On Mark Making and Leaving a Mark: Processing the Experience of Art Therapy with a Preschool Child', Pensri Rowe describes individual and dyadic art therapy with a four-year-old girl and her mother. Relational trauma, sexual abuse, identity and the mother-child relationship are explored. Rowe describes how she uses her countertransference images as reflective tools from which to gain greater perspective on the work and as reference points for exploring emerging themes. The images contain aspects of the strong transference and countertransference dynamics typical when working with this age group.

In '"Cheerful and Not Cheerful": Art Psychotherapy on a Paediatric Ward', Susan Rudnik presents an account of individual art therapy with a hospitalised four-year-old girl. The work described took place within the paediatric ward of a large inner-city London National Health Service (NHS) hospital. The importance and use of art making in containing and processing the experiences of hospitalisation are discussed, with an emphasis on thinking about the transference and countertransference in the work. In her role as the only art therapist on the ward, Rudnik describes working within a wider multidisciplinary team. The process of working in this complex environment is described, with particular consideration of the boundaries and maintaining the therapeutic space in such an unpredictable setting.

'"I Do Dots": Art Therapy with an Australian Aboriginal Preschool Child' is jointly written by art therapist, Judy King, and her supervisor, Celia Conolly.

The chapter describes moment-to-moment communications within the first two sessions of a short-term pilot art therapy intervention which was carried out by a White Australian art therapist with a three-and-a half-year-old Aboriginal girl. The setting was a preschool within an Aboriginal community in an inner-city suburb. The authors describe how the art therapist approached these sessions with a sense of her own lack of Aboriginal cultural knowledge, her consequent awareness of her own 'otherness' and her awareness of the girl's need to assert her Aboriginal identity, all of which created a huge cultural gap that lay between them. The authors describe how by remaining present and making use of her countertransference experiences, the art therapist could connect with the child and build a bridge between the two cultures. The art making, and the emerging relationship with her therapist, highlighted the child's struggles with identity, connection and 'otherness', and her ambivalence about her neediness. The sessions became an opportunity to explore their 'otherness' in the context of their connection, and her artwork opened up space for a 'third' in the therapeutic relationship, enabling shared thinking about the child's Aboriginal identity and her neediness.

Part 2: Family and dyad art therapy with infants, toddlers and their parents

This part describes art therapy in different settings where the common theme is that parents are active participants in their children's therapy. The relationship between the parent and the child is often the focus of the therapeutic intervention.

There are four chapters in this part, which begins with Chapter 5, Tessa Dalley and Jen Bromham's 'Transitions: Moving from Infancy to Latency through Symbolisation and the Acquisition of Language'. This is another chapter which has been written by an art therapist, Jen Bromham, and her supervisor, Tessa Dalley. The work took place in a specialist parent-infant project within an existing under-fives service in a child and adolescent mental health service (CAMHS) in a Sure Start children's centre. The approach was to place art making as a focus for the development of the relationship between mother and child. This approach was based on a model developed at the Parent Infant Project (PIP) at the Anna Freud Centre, London. Dalley and Bromham describe therapeutic work with a mother and her three-year-old child, who was diagnosed with complex speech delay. As language developed, the child became more able to articulate the struggles of his predicament. The combination of art work and play enabled verbal and non-verbal expression of feelings through development of symbolic functioning and thought. Reflections on the parallel processes between therapy, clinical supervision and family dynamics enabled significant shifts in the therapist, the therapeutic relationship and the child's progress. The art therapist was given a voice for the dilemmas and challenges that the work presented, using the supervision relationship to develop meaning and understanding.

In Chapter 6, 'The Imprint of Another Life: Assessment and Dyadic Parent-Child Art Psychotherapy with an Adoptive Family', Anthea Hendry describes the struggle of two adoptive parents to parent two newly placed preschool siblings who had a background of abuse, separation and loss. An attachment theory and adoption research-based CAMHS assessment highlights four priorities. One of these is a dyadic parent-child art therapy intervention with the adoptive mother and four-year-old daughter. This clinical work, using a 'joint engagement' approach to dyadic work, is described. The significance of the sensory nature of the art materials, the continuation of therapy outside the therapy sessions and the role of the therapist are examined in response to the therapeutic intervention.

In Chapter 7, 'Amazing Mess: Mothers Get in Touch with their Infants through the Vitality of Painting Together', Hilary Hosea expands on her earlier work (Hosea, 2006, 2011) and draws on ten years in the life of an art therapy parent-infant painting group within a Sure Start centre. Vignettes show how at the edge of mess and chaos parents and young children strengthen their attachment and tune in to each other as they use and explore the tactile, sensory and messy art materials together. The author refers to ideas from parent-infant psychotherapy, including video interaction and mentalising. The author develops the theme of circles of containment through which the messy feelings of parent and child become processed, digested and vital rather than being distorted and overwhelming.

In Chapter 8, 'The Crisis of the Cream Cakes: An Infant's Food Refusal as a Representation of Intergenerational Trauma', Julia Meyerowitz-Katz proposes that an infant's food refusal can be understood as a representation and communication of his own and his family's intergenerational trauma. She explores how the infant's and his mother's separate and shared unconscious wounds and traumas, held psychosomatically and therefore non-verbally, at a pre-symbolic level in their bodyminds, were expressed through art making. Art making lessened the grip of unrepresented trauma and the dyad were supported in rediscovering themselves and each other. Intergenerational patterns of trauma were significantly disrupted and the infant's recovery and return to health were facilitated. The author draws on Winnicott's concept of a 'psychosomatic partnership' and Jung's proposal of an unconscious bodymind structure and process, which he refers to as 'psychoid' experience. Psychoid experiences and processes are offered as a way of thinking about the integration of neurological systems, which are not only enskulled – that is, located in the head – but also embodied, extending throughout the body; as well as in embodied interpersonal communications. It is suggested that it is psychoid experience, the deeply unconscious bodymind structure and process, which is the enabling factor in art therapy.

Part 3: Group art therapy with infants and toddlers

This part focuses on contexts in which art therapists work with groups of toddlers in different settings – a family centre, an orphanage and a preschool. The art therapy described by Marcela Andrade del Corro and Julie Green occurred in a situation that is familiar to art therapists, where they find themselves working in contexts where there is little, if any, contact with the children's parents. Alice Rayment's chapter gives an account where she and a co-worker facilitated art therapy groups for children while a therapeutic parent support group ran in parallel.

Chapter 9, Andrade del Corro's 'Building a Fort: Art Therapy with a Group of Toddlers Going through the Adoption Process' describes the benefits of facilitating an art therapy environment for a group of toddlers living in a residential care home while awaiting adoption in Catalonia, Spain. They had all suffered a form of abuse and displayed disrupted attachment, behavioural issues, somatisation and a poor sense of self. The art therapy group proved to be a holding and containing environment that provided a secure base, becoming a symbolic family within which the toddlers functioned as siblings. The use of the art materials and the art-making process within the group acted as vehicles for communicating the children's changing needs, which could then be understood and supported. The author describes how disrupted attachment patterns were renegotiated, providing opportunities for the children to express and integrate painful feelings and experiences.

In Chapter 10, 'Making Waves: An Art Therapist's Retrospective Review of Countertransference Images and Case Material That Took Place in a Preschool Setting', Green examines the nature of countertransference paintings that she made in a preschool playground environment while children were playing around her. A retrospective view is taken of her paintings and is also applied to an art therapy relationship that developed at her 'station' within the playground with a four-year-old girl. Primitive states of mind are considered in relation to the behaviours of the two- to five-year-old children with whom she was working and the impact of these states upon herself. Developmental tasks are considered with particular regard to the shift from undifferentiated forms in painting to representations. The chapter focuses on the centrality of the art materials and transference and countertransference communications within the art therapy relationship.

Chapter 11 is 'Side by Side: An Early Years' Art Therapy Group with a Parallel Therapeutic Parent Support Group'. In this chapter Alice Rayment explores an innovative side-by-side model in which an early years' art therapy group for two- to three-year-olds ran in parallel with a therapeutic parent support group. The side-by-side model was developed over a number of years in a family centre that was part of a Jewish charity in London. Rayment describes how the development of the early years' art therapy group and parallel parental group was a joint enterprise involving a meta-family of a range of professionals who co-operated in thinking about the complex material, assessing risk and supporting the families attending the groups. The chapter focuses on therapy with two children and their parents. It describes layers of parallels and resonance between the children's group, the parents' group, the staff team and the families' home experience. The multilayered assessment of outcomes of this side-by-side model of art therapy intervention is presented. The therapy is contextualised in a discussion of relevant literature addressing art therapy groups with children and art therapy in the early years, as well as children and parent groups and simultaneous toddler and parent group work.

Conclusion

We began the project hoping that the book would contribute to the understanding and discussion about the way in which art materials and processes within a therapeutic relationship function to support emotional integration and development. We believed that art psychotherapists, who are attuned to their clients, and who are trained to sensitively track the moment-to-moment sequence of events in clinical settings, would be in a unique position to contribute useful understandings of what might be happening for infants, toddlers and their families when they made art.

In the conclusion to the book we focus on themes which relate to what is unique to art therapy: the role of the art materials, the artworks and the nature of the interactions and processes around them as they are described by our contributors. We explain how gathering these themes together and thinking about them have led us to propose that there is a fourth element to add to the traditional triangle of art therapist–client–art object. This is the complexity of the interpersonal and aesthetic responses around the processes of art making in an art therapy setting. Extending Schaverien's (1992, 1995, 2000, 2015) terms we have called this the 'life in and of the art making'. We further elucidate that when all the complex elements involved in art therapy are taken into account, it seems to us that art therapy offers a form of layered, embodied thinking which is inherently transformational and which provides the experience of a living, transformational psychosomatic object which can be internalised.

Note

1   Finding a Voice, Making a Mark, Goldsmith's London, 2013.

References

Ambridge, M. (2001) 'Using the reflective image within the mother–child relationship', in: Murphy, J. (ed.) *Art therapy with young survivors of sexual abuse: Lost for words.* Hove: Brunner-Routledge, pp. 69–85.

Arroyo, C. and Fowler, N. (2013) 'Before and after: A mother and infant painting group'. *International Journal of Art Therapy: Formerly Inscape*, 18(3), pp. 98–112.

Bat Or, M. (2012) 'Non-verbal representations of maternal holding of preschoolers'. *Arts in Psychotherapy*, 39(2), pp. 117–125.

Bion, W. (1962) *Learning from experience.* London: Heinemann Medical.

Bowlby, J. (1969) *Attachment. Attachment and loss (Vol. 1): Attachment.* London: Hogarth Press and the Institute of Psychoanalysis.

Bowlby, J. (1973) *Attachment. Attachment and loss (Vol. 2): Separation: Anxiety and anger.* London: Hogarth Press and the Institute of Psychoanalysis.

Bowlby, J. (1980) *Attachment. Attachment and loss (Vol. 3): Loss: Sadness and depression.* London: Hogarth Press and the Institute of Psychoanalysis.

Brazelton, T.B., Koslowski, B. and Maine, M. (1974) 'The origins of reciprocity: The early mother–infant interaction', in: Lewis, M. and Rosenblum, L.A. (eds.) *The effect of the infant on its caregiver.* New York: Wiley-Interscience, pp. 49–76.

Case, C. and Dalley, T. (Eds.) (1990) *Working with Children in Art Therapy*. London: Tavistock/Routledge.

Case, C. and Dalley, T. (Eds.) (2008) *Working with Children in Art Therapy*. London: Tavistock/Routledge.

Case, C. and Dalley, T. (eds.) (2014) *The handbook of art therapy*. Third Edition. London: Routledge, Taylor and Francis.

Choi, S. and Goo, K. (2012) 'Holding environment: The effects of group art therapy on mother–child attachment'. *Arts in Psychotherapy*, 39(1), pp. 19–24.

Chong, J.C.Y. (2015) 'Why art psychotherapy? Through the lens of interpersonal neurobiology: The distinctive role of art psychotherapy intervention for clients with early relational trauma'. *International Journal of Art Therapy: Inscape*, 20(3), pp. 118–126.

Dalley, T. (Ed.) (1984) *Art as therapy. An introduction to the use of art as a therapeutic technique*. London: Tavistock Publications.

Davies, J. (2003) 'Zero to one'. *Arts in Psychotherapy*, 30(1), pp. 43–49.

De Mause, L. (1976) (British Edition) *The history of childhood: The evolution of parent-child relationships as a factor in history*. London: Souvenir Press. First published (1974) New York: The Psychotherapy Press.

Deco, S. (1990) 'A family centre: A structural family therapy approach', in: Case, C. and Dalley, T. (eds.) *Working with children in art therapy*. London: Routledge, pp. 115–130.

Dubowski, J. (1984) 'Alternative models for describing the development of children's graphic work: Some implications for art therapy', in: Dalley, T. (ed.) *Art as therapy*. London: Tavistock, pp. 30–44.

Fraiberg, S., Adelson, E. and Shapiro, V.J. (1975) 'Ghosts in the nursery: A psychoanalytic approach to the problems of impaired infant-mother relationships'. *Journal of the American Academy of Child Psychiatry*, 14(3), pp. 387–421.

Frosh, S. (2013) *Hauntings: Psychoanalysis and ghostly transmissions*. Basingstoke: Macmillan.

Gerhardt, S. (2004) *Why love matters: How affection shapes a baby's brain*. London: Routledge, Taylor and Francis.

Gilroy, A. (2006) *Art therapy, research and evidence-based practice*. London: SAGE.

Gilroy, A. (ed.) (2011) *Art therapy research in practice*. Oxford: Peter Lang.

Gilroy, A. and Lee, C. (eds.) (1995) *Art and music: Therapy and research*. London: Routledge.

Hall, P. (2008) 'Painting together: an art therapy approach to mother infant relationships', in: Case, C. and Dalley, T. (eds.) *Art therapy with children from infancy to adolescence*. Hove: Routledge, pp. 20–35.

Hass-Cohen, N. and Carr, R. (eds.) (2008) *Art therapy and clinical neuroscience*. London: Jessica Kingsley.

Hill, A. (1945) *Art versus illness: A story of art therapy*. London: George Allen and Unwin.

Hosea, H. (2006) 'The brushes footmarks parents and infants paint together in a small community art therapy group'. *International Journal of Art Therapy: Inscape*, 11(2), pp. 69–78.

Hosea, H. (2011) 'The brush's foot marks: Researching a small community art therapy group', in: Gilroy, A. (ed.) *Art therapy research in practice*. Oxford: Peter Lang, pp. 61–80.

Jung, C.G. ([1931], 1954/1966/1982) *The practice of psychotherapy: Essays on the psychology of the transference and other subjects*, in: *Collected Works*. Vol. 16. Bollingen Series 20. Princeton: Princeton University Press.

Kandel, E.R. (2012) *The age of insight: The quest to understand the unconscious in art, mind and brain*. New York: Random House.

Kramer, E. (1971) *Art as therapy with children*. New York: Schocken Books.

Kramer, E. (1977) *Art therapy in a children's community*. New York: Schocken Books.

Kramer, E. (1979) *Childhood and art therapy: Notes on theory and application*. New York: Schocken Books.

Laplanche, J. (1999) *Essays on otherness*. New York: Routledge.

Malloch, S. and Trevarthen, C. (eds.) (2009) *Communicative musicality: Exploring the basis of human companionship*. Oxford University Press.

Metzl, E.S. (2015) 'Holding and creating: A grounded theory of art therapy with 0–5 year olds'. *International Journal of Art Therapy Inscape*, 20(3), pp. 93–106.

Meyerowitz-Katz (2003) 'Art materials and processes. A place of meeting: Art psychotherapy with a four-year-old boy'. *Inscape*, 8(2), pp. 60–69.

Milavic, G. and Fenton, M. (1995) *The Greenwich nursery project: An enquiry into the therapeutic use of art, music and movement in the nursery setting*. London: The Cicely Northcote Trust.

Murphy, J. (ed.) (2001) *Art therapy with young survivors of sexual abuse: Lost for words*. Hove: Brunner-Routledge.

O'Brien, F. (2004) 'The making of mess in art therapy – attachment, trauma and the brain'. *Inscape*, 9(1), pp. 2–13.

O'Brien, F. (2008) 'Attachment patterns through the generations: Internal and external homes', in: Case, C. and Dalley, T. (eds.) *Art therapy with children from infancy to adolescence*. Hove: Routledge, pp. 36–53.

Prokofiev, F. (2013) 'Allowing the artwork to speak: The use of a visual display as research method in a retrospective study of four years' artwork in art therapy with a four-year old boy'. *ATOL: Art Therapy Online*, 4(1), pp. 1–5. Available at: http://journals.gold.ac.uk/497/1/Prokofiev_Atol4(1)V2.pdf (Accessed 08.11.15.)

Proulx, L. (2003) *Strengthening emotional ties through parent-child-dyad art therapy: Interventions with toddlers and preschoolers*. London: Jessica Kingsley.

Reddick, D. (1999) 'Baby-bear monster'. *Inscape*, 4(1), pp. 20–28.

Robertson, J. (1953) *A two-year old goes to hospital*. London: Tavistock Child Development Research Unit. New York University Film Library.

Rubin, J. (1978/1984) *Child art therapy: Understanding and helping children grow through art*. Second Edition. New York: Van Nostrand Reinhold.

Schaverien, J. (1992) *The revealing image: Analytical art psychotherapy in theory and practice*. London: Tavistock/Routledge.

Schaverien, J. (1995) *Desire and the female therapist*. London: Routledge.

Schaverien, J. (2000) 'The triangular relationship and the aesthetic countertransference in analytical art psychotherapy', in: Gilroy, A. and McNeilly, G. (eds.) *The changing shape of art therapy: New developments in theory and practice*. London: Jessica Kingsley, pp. 55–83.

Schaverien, J. (2015) *Boarding school syndrome: The psychological trauma of the 'privileged' child*. London: Routledge, Taylor and Francis.

Schore, A.N. (1994) *Affect regulation and the origin of the self: The neurobiology of emotional development*. Hillsdale, NJ: Lawrence Erlbaum.

Shimamura, A.P. and Palmer, S.E. (eds.) (2014) *Aesthetic science: Connecting minds, brains and experience*. Oxford: Oxford University Press.

Siegel, D.J. (2012) *The developing mind: How relationships and the brain interact to shape who we are*. London: Guilford Press, Second Ed.

Stern, D.N. (1985) *The interpersonal world of the infant: A view from psychoanalysis and developmental psychology*. New York: Basic Books.

Waller, D. (1991/2013) *Becoming a profession: The history of art therapy in Britain 1940–1982*. London: Routledge, Taylor and Francis.

Westwood, J., Keyzer, C. and Evans, J. (2010) 'Art therapy, children 0–6 years and their families: A research project surveying the Sydney region of New South Wales, Australia'. *The Australian and New Zealand Journal of Art Therapy*, 5(1), pp. 17–28.

Willemsen, H., and Anscombe, E. (2001) 'Art and play therapy for pre-school children infected and affected by HIV/AIDS'. *Clinical Child Psychology and Psychiatry*, 6(3), pp. 339–350.

Winnicott, D.W. (1957/1964) *The child, the family, and the outside world*. Middlesex: Penguin Books.

Winnicott, D.W. (1960/1965) 'The theory of the parent–infant relationship', in: *The maturational processes and the facilitating environment*. London: The Hogarth Press and the Institute of Psychoanalysis, pp. 37–55.

Zornado, J. (2006) *Inventing the child, culture ideology and the story of childhood*. New York: Routledge.

PART 1

Individual art therapy with infants and toddlers

1

AN ODD MIRROR

Dean Reddick

Introduction

Simon, and his twin, Peter, were born at twenty-five weeks whilst their mother, Carla, was visiting relatives in her home country. Simon was the smaller and second-born twin. He was born blue and resuscitated at birth. An intensive-care infant unit separated Simon from his family. He was 'stuck' in hospital for the first five months of his life and Carla and the twins were 'stuck' overseas for eighteen months before returning home to the UK and to Steven, the twins' father. Simon received repeated surgical interventions as a baby, including operations on his eyes, kidneys and stomach. He achieved oral feeding but after a stomach operation in his second year required a gastronomy button and tube. At the age of three and a half he had not returned to eating orally.

I use Simon's own idea of being 'stuck' as a representation of his traumatic start to life, where 'Trauma implies the baby has experienced a break in life's continuity' (Winnicott, 1971, p. 131), with subsequent defences against 'unthinkable anxiety' and the return to defensive confusional states (Winnicott, 1971, p. 131). I refer to Tustin's idea of 'psychogenic autism' (Tustin, 1992), when 'awareness of bodily separateness had been traumatic' leading to 'autistic reactions' (Tustin, 1992, p. 11). I draw on Ogden's concept of the 'autistic contiguous position', which is 'a sensory-dominated, presymbolic area of experience in which the most primitive form of meaning is generated on the basis of the organization of sensory impressions at the skin surface' (1992, p. 4). It is 'a psychological organisation more primitive than either the paranoid-schizoid or depressive position' (Ogden, 1992, p. 81).

In addition, Ogden's notion of non-linear and interrelated developmental stages is a central theme. Ogden (1992) states that the different experience-generating modes (positions) (autistic contiguous, paranoid schizoid and depressive) 'stand in a dialectical relationship with each other' (Ogden, 1992, p. 10). Each mode has its

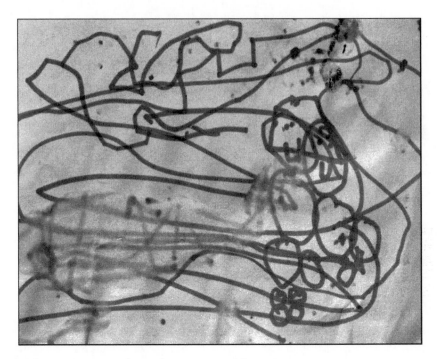

FIGURE 1.1   Drawing of twins by Simon, aged five.

own form of defence and symbolisation, and there is always a part of the patient functioning in the depressive mode. However, in psychopathology (e.g. that caused by trauma) there is a 'collapse' towards one of the modes. Furthermore there are areas of experience which are 'defensively foreclosed from the realm of the psychological, for example . . . forms of "non experience"' (Ogden, 1992, p. 39).

The dynamic processes of twinning are explored; 'twinship offers a narcissistic refuge' (Lewin, 2009, p. 68), a refuge lacking containment (Bion, 1962, 1963) and which prevents development (Lewin, 2009) due to the absence of a generational gap between twins. 'Twins are often premature and often surrounded by medical paraphernalia' (Lewis and Bryan, 1988, p. 269). Children born prematurely can experience a range of medical and developmental issues, such as 'post traumatic feeding disorders' (Acquarone, 2003, p. 290). The developmental picture for a premature twin may be complicated and unequal with a 'jumbling of developmental phases' (Tustin, 1992, p. 97). The child's experiences of invasive medical treatment is likened to abuse (Lillitos, 1990), and the hospitalised baby, with multiple caretakers, is at risk of emotional deprivation (Bowlby et al., 1956, Harris, 2005, Robertson and Robertson, 1989). Bonding with a premature baby is more difficult than with a full-term baby (Harris, 2005).

The nursery school and children's centre

Simon was referred for art therapy by his nursery school when he was three years old. The school provides free nursery places for children from the age of two years in the local community and marketed places for babies and children from six months of age. The children's centre provides universal services, such as group play sessions, and targeted services, such as family support to families with young children in the local area. Art therapy is well established in the setting. I offer supervision to the nursery team and individual, dyadic, family and group art therapy to children and their families. The art therapy initially took place in the nursery school and later in Simon's primary school and is ongoing at the time of writing. Names and some details have been altered to protect confidentiality.

Referral and initial meeting with Simon and his parents

The referral noted Simon's experiences of being separated from his family at birth and the many medical procedures that he had undergone. His intolerance of food and feeding with a gastronomy tube and his tendency to gag when touching viscous materials, such as sand or paint, were described. He experienced communication difficulties and had recently had grommets fitted. He was still wearing nappies.

In the initial meeting with Carla and Steven, I heard about how traumatic the first eighteen months of Simon's life had been for all the family. The common complications of parenting twins (Lewin, 2009) were magnified by Simon's prematurity, hospitalisation and the geographical separation between his parents. Carla movingly told me that Simon had been an unresponsive baby and she had to wait to fall in love with him (Harris, 2005). By the time I met the family there were strong, loving relationships between Simon and Peter and both parents.

I learned that Simon's developmental situation was complex, and his social development was affected. He had little interest in his peers at an age when peer relationships are beginning to blossom for most children. The capacity to develop peer relationships is a developmental achievement linked to movement through the Oedipus complex and 'the twin relationship may profoundly affect the resolution of . . . oedipal conflicts' (Lewin, 2009, p. 68).

Simon had an almost permanent smile and a stiffness to his body movements. He would repeat his name as though it were a shield to manage contact with those around him (Sinason, 1992). Despite these difficulties he was a determined toddler. He had settled surprisingly well into nursery school given the intense separation issues that premature, incubated babies face (Acquarone, 2003, Baradon et al., 2005, Case, 2005, Harris, 2005, Lewis and Bryan, 1988, Mintzer et al., 1984).

Assessment period: the first four sessions

I met Simon in the nursery school garden. It took a few minutes for him to agree to come with me so we could 'do art and think about his feelings'.

Simon explored the art room and took a pencil and paper. He made a small drawing, saying his name as he did so. He tried to pull the end off the pencil as though it were a lid. I wondered if this indicated some sort of confusion about how things came apart and fitted together and how we might fit together (Alvarez, 1992, Case,

2005, Tustin, 1992). He heard an adult voice outside and asked 'Mummy?' in a pensive voice that made me feel sad. I wondered aloud if he was missing his mummy.

In the following three sessions Simon communicated more detail about loss and absence. He told me his mummy and daddy were 'gone' and pointed to an empty chair. He frequently sighed, 'Oh, no,' but did not seem to expect me to respond. When I tried to capture the feelings behind these sighs Simon frowned at me as though my attempt to relate to his feelings was uncomfortable (Bion, 1959). In this way, he let me know that he could communicate but that thinking about feelings was problematic (Bion, 1959).

In the fourth session Simon drew 'Mummy car stuck' and made sounds which made me think about being constipated. Alongside being stuck there was a lot of messy water play where he repeatedly spilt water over himself and the room in a self-soothing activity which did not seem to need me to be present. This reminded me of the closed and sensory world of autism (Tustin, 1992) with its 'machinelike predictability' (Ogden, 1992, p. 59), omnipotence and lack of potential space (Winnicott, 1971).

In the assessment review meeting Simon's parents told me he played with water when he felt anxious. We thought about him being 'stuck'; both parents recognised this and told me how he could get stuck in oppositional or withdrawn moods for days. We thought about trauma related to Simon's birth and medical interventions and about how he needed help to emerge from being stuck, withdrawn and hard to reach. His parents were keen for art therapy to proceed and we agreed for Simon to attend individual weekly sessions with regular reviews. We also communicated by email: Simon's parents kept me up to date with any medical issues, absences and periods of ill health.

A dry and wet baby

The theme of water play continued into the fifth session. A daddy doll was placed in a pot of water and was 'stuck'. Being 'stuck' reminded me of autism, characterised by a lack of change, the dominance of auto-sensory experience and truncated or underdeveloped symbolic capacities (Tustin, 1992). The experience of 'stuck' induced a sense of panic in me. Perhaps panicked parts of Simon were 'stuck' in the incubator and developmentally stuck in an omnipotent identification through twinning (Lewin, 2009) with an autistic, machinelike world of surfaces (Bick, 1968, Ogden, 1992).

Simon, born at just twenty-five weeks and incubated for five months, lost the deep connection with his mother's body and with his twin, with whom he shared the womb (Piontelli, 1992). Tustin describes the baby's traumatic loss of body connectedness with his mother as 'a black hole catastrophe' (Tustin, 1992, p. 18) which can lead to autistic defences as the infant desperately tries to fend off the horror of being disconnected (Dalley, 2008, Lewin, 2009, Ogden, 1992, Piontelli, 1992, Roberts, 2009, Tustin, 1992). This aspect of the water play could then be understood as an autistic behaviour, desperately creating sensation at the skin boundary (Bick,

1968) as a way of providing a fundamental experience of being a boundaried self. In this way the water play was life-sustaining but, paradoxically, it was simultaneously a turning away from relating and therefore in the realm of the death instinct, a return to the inanimate (Freud, 1920).

In contrast, Simon also used water in more relational play, as the following vignettes show.

Simon splashed water aggressively and tipped pots of water over the table. There seemed to be an aspect of the water play consistent with paranoid schizoid functioning – the quality of 'attack' in the deliberate spilling of the water and a subsequent countertransference wish in me to control this behaviour and to tidy up the mess (Aldridge, 1998, Case, 2003, Lillitos, 1990, Meyerowitz-Katz, 2003, Murphy, 1997, O'Brien, 2004, Reddick, 1999, Sagar, 1990).

In the following sessions I had an association that Simon's water play represented something vital and alive. I was aware that he did not eat orally and his mouth and lips appeared dry. In my mind there was a link between the water and life-sustaining amniotic fluid. Previously, I had thought of him as a 'dry baby'. This seemed to be a representation of his traumatic birth and of his premature emergence from an oce-anic, womb-like feeling (Tustin, 1992, p. 98) into the dry incubator. But this new association with the water seemed to signal something different.

The mud game

Five months into the therapy Simon made his first clear representational draw-ing and said, 'Baby Simon.' I said, 'Hello, baby Simon, how are you feeling?' Baby Simon replied, 'Sad.' Simon stood in some spilt water and said it was mud. He cried out to me, 'Help.' He held his hands out to me, and I reached out and took his hands and played at pulling him out of the mud. He laughed hysterically at this activity but I felt a terrible sadness, echoes of which are still present as I write. Simon wanted help out of being stuck, but this help seemed to fill him with dreadful anxiety.

The following week more 'mud' appeared. I set a limit to the amount of water and paint allowed on the floor. Simon reacted angrily, shouting, 'No!' Perhaps the limits I set were an affront to his omnipotence. When Simon put his hands in the 'mud', he retched. We played the 'pulling out of the mud game' again, a game full of anxiety and panic, reminiscent of the terror associated with the catastrophe of the black hole and the 'horror of bodily separateness' (Tustin, 1992, p. 33). The mud game seemed to be a representation of Simon's life-and-death struggle to manage feelings of emerging, of becoming a separate person and of his need for another person to connect with to pull him out of the cloying, sickening mud.

Following this game Simon stormed around the room, knocking over chairs and raging, shouting, 'No!' – a display of potency and aggression which left me shaken as though his 'bottled up' (Tustin, 1992, p. 30) feelings were exploding out of him. During these moments there was little sense of the safety of an autistic contiguous sensory floor holding him together (Ogden, 1992).

In the same session Simon found a lolly stick which he used as a tongue depressor. He told me to say, 'Ahh' and I opened my mouth; in went the stick so that I gagged. He gave me a stick and I pretended to put it in his mouth and look inside. This game went round several times and he seemed excited. I asked what the doctor saw. Simon said I needed medicine. I found a little pot but he took a pen and, syringe-like, tried to jab it into my mouth. He passed wind loudly and then retched, evidence of his confusion where oral experiences seem to be tangled up with feelings in his stomach and anus. He drew a car, shouting, 'Help baby Simon, help baby Peter.' I asked where the car was going. Simon shouted, 'Help Doctor,' communicating a strong sense of his terror and panic. I said, 'The babies need a doctor, they need help.' Simon rushed over to me and grabbed me in an aggressive hug as though gluing himself to me in order to fend off the terrible threat of separation. This was perhaps an enactment of adhesive identification with its lack of a phantasy of an internal space, a form of two-dimensional, autistic relating (Bick, 1968, Meltzer, 1975).

Tustin (1992) describes how the sensuous experience of the 'nipple in the mouth' provides the infant with a feeling of 'rootedness' which replaces the umbilical connection to the placenta of the mother. The life-giving nipple also 'mediates sanity to the infant' (Bion, 1962) without which the infant is 'unrooted' and at the mercy of primitive anxieties. Tustin describes how the 'nipple in the mouth' leads to other sensuous developmental progressions, such as 'faecal stool in anus' (Tustin, 1992). I think Simon had achieved a tentative sense of 'rootedness' after he left intensive care and the umbilical care of the incubator. His rootedness was then repeatedly disrupted by traumatic hospitalisations at developmentally sensitive moments, such as weaning.

After this session, and unusually for me, I cried as I wrote my notes. The 'syringe' penetrating my mouth, a representation of invasive, painful, phallic and mechanical care, replaced the nipple in the mouth experience and represented emergency medical help in lieu of a containing maternal object. It represented the treatment of the body as a thing and not as a person (Orbach, 2004). Simon's desperate attempt to communicate his terror and urgency through projective identification (Bion, 1962) left me tearful and shaken; this was a powerful countertransference experience.

Separation and the summer break

Simon was now four and a half years old. As we headed towards the long summer break and his move to primary school he continued to play 'stuck in the mud' and 'doctor' games. He blocked my attempts to talk about leaving nursery and the summer break by counting out loud. He turned the light on and off, and I spoke about going to bed and waking up. We played hide-and-seek. Simon told me to count to one hundred. This felt too long for him to be hidden, eloquently communicating our fear that the break would be too long and that his struggle to emerge from his traumas would be compromised. In the final few weeks before the break Simon developed a new game. I was to pretend to go to sleep. I did so and was woken by a shocking, piercing scream. This game was played repeatedly and I found it harrowing, as though he was trying to tell me about the horror of waking up, of being born before he was ready and of the pain of his psychological birth (Mahler et al., 1975, Tustin, 1992).

At a review with the parents we agreed to continue art therapy at Simon's new school. We arranged for one extraordinary session for Simon during the summer holiday to shorten the length of the break from treatment.

Becoming an unstuck twin

In art therapy at primary school Simon's twin played an increasingly important part in his therapy as separation issues came into focus. Peter went to a different school. Simon explored his twin's absence symbolically in his play, driving toy cars with his dad taking Peter to one school and Simon another. In the second session of term, Simon made a microphone from tape and a glue stick. He sang a song for Peter, a heavy, melancholic song with the words 'Goodbye, Peter' repeated throughout. I was told to sing a 'goodnight song', and Simon played at going to sleep only to suddenly wake up screaming. The songs were symbolic processes, achievements of the depressive position, expressions and communications of sadness, loss and mourning and are especially apt when confronting moments of separation (e.g. parents sing their babies to sleep). I think Simon was negotiating separating from his twin and from the safe-feeling but developmentally stuck state of twinning – the 'narcissistic refuge' (Lewin, 2009). The symbolic quality of these communications was shattered, on waking, by the screaming, when Simon seemed to have lost both his twin as a pseudo-container and his sense of me as a maternal container.

Simon squeezed together a toy cage and a toy table as though they were fused uncomfortably, not fitted together in a coherent way like a mother and a baby or a nipple and a baby's mouth. The toys were pulled apart and one of them flew into space. This play seemed to represent his experience of the sudden and catastrophic loss of his twin. This idea was reinforced further when Simon played with a bunk bed toy, a twin image of 'two in one' which he violently tore apart so that one piece could go into space. During these times I really felt as though he was going away from me. I imagined space as a freezing void with no people, a truly terrifying autistic place to be in but perhaps less terrifying than staying on earth, where catastrophic loss or perhaps 'lack' threatened his sense of being. Going into space was then perhaps a retreat to the incubator space. I found myself calling him back to earth.

Simon introduced a third toy, squeezing the now separated parts of the bunk bed into a box. I thought of the box as a container (Bion, 1962); but this was not a soft, flexible maternal container – it was hard, sharp and unyielding and did not change shape to accommodate the separated twins; it was not 'alive' (Alvarez, 1992). Without a capacity for reverie this container couldn't offer an 'apparatus for thinking' (Bion, 1962). It reminded me of an incubator and of Simon's experience of containment (or more correctly 'management') by machines in hospitals, experienced perhaps as a prototype for rigid mechanical ways of relating (Alvarez, 1992, Bion, 1967). I wondered if Simon was trying to recreate a primitive sense of safety and coherence, an experience of an 'autistic shape', a hard, protective sensation used to fend off the awareness of bodily separation (Tustin, 1992, p. 18) consistent with experience generated in a predominantly autistic contiguous developmental position (Ogden, 1992).

In a session before a break Simon grabbed at me aggressively and played with a toy lion and a toy picnic hamper, with his back to me. I felt he had gone away from me. I spoke to him about this and I felt he was angry with me, so I offered this idea to him. Simon shouted, 'No!' and he stomped around the room, his body stiff. I said, 'Perhaps Simon is angry like a lion,' and he ran at me and roared in my face. He took two toy lions to bite me and at one point he used his teeth to bite me. I pulled away and Simon said, 'The lion is naughty.' I said, 'The lion wants to bite me.' He shouted, 'Yes!' It seemed to me that Simon's angry, oral aggression had broken through his autistic withdrawal. At the end of the session and consistent with this healthy paranoid schizoid communication Simon told me that I was stuck in a pit; I was to suffer for abandoning him during the forthcoming break in the therapy and Simon was to be a lion, the aggressor (Case, 2005).

Simon missed the next session through illness and when he returned we played the going-to-sleep game again. This time I was woken up by the sound of a crying baby who wanted his mummy. The crying baby is more consistent with the mourning of depressive functioning compared to the projective, paranoid schizoid process of screaming in the earlier sleep–and–wake games. Simon found a doll baby and carefully put it to sleep. He pointed to its belly button and said the baby had done a pee, referring to his confusion about how bodily processes work and trying to make sense of what is inside and what is outside. Simon pretended to change the baby's nappy, showing a lot of care and nurture in his play. I felt Simon was showing me about his feelings of being looked after, a transference representation of the maternal care that his baby self was receiving in art therapy.

However, trauma erupted in the play as though Simon catastrophically lost contact with me as a live container. The baby got stuck and together we freed the baby. Simon then soothed the baby as the emergency passed. The whole traumatic scene was repeated (Fraiberg, Adelson and Shapiro, 1975, Freud 1920). Perhaps these communications represented the trauma of being returned to the incubator after being held by his mother and/or of going back into hospital after time at home.

I spoke to Simon about how he had been a baby who had needed lots of help, even though putting this into words felt dangerous. Simon said the baby needed to go to the toilet. Then he said he needed to go to the toilet. I offered to escort him but he said he did not need to go. The emergence of the thought of the need to pee is absent in autistic functioning (Tustin, 1992), which is characterised by a lack of phantasy and projective processes of being able to get rid of intolerable feelings (Klein, 1946). In this play it seemed that Simon represented that he was no longer just stuck as the terrified baby in need of help, that he understood that he and I were tenderly caring for his baby self and that he had a growing sense of his own insides.

Twin words

Returning after a Christmas break, Simon, aged five, used paint messily, putting his hands in and dripping paint on the floor and table. He did not gag or retch and he talked about Peter, who he said was 'little'. Representations of twins continued to emerge in the work (Figure 1.2). Simon talked about digraphs (he had learned a lot about phonics at school), 'A group of two letters expressing a simple sound of speech' (Oxford English Dictionary, 2015), and made rhyming pairs, such as 'Simon is sad' and 'Peter is glad.' I also felt Simon was trying to control me as his twin, to deny our separateness. In these sessions I felt stifled and uncreative – a counter-transference response to twinning in the transference (Lewin, 2004, Roberts, 2009).

Three sessions after the Christmas break Simon made a drawing he called 'Zig and Zags' (Figure 1.3), a twin image that allowed for some difference between the twins. The spiky lines reminded me of a biting mouth. When I offered this interpretation to Simon he made angry biting movements with his mouth. He suddenly needed to go to the toilet. This suggested some link between his oral aggression

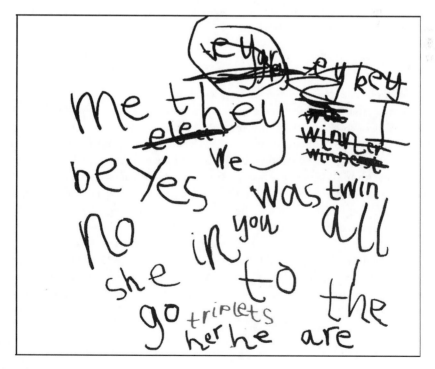

FIGURE 1.2 Twins and triplets.

FIGURE 1.3 Zig and zags.

and the sensation of needing to urinate and implied the development of a phantasy world in between the two sensations.

Symbolic birth

Simon continued to make symbolic representations of the stuck baby. I pulled baby Simon out from between two big cushions with a rope (a piece of string). Baby Peter also got stuck, and it is hard not to see these as representations of Simon's birth trauma. I spoke about Simon and Peter being in Mummy's tummy together and about coming out early. Simon put his head inside my jumper as though I were pregnant with him. These were intense, frightening scenes in which Simon would gag as the terror of his feelings overwhelmed him and his capacity for symbolic communication would collapse as the play became frightening (Winnicott, 1971). The rope seemed to offer an umbilical link between us, a lifeline with which to maintain relating in these extreme moments when Simon was teetering on the edge of the 'black hole' (Tustin, 1992). In contrast to these highly emotional states Simon continued to go into space. At these times I felt as though even the umbilical cord connection was lost as he drifted into an autistic state where feelings could not touch him.

An odd mirror

An 'odd miror' [sic] (Figure 1.4) is five-year-old Simon's poetic description of his experiences of the mirroring of his infancy, where in the normal course of

FIGURE 1.4 Odd miror (identifying material removed).

development, the mother gives 'back to the baby the baby's own sense of self' (Winnicott, 1971, p. 158). Born very early, he lost the containment of the womb and his twin as a mirror and experienced instead an incubator-mirror. It is not possible to know what this was like for Simon, but I imagine the losses were catastrophic and that in an attempt to 'hold himself' together Simon had to attach himself to the incubator-mirror. These experiences were represented in his umbilical and autistic organisations which emerged in relation to threats (real and imagined) of separation. I do not consider Simon to be autistic as he did not exhibit 'psychogenic autism' based on a delusional situation as described by Tustin (1992). However, disruptions in Simon's 'autistic contiguous' development, which is dependent on bodily being and 'the rhythm of sensation particularly at . . . the skin surface' (Ogden, 1992, p. 31), produced corresponding autistic defences. These defences function to fend off the terror of the 'black hole', a terror of bodily disconnectedness in which even space and time are annihilated.

Simon communicated his traumatic situation and his struggle to stay connected through being 'stuck'. Re-enactments which pointed to birth trauma filled me with panic and grief and my body reacted with sudden, sharp tears (Orbach, 2004). These intense, feeling-filled dramas operated as symbolic equations (Segal, 1950) where there was almost no difference between the experience and the representation of the experience. In my countertransference I experienced the claustrophobia of being stuck together with Simon, twinned in frightening experiences evocative of being inside the non-containing environment of an incubator. Being twinned in the transference in these moments was a necessary part of our relationship, a sticking together in the face of unthinkable anxiety. The form of containment operative here is bodily containment in relation to Simon's 'body-ego' (Adler, 2007, Freud, 1923), containment of 'somato-sensory memories and proto-phantasies' (Adler, 2007, p. 188) that have failed to be represented in the 'mind ego' due to a lack of containment leading to disruption in the psyche-soma (Winnicott, 1949) and disruptions in autistic contiguous development (Ogden, 1992). Simon's uncontained anxieties were expressed somatically by gagging and 'his striking indifference and lack of enthusiasm toward the breast' (Adler, 2007, p. 188).

These body-to-body transference phenomena (Orbach, 2004) also point to the concreteness of symbolic equation functioning. In these moments real physical contact between our bodies (e.g. my taking his offered hands) seemed essential. Art materials such as wet sand and paint were also experienced concretely when Simon gagged as he touched them. The sand and paint did not remind Simon of something sickening; they were felt by him to be *really* sickening. At other times (e.g. in his drawings) Simon demonstrated 'symbol formation proper' (Segal, 1957), an achievement of the depressive position where the symbol represents and is different from that which is symbolised.

Ogden believes that there is always some part of the client operating from a depressive mode and therefore able to make use of verbal symbolic communication (Ogden, 1992). Ogden's non-linear, dynamic view of an interplay between developmental experience-generating positions allows for an understanding of Simon's varying symbolic capacity. For example it is possible to consider Simon's autistic defences without collapsing into thinking of him as an autistic child; his capacities for symbolic play demonstrated that he was not autistic.

The duration of Simon's art therapy is also important. Winnicott (1971) stresses that play takes time. Simon needed time to work through his traumas and to begin to emerge from confusional states. Autistic defences were one aspect of Simon's confusion. He also had a deep confusion about his body and about how parts of his body linked up. In his nascent mind-emerging-from-body (Freud, 1923, Winnicott, 1949), there appeared to be a disruption of the autistic contiguous sense of being a coherent self.

Symbol formation begins with the body and the organs (parts) of the body and through phantasy eventually leads to a commonality of shared symbolic meaning (Klein, 1930). Simon's experience of his body's coherence was disrupted and saved by many surgical interventions, and this played a significant part in his confusional states. His phantasy of commonality was disrupted at a bodily level – for example in his mechanical relationship to his 'gastronomy tube as umbilical cord' instead of the more rooted and post-natal experience of 'nipple in the mouth.'

Being a twin contributed to Simon's confusion about himself as a separate person. This created a complex, multilayered transference where the ordinary developmental processes of individuation were impacted on by twinning. Lewin considers that separating from a twin is more difficult (and potentially catastrophic) than separating from a mother due to the strength of the narcissistic identification in twinning (Lewin, 2009). Simon's twin, Peter, like the incubator, could not offer the transformative experience of a live mother's effective containment.

The more split aspects of twinning were also present. For example Carla spoke about how she carried the fear that Simon would die as a baby whilst Steven actively sought the best medical interventions for Simon. The fact of my being a male therapist and the strength of a 'rescuing' (Gerrard, 1992) paternal transference are present in Simon's drawing (Plate 1) where Simon drew his father next to himself in an incubator in the absence of a live maternal container (Gerrard, 1992). There are also representations of intrusive, phallic experiences in Simon's doctor play, where I am represented as a penetrative male object in the transference.

In supervision we thought about twinning with Simon in the transference – a process through which the therapist unconsciously denies the pain of separateness and identifies with being in a 'special' twin relationship (Lewin, 2004, 2009). Instances of twinning in the transference can be discerned by a departure from normal therapeutic technique. I offered extraordinary sessions during a holiday, and I subsequently introduced food into the art therapy. Supervision was essential in thinking about differentiating between a therapeutic, attuned, flexible response and what might have been an aspect of transference twinning. My role as a container, able to receive and transform Simon's primitive communications (Bion, 1962), was dependant on not becoming stuck as a transference twin.

Postscript

Simon, now six years old, continues to attend weekly art therapy. He has used paint and water to create 'poo and pee' messes, which he gradually became able to clean up and manage. These messy art therapy processes are familiar to me and are well documented in British art therapy literature (Aldridge, 1998, Case, 2003, Meyerowitz-Katz, 2003, Murphy, 1997, O'Brien, 2004, Reddick, 1999, Russell, 2011, Sagar, 1990). He has achieved toileting. After discussions in supervision and in consultation with his parents and the wider team, real food was introduced into the art therapy sessions. Simon began to tolerate having food in his mouth and has recently begun to eat orally.

Simon's drawing (Plate 1) shows baby Simon in hospital, in an incubator-like object with his dad next to him. There is a huge monster in the room. It is a complex and symbolically rich drawing representing the original trauma, the predicament Simon was stuck in and the therapeutic relationship and process that enabled him to emerge from it.

References

Acquarone, S. (2003) 'Feeding disorders', in: Raphael-Leff, J. (ed.) *Parent-infant psychodynamics wild things, mirrors and ghosts*. Bodmin: MPG Books Group, reprinted 2011, pp. 283–293.

Adler, J. (2007) 'The feeding relationship, ambivalence and the psyche-soma of the infant: A study based on infant observation'. *Infant Observation: International Journal of Infant Observation and Its Applications*, 10 (2), pp. 183–194.

Aldridge, F. (1998) 'Chocolate or shit: Aesthetics and cultural poverty in art therapy with children'. *Inscape*, 3 (1), pp. 2–9.

Alvarez, A. (1992) *Live company.* London: Routledge.

Baradon, T., Broughton, C., Gibbs, I., James, J., Joyce, A. and Woodhead, J. (2005) *The practice of psychoanalytic parent-infant psychotherapy: Claiming the baby.* Hove: Routledge.

Bick, E. (1968) 'The experience of skin in early object relations'. *International Journal Psychoanalysis*, 49, pp. 484–486.

Bion, W. (1959) 'Attacks on linking'. *International Journal of Psychoanalysis*, 40, parts 5–6.

Bion, W. (1962) *Learning from experience.* London: Heinemann Medical.

Bion, W. (1963) *Elements of psycho-analysis.* London: Heinemann.

Bion, W. (1967) *Second thoughts.* London: Heinemann.

Bowlby, J., Ainsworth, M., Boston, M. and Rosenbluth, D. (eds.) (1956) 'The effects of mother child separation. A follow up study'. *British Journal of Medical Psychology*, 29 (3–4), pp. 211–247.

Case, C. (2003) 'Authenticity and survival: Working with children in chaos'. *Inscape*, 8 (1), pp. 17–27.

Case, C. (2005) *Imagining animals: art psychotherapy and primitive states of mind.* Hove: Routledge.

Case, C. and Dalley, T. (eds.) (2008) *Art therapy with children: From infancy to adolescence.* Hove: Routledge.

Dalley, T. (2008) 'The use of clay as a medium for working through loss and separation in the case of two latency boys', in: Case, C. and Dalley, T. (eds.) *Art therapy with children: From infancy to adolescence.* Hove: Routledge, pp. 69–85.

Fraiberg, S., Adelson, E. and Shapiro, V. (1975) 'Ghosts in the nursery: A psychoanalytic approach to the problems of impaired infant-mother relationships'. *Journal of the American Academy of Child & Adolescent Psychiatry*, 14 (3), pp. 387–421.

Freud, S. (1920) 'Beyond the pleasure principle', in: Strachey, J. (ed.) (2001) *The standard edition of the complete psychological works of Sigmund Freud.* Vol. 18: *Beyond the pleasure principle, group psychology and other works.* London: Vintage Books. The Hogarth Press and The Institute of Psychoanalysis, pp. 1–64.

Freud, S. (1923) 'The ego and the id', in: Strachey, J. (ed.) (2001) *The standard edition of the complete psychological works of Sigmund Freud.* Vol. 19. London: Vintage Books. The Hogarth Press and The Institute of Psychoanalysis, pp. 19–27.

Gerrard, J. (1992) 'Rescuers and containers; mothers and fathers?' *British Journal of Psychotherapy*, 9, pp. 15–23.

Harris, J. (2005) 'Critically ill babies in hospital-considering the experience of mothers'. *Infant Observation: International Journal of Infant Observation and Its Applications*, 8 (3), pp. 247–258.

Klein, M. (1930) 'The importance of symbol formation in the development of the ego', in: Mitchell, J. (ed.) *The selected Melanie Klein.* New York: Free Press, pp. 95–114.

Klein, M. (1946) 'Notes on schizoid mechanisms', in: Klein, M. (ed.) *Envy and gratitude.* London: Hogarth Press, pp. 1–24.

Lewin, V. (2004) *The twin in the transference.* London: Whurr.

Lewin, V. (2009) 'Twinship: A unique sibling relationship', in: Lewin, V. and Sharp, B. (eds.) *Siblings in development: A psychoanalytic view.* London: Karnac, pp. 63–74.

Lewis, E. and Bryan, E.M. (1988) 'Management of perinatal loss of a twin'. *British Medical Journal*, 297, pp. 1321–1323, in: Raphael-Leff, J. (ed.) *Parent-infant psychodynamics: Wild things, mirrors and ghosts.* London: Whurr, pp. 268–282.

Lillitos, A. (1990) 'Control, uncontrol, order, and chaos: Working with children with intestinal motility problems', in: Case, C. and Dalley, T. (eds.) *Working with children in art therapy.* London: Routledge, pp. 72–88.

Mahler, M., Bergman, A. and Pine, F. (1975) *The psychological birth of the human infant.* New York: Basic Books.

Meltzer, D. (1975) 'Adhesive identification'. *Contemporary Psycho-Analysis*, 11, pp. 289–310.

Meyerowitz-Katz, J. (2003) 'Art materials and processes – A place of meeting: Art psycho-therapy with a four-year-old boy'. *Inscape*, 8 (2), pp. 60–69.

Mintzer, D., Heidelise, A., Edward, Z., Tronick, E.Z. and Brazelton, T.B. (1984) 'Parenting an infant with a birth defect – the regulation of self-esteem'. *Psychoanalytic Study of the Child*, 39, pp. 561–589.

Murphy, J. (ed.) (1997) 'Art therapy with sexually abused children and young people'. *Inscape*, 3 (1), pp. 10–16.

O'Brien, F. (2004) 'The making of mess in art therapy: Attachment trauma and the brain'. *Inscape*, 9 (1), pp. 2–13.

Ogden, T. (1992) *The primitive edge of experience*. London: Karnac. First published 1989. New Jersey: Jason Aronson.

Orbach, S. (2004) 'What can we learn from the therapist's body?' *Attachment and Human Development*, 6 (2), pp. 141–150.

Oxford English Dictionary (2015) Available at http://www.oed.com/. Accessed on 2 September 2015. Oxford University Press.

Piontelli, A. (1992) *From foetus to child an observation and psychoanalytic study*. London: Routledge.

Reddick, D. (1999) 'Baby-bear monster'. *Inscape*, 4 (1), pp. 20–28.

Roberts, E. (2009) 'Tsunami boy', in: Lewin, V. and Sharp, B. (eds.) *Siblings in development: A psychoanalytic view*. London: Karnac, pp. 23–36.

Robertson, J. and Robertson, J. (1989) *Separation and the very young*. London: Free Association Books.

Russell, E. (2011) *Swimming against the tide: Trauma and mess in art therapy with a 3 year old girl*. Unpublished MA thesis. Goldsmiths College London.

Sagar, C. (1990) 'Working with cases of child sexual abuse', in: Case, C. and Dalley, T. (eds.) *Working with children in art therapy*. London: Routledge, pp. 89–114.

Segal, H. (1950) 'Some aspects of the analysis of a schizophrenic'. *International Journal of Psycho-analysis*, 31, pp. 268–278.

Segal, H. (1957) 'Notes on symbol formation', in: *The work of Hanna Segal*. New York: Aronson (1981), pp. 49–64.

Sinason, V. (1992) *Mental handicap and the human condition: new approaches from the Tavistock*. London: Free Association Books.

Tustin, F. (1992) *Autistic states in children* (Revised edition). London, New York: Routledge.

Winnicott, D.W. (1949) 'Mind and its relation to psyche-soma', in: *Through paediatrics to psycho-analysis*. London: Hogarth, pp. 243–254.

Winnicott, D. (1971) *Playing and reality*. London: Tavistock.

2

ON MARK MAKING AND LEAVING A MARK

Processing the experience of art therapy with a preschool child

Pensri Rowe

Introduction

In my experience, there is an explosive, all-consuming quality to what is brought by preschool children to the art therapy room. Intense, preverbal expériences are brought to the therapy space, enacted in the art making and play and communicated through projective processes in the transference (Meyerowitz-Katz, 2003, Reddick, 1999). When I first began working with this age group, I was flooded with intense feelings and at times overwhelmed by the chaotic mess that the children made. O'Brien (2008) writes of countertransference to the dissociated child as consisting of feelings of being overwhelmed by chaos, loss of skill and disconnectedness during seemingly mindless play brought to therapy. The therapist's role is to hold the space and take in these emotions, think about them and reflect them back to the child in a digestible way, so that the child has the experience that his or her emotions are witnessed and can be taken back meaningfully (Dalley, 2007).

Four-year-old Lara brought her relational experiences and traumas to the therapeutic space through the use of art materials and processes. Her mark making with the materials left corresponding symbolic and transferential marks on me. In this chapter I describe how her therapy unfolded, how I managed the intensity of my countertransference experiences and how I worked with her mother, Melissa, in order to support the mother-child dyad.

Art making as mark processing

Making art after each session helped me begin to discharge and process some of the projections I had received in the art therapy sessions. These projections were understood as countertransference experiences that signalled primitive non-verbal communications (Case, 1994). The images were usually made directly after the

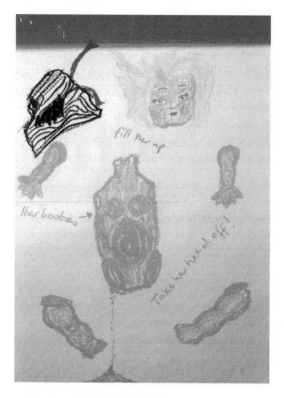

FIGURE 2.1   Art response to third session with Lara.

session in the therapy room, using materials available in the space. This was followed by further reflection through note writing and fortnightly supervision.

Images created immediately after sessions are useful reference points for supervision in addition to the child's imagery (Case, 1994). While the child's artwork often contains elements of the transference (Schaverien, 1999), the therapist's image contains elements of the countertransference (Case, 1994/2007, Brown et al., 2007, Meyerowitz-Katz, 2013). They add another element to Schaverien's (2000) triangle. They represent what Isserow (2008) names 'triadic relating': the supervisee, supervisor and supervisee's art response. Through paying attention to and understanding the countertransference as it is represented in the images made by therapists, we may deepen our insight into the nature of what is being communicated in the therapy (Meyerowitz-Katz, 2013).

Rogers (2002) argues that the therapist's art making is a language through which we gain deeper understanding about and empathise with our clients' experience. She comments that art making coupled with supervision can enhance our ability to be conscious and present with our clients. Brown et al. (2007) propose that by employing the aesthetic tools of our profession in supervision, we can enhance and deepen our understanding of clinical work, offering another medium through which to communicate and process emotional experience. Case suggests that it is in the additional images we create in response to our clinical work that our 'understanding of the client hovers on the edge of awareness' (Case, 2007, p. 96).

Drawing on Winnicott's (1971) 'good enough mother' in relationship to holding the therapist in supervision, Dalley (2007, p. 65) notes that supervision is particularly important when working with children given the 'chaotic and primitive feelings and thoughts' they bring to therapy. She suggests that supervision provides the space where thinking takes place and undigested, unprocessed thoughts and feelings are understood, allowing meaning to take place.

I have struggled to write this chapter. This struggle represents my countertransference to this work and includes the difficulty in bringing words to such intense primitive communications – a reflection of the difficulty that Lara had in managing her own primitive experience. Matthews writes,

> These apparently chaotic actions form the basis of all later symbolic and representational thinking . . . that this development requires a special kind of support from the interpersonal and social environment if it is to fully flourish. Lacking these certain optimal conditions for growth, we jeopardize children's intellectual and emotional development.
>
> *(Matthews, 1999, p. 4)*

Organisational context

The setting is a charitable organisation with five early childhood education and care (ECEC) centres, located in Sydney's Western suburbs in a culturally diverse area. Some families are migrants whose children have been born in Australia, and others have come with children from their original countries. Thirty per cent of the families that access the centres are identified as vulnerable in some way (Wall, 2010). The staff within the organisation also come from diverse backgrounds and speak a variety of languages other than English. These include Vietnamese, Mandarin, Cantonese, Hindi, Bengali, Korean, Malaysian, Burmese, Greek, Italian and Spanish.

The organisation is working towards integration, offering ECEC as well as allied health services in each centre. A multidisciplinary allied health team (AHT) includes social workers, occupational therapists, speech pathologists and a child and family health nurse. We work together with educators to consider how to best support the children's needs, as well as liaising with each other regarding the families that we work with.

The priority for my work is to focus on children in the preschools who will be going to primary school the following year. I work in a therapy room that is within the grounds of the larger organisation, though separate from the actual centres. I collect the children from their centre, sign them out and escort them to the art therapy room, which is approximately fifty metres from the centres in a separate building. This separation supports a psychological separateness for the children (Greenwood and Layton, 1987).

The room has a small table and chairs for art making, as well as a shelf for art materials, including paint, clay, play dough, collage and drawing materials. There is a sand tray, and toys for use in the sand tray. The room also has a doll's house, dolls and puppets. I have a cupboard in which I store the children's artworks between sessions.

Referrals

Referrals for individual art therapy or parent–child dyad sessions are made by either the director of a centre, an educator, a member of the AHT or by myself. If I do not already have a relationship with the child through running open drawing groups or supporting a particular child on the floor within the centres, with the family's consent I observe the child within the centre. Observational visits give me insight into the child's experience and provide opportunities for the child to familiarise themselves with me in order to support their transition to therapy.

Depending on the needs of the child and the capacity of the parents, I decide whether dyad sessions would be of greater benefit, or if the child would benefit more from individual sessions. I make this decision on the basis of the child's capacity to engage with me on their own or if they respond better with the support of their parent, as well as the parent's capacity to consistently attend and engage in the process. Sometimes this becomes apparent only retrospectively, with some families struggling to support or engage in the process. In such an instance individual sessions offer a therapeutic space for the child without the pressure of dyadic sessions.

When working with parents, I use the Circle of Security (COS) parenting programme (Powell et al., 2014), attachment-based psycho-education. It simply and concretely describes how to create security in relationships and supports the development of the parent's reflective capacity to provide a secure attachment with his or her child.

The difficulty of repairing marks left

Lara began a fourteen-month period of weekly art therapy when she was four years old. Her challenging behaviour and stressful family events led the director of the ECEC centre, where she attended five days a week, to refer her for individual art therapy. A referral to our speech pathologist for assistance with her speech and language development had been successful, and Lara's development in this regard was going well. However, there was a feeling that she needed additional support to express her thoughts and feelings about her experiences in a safe environment. She was particularly preoccupied with her identity in relation to the difference in her skin colour to her mother's. Lara had not met her father, who was African. Her mother, Melissa, was of Anglo-Australian descent.

Melissa and Lara lived locally in a small two-bedroom housing commission property. Melissa had little or no contact with her biological family. She had had a very conflictual relationship with her mother with whom she lived until she was thirteen, at which time she left home as she felt unsafe and unwanted. Melissa's mother had been emotionally and physically abusive, often targeting her and favouring her two younger children. After leaving home Melissa lived on the streets and began to use drugs.

Lara and Melissa were considered to be a family that required additional support in regards access to social work and other allied health services within the organisation. Melissa's drug use had resulted in the involvement of the Department of Family and Community Services. She had complied with a mandate to attend a two-year, weekly dialectical behaviour therapy group.

Melissa struggled with being a mother; she struggled with physical intimacy and overestimated what was appropriate for her daughter's age and stage of development. She described how she would let Lara hug her leg if she needed, as this felt manageable. She experienced other displays of affection as intrusive and uncomfortable. Melissa had a very brief relationship with Lara's father. The pregnancy was unplanned. He had made it clear that he did not want to acknowledge Lara as his child. He had had no contact with Lara and limited, abusive contact with Melissa.

Before beginning the art therapy, I made three observational visits to the centre. During these visits I observed that Lara was interested in connecting with her peers but struggled to share resources. When a rupture would occur with her friends over a toy or play idea, she appeared to want to reconnect, but did not know how to go about this, nor how to negotiate a repair after the conflict (Powell et al., 2014).

Being with Lara

From the first session I experienced a positive maternal transference, feeling loving and protective towards Lara, even though she took on a parental role and was highly directive; she wanted me to be the child and follow her lead from the beginning of our work together. While exploring the room and its contents she would glance at me, vigilant to my emotional state and expressions. In this way, a theme of confusion and ambivalence around looking and being looked at emerged in this first session.

In the third session she engaged in painting, adding white to different colours. I silently wondered about the symbolism of this in regards to her questioning of her genetic heritage, the mixing of her Anglo/African heritage. She also began to play with the baby dolls, and used a baby voice; she became quite erratic and chaotic. She undressed and dismembered a doll, pulling off its arms, legs and head and filling the parts with sand. This was very disturbing to watch. I felt like I was witnessing abuse. It seemed that she was re-enacting abuse by taking on a perpetrator's role, identifying with the aggressor (Freud, 1937) and sharing her wounds and hurts with me. From this session, and for the remainder of our time together, she struggled with the endings of our sessions, often refusing to finish, becoming distressed and acting out with the materials and toys.

Several months before she came to therapy Lara had been sexually abused by her twelve-year-old uncle. This occurred during a family holiday with Melissa, at her maternal grandfather's house in the country, with his new partner and their son. I was not informed of this until it emerged in Lara's third session.

In response to this session I made an image of the dismembered doll (Figure 2.1), which reminded me of the way in which trauma is stored as visual or somatic fragments (Van Der Kolk and Fisler, 1995). My image suggests this disintegrated experience. I subsequently learned that Lara had told her mother of what had happened immediately after the abuse. Melissa had acted promptly, speaking to her father's partner about what Lara had disclosed and leaving her father's house. Once Melissa returned to the city, she took Lara to a children's sexual assault clinic for an examination.

Two sessions later, Lara requested the doll, which I had safely stored for her, saying she wished to put it back together. Though she tried to repair it, she put the hand where the head should go. Perhaps this was Lara's way of communicating the internal confusion and the disorganisation she experienced as a result of the abuse. She then noticed sand inside the parts of the doll that she had added two sessions before and referred to how it was 'dirty inside'. Because the art materials and toys were stored safely for her in between sessions, and available in each session, Lara was able to make use of them to develop linking capacities and build connections between her internal and external experience (Bion, 1962).

She left the doll and moved onto cutting and sticking pink cellophane, telling me to stay away and warning that she might cut me. Lara said that her mother told her to stay away while she was using scissors. I wondered if this was about Melissa's unconscious fears of what she might do to her child – that she needed to keep her distance so as not to perpetuate the abuse she had experienced from her own mother. Lara was letting me know that her experience of intimacy was that people get hurt, and repairing this damage was difficult and confusing. Kalsched writes, 'We have to realise that trauma is an attachment disorder – it's about a rupture in a life-sustaining early relationship now being remembered in the transference' (Kalsched, 2003, p. 1490).

My countertransference changed. Having initially experienced a strong positive countertransference, I began to feel helpless and questioned my ability as a therapist to be of value to Lara. I was feeling Lara's despair that intimacy was hurtful and difficult to repair; she was communicating her fear that we would hurt each other and make each other dirty inside like the doll. We were swept up in a shared helplessness in the face of the damage that people do to each other, a *participation mystique* (Jung, [1921] 1971, para. 781) of mutual contamination and infection (Meyerowitz-Katz, 2013).

Lara engaged in dramatic play with baby dolls and a larger doll that she called the big sister, who was labelled 'naughty'. When I gave voice to the doll, 'I'm the big sister and I like being naughty', Lara hung her from the doorknob and kicked her, and also invited me to kick the doll. I declined, feeling that joining in this attack would be confirming the punitive reproach of Lara's 'bad' or 'naughty self'. Lara then used a noise from outside the session as an inspiration to hide, explaining that it was the police and that we needed to be quiet or they would come and get us. She gave me a gun and a drink, and demonstrated, using her hair bands, how police handcuff people.

The police and the witches

I was left wondering what experience Lara had of the police. I subsequently learned that they had been to her house when a thirteen-year-old family friend had been returned to their house after having run away from home. Melissa had also used the police as a threat to control Lara's behaviour; she claimed that the police would lock Lara up if she misbehaved. The police in Lara's play were driven away by witches. It seemed that the daimonic spirits (Kalsched, 2003) or ghosts (Fraiberg et al., 1975) of early trauma were haunting her ambivalently, being both helpful and persecutory.

The witches became a recurrent theme of her play and she returned to this idea week after week. It became a way to break up the intensity of the sessions. It felt like a way to discharge anxiety through playing, when we hid from the witches together. It was a way to be unified at times, for Lara to take back control, shifting away from moments of conflict when she pushed the boundaries of what was safe in the space, or acceptable in regard to mess. Sometimes we would hide from the witch together, and sometimes Lara would become the witch. At other times I was directed to play the witch. This repetition in the transference is a way of remembering; it 'may actually lead to the potential healing of trauma', provided that the therapist and client can survive the dynamic brought to therapy (Kalsched, 2003, p. 157).

I made Figure 2.2 in response to Lara's ninth session. The image shows two small birds on a snow-spotted branch, looking with googly eyes at a pink swirl shape–painted area. In the corner there are the words from the postcard from which the collage birds were cut; it explains that these birds travel in family groups. During

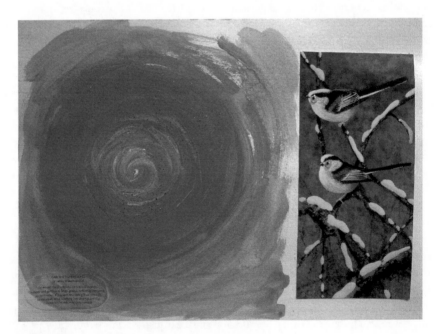

FIGURE 2.2 Art response to ninth session with Lara.

the session, Lara explored cultural norms within her relationship with her mother. She referred to her absent father and her own identity, explaining that she and her father were from Africa. My own 'whiteness', like that of Melissa, made the therapeutic relationship ripe for Lara's maternal transference and harder to uncover the paternal transference.

Lara found my gaze overwhelming, saying that staring was rude; and that you could go to gaol for staring, adding that she and her mother didn't stare at each other. Did Lara experience my gaze as shaming, exposing her 'dirty insides'? This tension was present in many sessions. It evoked my wondering about the maternal gaze and how much this would have been a struggle for Melissa. I thought about how such intimacy would have been difficult for her, having lacked a supportive relationship with her own mother.

The countertransference image contains layers of meaning. The pink shape has a maternal quality to it: given its colour and shape, it is almost breast-like, with the white nipple swirl in the centre, perhaps like a whirlpool that you cannot escape, a breast that is both benign and dangerous. I wondered if the birds represented Lara and me as observers, curious about her art making and play in the session. The two birds could also represent Lara and her mother. It seemed that each was separated from a longed-for connection, that they were somewhat out in the cold, on the snowy branches. There is a tension in the gaze, a split between the breast and the birds.

Lara continued to explore the theme of identity and difference in her art making in the following session (Figure 2.3). Making a mixture with paint and glue, and adding googly eyes and stars to the mixture, she used her hands to spread the mixture on the page as well as smearing it onto my hands. Perhaps the eyes represent Lara's confusion about looking and being looked at. Lara's painting has two formless messy shapes that are connected, one with sparkles; perhaps they represent her and me in the session. The mixture had a poo-like quality (Aldridge, 1998). The paint also referenced Lara's brown skin colour. During this session she said that she was 'blacker' than one of the baby dolls in the room and also 'blacker' than her father.

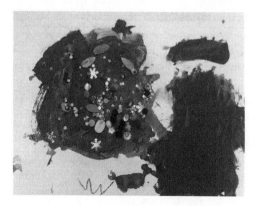

FIGURE 2.3 Lara's artwork from the tenth session.

Lara was exploring her identity and sharing her process with me, helping me feel what it was like for her. It felt chaotic and out of control, yet when Lara put the paint on my hands, there was a care and reverence in this act. It felt significant, and I felt as though I was joining in her ritual. Lara was making me as dirty as she felt inside, I wondered if she was acknowledging that the therapy was helping her with her internal mess. It seemed that she needed this to be experienced and felt by me, not just thought about, in order to be understood and that we were in this confusion together. She was leaving her mark on me both physically and psychically. Meyerowitz-Katz (2013) describes the importance of mutual 'contamination and infection' occurring within the therapy for it to be effective. I wondered if perhaps Lara was also making me black like her father to explore her paternal transference.

Plate 2 was created in response to the tenth session with Lara. Brown et al. (2007) discuss the use of image making to deepen understanding of embodied images by imitating a client's process of art making to gain greater consciousness of the client's communications and experiences. In this image I employed some of the materials Lara used and explored my experience of being brought into her art-making process as she smeared it onto my white hands. The leftover materials were used to concretely contain and process mess created in the session.

In my image, 'sssshhhh' references Lara's desire to control my responses, and maintain authority within the space, attempting to inhibit my thinking. It is also the beginning of the word 'shit', which references Lara's ambivalence as to whether the brown paint is a reference to Black skin and Black identity or whether is it is something dirty and possibly abusive. Perhaps she was feeling intruded upon (Winnicott, 1958) by my responses, or expressing an inhibiting part of herself. Perhaps the image echoes her communication about my gaze having been too much during the last session, as well as confusion about the abuse while also attempting to repair her wounds.

O'Brien (2004) conceptualises mess as a kind of dissociation and means of retreat from being with another (see Plate 3). She suggests that children who have experienced early relational trauma, in particular sexual abuse, often generate chaotic mess. Even those children who are capable of creating aesthetically pleasing drawings appear unable to resist such chaotic pouring, mixing and emptying of paint, water and clay within the art therapy session. O'Brien proposes that the mess making may be a way of reconnecting neural pathways by activating parts of the brain through a visual process that retrieves emotional experience, damaged by early relational trauma and insecure attachments to caregivers. She writes of inter-generational insecure attachment, that 'Patterns seen in practice may involve paints, mixed and spread over hands, paper and table in ways that feel hard to contain' (O'Brien, 2008, p. 41).

A premature move to dyad sessions

In consultation with the allied health team an idea emerged that dyad sessions would best support the relationship between Melissa and Lara. In order to prepare

Lara, I introduced the idea of Melissa coming to our sessions some weeks in advance. She was excited by this idea and agreed to having her mother join the session. However, in retrospect this became a parallel process of external destructive forces on the therapeutic relationship, an enactment of the intrusiveness of abuse. By enactment I am referring to an interaction within the therapeutic relationship which is motivated by strong unconscious affect and proceeded by mutual projective identification (Bion, 1962, Maroda, 1998).

In the dyadic sessions, Melissa engaged with Lara by becoming very directive and controlling. When Lara did not respond to this and challenged her, Melissa threatened to leave and said that she wouldn't come back. I really felt for Lara, given that the space and the boundaries of the therapy had been changed. I also felt for Melissa, who was clearly struggling and at times appeared scared of her child. Lara struggled with words, becoming erratic, hyperactive and regressive. O'Brien (2008) suggests that the child can attempt to maintain safety by using activity to prevent thinking when relationships have been abusive.

I felt as though I had let them both down and wondered how we could repair this experience. I wondered how Lara would respond in our next session. In particular I was interested in what this experience of my having witnessed the struggle between her and her mother had been like for her. While she had brought much of her struggles to the therapeutic space in her play and art making, to physically have her mother and their relationship present and witnessed by me felt to me to be devastating and shaming. Through supervision I understood this as a countertransference enactment in the therapy that offered me an experience of what it was like to be Lara, who had experienced rupture, sexual abuse and penetrating damage to her going-on-being (Winnicott, 1956). The therapy's going-on-being was damaged and needed repair.

The initial dyad session gave a clearer sense of the difficulties within Melissa and Lara's relationship. It was intolerable for Melissa to be in the room. At the time, within the organisation there was not another therapist available to work with Melissa, so I also took up this role. I decided to work with her separately and to employ the COS programme as a framework to structure these sessions.

I continued to see Lara individually. It was anxiety-provoking for her that I was seeing her mother separately as well. I explained to Lara that we spoke about ways for Melissa to best support her needs. While working in this way had its challenges, I also found that seeing mother and child separately offered me far greater insight into their relationship. I focused on Melissa's parenting of Lara, with my primary concern being Lara's well-being, and I supported Melissa to acknowledge the ghosts of her early experience and negate their repetition (Fraiberg et al., 1975, p. 171).

Individual sessions with Lara

I felt a deep sadness after our initial dyad session. I wondered if this sadness was about the difficulty Lara and Melissa had in connecting with each other. I had noticed that sadness was something from which both of them seemed to protect themselves. While I felt dyad work with Lara and Melissa would be the most beneficial to support their relationship, I realised in retrospect that this was not yet possible. Melissa could not tolerate the uncertainty of the therapeutic space with her daughter. Perhaps Melissa felt envious (Fraiberg et al., 1975, p. 190) of Lara in the session and was struggling to share me as she had not had the experience of an adult joining her in play as a child. In the session, Melissa had struggled to take on the role of parent to Lara and to trust me, having not developed a relationship with me prior to joining the space that Lara and I had shared for some time. I wondered if Melissa was threatened by the capacity for Lara and me to play, something with which Melissa struggled.

Lara was beginning to explore her Oedipal fantasies of having a parental couple and her despair and confusion about how parents and children do or don't fit together. During the sixteenth session Lara made a portrait of her mother and explained that there were cracks in it and that there were flames on her mother. This, like most of Lara's artwork, was complex, embodied imagery (Schaverien, 1999) that was hard to put into words, and seemed to contain much of her non-verbal, pre-symbolic experience.

I wondered if this was Lara's way of expressing the undercurrent of rage within her mother which I had felt in my sessions with Melissa. Or perhaps this was a transference image of me as a cracked mother, a cracked mother/therapist who, by allowing Melissa into her space prematurely, hadn't held the space for her. In addition, perhaps the image also symbolised Lara's fear at what her rage at me for having allowed Melissa in would do.

She then made a portrait of herself with her mother and father, explaining that her father was rude to her mother. I acknowledged that she seemed sad. Lara expressed that she was sad that her father had never touched her. I acknowledged that this was sad that she had never hugged her dad.

I wondered about Lara's sense of intimacy – if it was skewed by her abuse, if feelings of longing for a relationship with her father were mixed up with being sexualised by her uncle, particularly in the absence of much physical affection from her mother, nor any supportive male role models. Reddick (1999) quotes Gerrard (1992): 'The more a mother is experienced as unable to be sensitive to her child's needs or unable to contain unbearable feelings the greater will be the child's need to look for a father (or father figure) to rescue him/her from the relationship with this mother' (Gerrard, 1992, p. 16). Lara's experience of a lack of maternal attunement (Stern, 1998) was further complicated by her experience of sexual abuse by her young uncle.

Parenting sessions with Melissa

I met with Melissa weekly for approximately twenty sessions. We were able to reflect on how her own early experiences were impacting on her parenting of Lara. She had enrolled Lara for five days a week at the centre in order to limit the amount of time she spent with her. I often felt on edge, anxious that I would say the wrong thing or provoke Melissa in some way. I wondered if this was how Lara felt and if this also mirrored Melissa's experience as a child with her own mother. Through the sessions Melissa was able to acknowledge that she was being triggered by Lara's emotional needs and the challenge of being able to provide a safe haven (Powell et al., 2014) for Lara to return to when she needed closeness and support.

Return to dyad sessions

After completing the Circle of Security parenting material and our sessions together, Melissa was able to join her daughter in the art and play room and participate in three dyad sessions. Following this, Lara left the centre to attend primary school. Melissa was much more comfortable in the space with her daughter than she had been during our first dyad session. She was able to tolerate the uncertainty of the space and follow Lara's lead. While Melissa needed some prompting to join in with Lara's play ideas, she was eventually able to take these up and engage. I feel the parent sessions had allowed Melissa to develop trust and a relationship with me, and they had fostered a belief that I was there to help rather than judge or make further reports to the Department of Family and Community Services. Developing this trust allowed Melissa to join with Lara in the play, safe in the knowledge that I was holding the space for both of them.

In the first of the final dyad sessions Lara instructed Melissa to find the treasure and helped her join in the play by suggesting what to use. Melissa took a box from the shelf, adding some toys as instructed, and placed it on the rug. Lara then covered it with a sheet and gave Melissa and me each a map with which to find the treasure. Together they found something precious in the therapeutic space, poignantly symbolising the impact that the therapy had on their relationship.

Lara gave Melissa a piece of paper and asked her to write all the names of the members of her family, which Melissa did. Melissa included many of her friends, who Lara referred to as Aunty or Uncle. In the absence of extended family, Melissa had adopted friends as family. Lara requested that Melissa write my name on their list. It seemed that Lara had been able to internalise some of the holding, feeling and thinking about her through our sessions together. Lara made two small final artworks and stuck them on the art therapy room door before leaving the last session. She left her mark on the space.

Conclusion

Negotiating the boundaries of working separately and dyadically with parent and child has generated challenges in this treatment, as well as providing clinical learning for use in future practice. The individual art therapy with Lara offered her a space to explore her relational trauma, sexual abuse and identity. Being together in the room, mother, child and therapist, was impossible at first. The gaze of the father, who I symbolised at times, should function to contain the mother–child dyad (Winnicott, 1960), yet the father was absent or experienced as critical and shaming. Had I had the choice I would have continued the second series of dyadic session with Lara and Melissa; however, the limitations of the service provision prevented this. I feel the therapy was of value in fostering Melissa's awareness of the impact of her own early experiences on her parenting and in bringing her into a more playful relationship with her child.

I have at times found it challenging to put into words the experience and primitive feelings brought to therapy by the preschool children I have worked with. O'Brien (2008, p. 45) writes, 'the process of therapy throws up an intuitive knowing that is creative in its communication.' Engaging in my own art making in response to sessions with preschool children has helped me to access multiple levels of this intuitive knowing. In the work with Lara and Melissa, the concreteness of the art materials supported the containment of my process so that it could be metabolised and fed back to them. Exploration of my countertransference through image making and supervision provided invaluable insight into Lara and Melissa's experiences. These countertransference images had layers of meaning and led to new thoughts about the clinical work. Through her mark making and her leaving a mark on me, transformation of Lara's struggles has been made possible.

References

Aldridge, F. (1998) 'Chocolate or shit. Aesthetics and cultural poverty in art therapy with children'. *Inscape*, 3 (1), pp. 2–9.

Bion, W. (1962) *Learning from experience*. London: Heinemann.

Brown, C. Meyerowitz-Katz, J. and Ryde, J. (2007) 'Thinking with image making in supervision', in Schaverien, J. and Case, C. (eds.) *Supervision of art psychotherapy – A theoretical and practical handbook*. East Sussex: Routledge, pp. 167–182.

Case, C. (1994) 'Art therapy in analytical advance/retreat – in the belly of the spider'. *Inscape*, 1, pp. 3–10.

Case, C. (2007) 'Imagery in supervision: The non-verbal narrative of knowing', in Schaverien, J. and Case, C. (eds.) *Supervision of art psychotherapy – A theoretical and practical handbook*. East Sussex: Routledge, pp. 95–116.

Dalley, T. (2007) 'Piecing together the jigsaw puzzle: Thinking about the clinical supervision of art therapists working with children and young people', in Schaverien, J. and Case, C. (eds.) *Supervision of art psychotherapy – A theoretical and practical handbook*. East Sussex: Routledge, pp. 64–79.

Fraiberg, S. Adelson, E. and Shapiro, V. (1975) 'Ghosts in the nursery: A psychoanalytic approach to the problems of impaired infant-mother relationships'. *Journal of the American Academy of Child Psychiatry*, 14, pp. 387–422.

Freud, A. (1937) *The ego and the mechanisms of defence*. London: Hogarth Press and Institute of Psycho-Analysis.

Gerrard, J. (1992) 'Rescuers and container: Mothers and fathers?' *British Journal of Psychotherapy*, 9, pp. 15–23.

Greenwood, H. and Layton, G. (1987) 'An out-patient art therapy group'. *Inscape*, Summer, pp. 12–19.

Isserow, J. (2008) 'Looking together: Joint attention in art therapy'. *International Journal of Art Therapy*, June, 13 (1), pp. 34–42.

Jung, C.G. ([1921] 1971) *Collected works*. Vol. 6. *Psychological types*. Princeton, NJ: Princeton University Press.

Kalsched, D. (2003) 'Daimonic elements in early trauma'. *Journal of Analytical Psychology*, 48, 145–169.

Maroda, K. (1998) 'Enactment when the patient's and analyst's pasts converge'. *Psychoanalytic Psychology*, 15 (4), pp. 517–535.

Matthews, J. (1999) *The art of childhood and adolescence: The construction of meaning.* London: Falmer Press.

Meyerowitz-Katz, J. (2003) 'Art materials and processes: A place of meeting art psycho-therapy with a four-year-old boy'. *Inscape*, 8 (2), pp. 60–69.

Meyerowitz-Katz, J. (2013) 'Consciously forgotten, unconsciously remembered relationships made visible'. Unpublished Paper ANZATA Conference, Sydney.

O'Brien, F. (2004) 'The making of mess in art therapy – Attachment, trauma and the brain'. *Inscape*, 9 (1), pp. 2–13.

O'Brien, F. (2008) Attachment patterns through the generations: Internal and external homes', in: Case, C. and Dalley, T. (eds.) *Art therapy with children: From infancy to adolescence.* London: Routledge, pp. 36–44.

Powell, B. Cooper, G. Hoffman, K. and Marvin, B. (2014) *The Circle of Security intervention: Enhancing attachment in early parent-child relationships.* New York: Guilford Press.

Reddick, D. (1999) 'Baby-bear monster'. *Inscape*, 4 (1), pp. 20–28.

Rogers, M. (2002) 'Absent figures: A personal reflection on the value of art therapists' own image-making'. *Inscape*, 7 (2), pp. 59–71.

Schaverien, J. (1999) *The revealing image: Analytical art psychotherapy in theory and practice.* London: Jessica Kingsley.

Schaverien, J. (2000) 'The triangular relationship & the aesthetic countertransference in ana-lytical art psychotherapy', in Gilroy, A. and McNeilly, G. (eds.) *The changing shape of art therapy: New developments in theory & practice.* London: Jessica Kingsley, pp. 55–58.

Stern, D. (1998) *The interpersonal world of the infant.* London: Karnac.

Van Der Kolk, B. and Fisler, R. (1995) 'Dissociation and the fragmentary nature of traumatic memories: Overview & exploratory study'. *Journal of Traumatic Stress*, 8 (4), pp. 505–525.

Wall, J. (2010) *Ethics in light of childhood.* Washington, DC: Georgetown University Press.

Winnicott, D. W. (1956) 'Primary maternal preoccupation', in *Through paediatrics to psychoa-nalysis: Collected papers.* London: Karnac, pp. 300–305.

Winnicott, D. W. (1958) *Through paediatrics to psycho-analysis.* London: Hogarth Press and the Institute of Psychoanalysis.

Winnicott, D. W. (1960) 'The theory of the parent-infant relationship'. *International Journal of Psycho-Analysis*, 41, pp. 585–595.

Winnicott, D. (1971) *Playing and reality.* London: Tavistock.

3

'CHEERFUL AND NOT CHEERFUL'

Art psychotherapy on a paediatric ward

Susan Rudnik

Introduction

This chapter describes my work on a paediatric ward within a large hospital in a central London National Health Service (NHS) trust. I will use the clinical material from twenty-four sessions with a four-year-old girl called Rosie, who had a congenital heart defect, in order to illustrate the function of art psychotherapy on a children's ward. The title of this chapter refers to Rosie's coping with and thinking about the sad and frightening aspects of being in hospital and her making sense of what was going on in her body through her art making within the therapeutic relationship.

The importance of giving the 'not cheerful' feelings space in the artwork, and allowing them to be contained, thought about and understood through the analysis of the transference and countertransference, is central. This lies alongside my understanding of the potential for properties inherent in art materials to enable very young children to express unconscious distress and to give language to their feelings (Meyerowitz-Katz, 2003).

The containing function of the art making within the therapeutic relationship in holding intolerable and unbearable feelings (Dalley, 2000) is further discussed and focused on through Bion's concept of container/contained (Bion, 1962). Bion conceptualised that the baby does not have the function for thinking at the beginning of its life (Caccia, 1984) and that therefore any unpleasant and intolerable feelings are projected into the mother to be converted from meaningless bodily feelings to thoughts. This Bion calls 'alpha function' (Bion, 1963). In other words the mother (the container) holds and digests the baby's projections (the contained), making sense of them for the infant through her thinking. She then returns them to her baby in a consequently more manageable form so that they are no longer overwhelming. Through the container/contained process, she also provides the baby with an 'apparatus for thinking' so that, over time, the baby develops the capacity to think independently.

When faced with life-limiting illness, extraordinary medical procedures and interventions, the need for containment and processing of the bodily and emotional experience of illness is fundamental for a child. This is particularly true for young children who may not have the verbal skills to communicate or understand their distress and what is happening to them physically.

The hospital setting

My post is predominately ward-based. Consequently, I am often at the frontline of children's and families' distress. I meet with families in states of despair after a shock diagnosis or tragic accident, as well as those children and families that are coping with ongoing, lifelong ill health. As the therapist I witness the child's experience of illness and bear painful and distressing feelings in the countertransference. This allows for some containing of the child's distress, be it over several months or in a single session. Segal (2010) identifies the role of the psychotherapist within the hospital setting as offering 'containment of unbearable feelings'; she continues: 'the hope is to minimise the psychological effects and to foster the capacity for resilience by believing that being able to make sense of the experience [of hospitalisation] helps the child's or adolescent's coping mechanism' (Segal, 2010, p. 175). As well as engagement with the materials providing opportunities for the expression of unconscious distress (Meyerowitz-Katz, 2003), I believe the artwork functions as a container allowing for the 'un-nameable fears' of hospitalised children to be held, processed and thought about, leading to the experience of being contained (Dalley, 2000).

Despite the clear advantages of offering art-based therapy to children in hospital there is very little written about art therapy in paediatric inpatient services in the UK (Hill, 1986, Lillitos, 1990, Bissonnet, 2015, Clifton, 2015, Fischer, 2015). The lack of literature is also a reflection of the limited services in this area, and I concur with Bissonnet (2015) on the need to support children and families coping with the enormity of physical illness. Fischer (2015) identifies a larger body of literature and subsequent services in America and Canada (Malchiodi, 1999) where art therapy within paediatrics is a well-established field.

In my experience, the modern-day children's ward is a busy and bustling place. Doctors, nurses, play specialists, psychologists and teachers all come to support the sick children and families on the ward. Alongside the numerous medical treatments, tests and procedures there are often fun activities, with visits from celebrities and local premiership football teams. It is a hub of almost constant activity. Skogstand (2000, p. 120) talks of the 'liveliness and manic excitement' of an adult cardiology ward as a 'reassurance against the fear of death'. This is ever present on the children's ward.

The setting requires a flexible approach from the art therapist; boundaries that so often offer containment in the therapeutic session are challenged and broken. On a practical level there is no set space for the art therapist to use. I sometimes see patients by their beds with the curtain drawn, or in their cubicle if they have one. I use the playroom on the ward but mostly a small room belonging to the school just off the ward. None of these spaces are textbook art therapy rooms – they are small, multi-use spaces. Tables often need to be cleared of food and medicine to make just enough room for a piece of paper as I juggle paint and water containers. Interruptions are frequent and at times necessary in order to attend to the medical needs of the children. Some sessions involve the parents or siblings or even grand-parents. There is an almost constant need to explain and introduce the purposes of art therapy on the ward to the changing patient population.

Judd (2010) refers to the frequently flimsy setting of the hospital ward with the importance of the therapist's mind in holding the consistent frame. I have also found that the concrete containers in art therapy hold ever more importance: the child's art therapy folder, the materials box, the trolley I use, the materials themselves, even the clock I use. These are concrete things that stay the same, offer continuity and allow a sense of trust and containment to develop even in the briefest of therapeutic encounters. They can also hold some of my own anxieties amongst the chaos.

Referrals are given verbally in handover meetings from nurses, teachers, psy-chologists and the children or parents themselves, who may have seen a leaflet on the ward. There is no complicated paperwork or waiting lists; the child is referred and usually seen on the same day. Children are mainly referred for emotional sup-port in coping with a challenging, traumatic or life-limiting medical condition. The multidisciplinary team has usually noticed withdrawn or angry behaviour or a gen-eral disengagement from activities, and some children are known to have complex social issues. Sometimes the team just feels intuitively that a child seems to need extra space for his or her feelings and for processing something of his or her experi-ence in a therapy not reliant on verbal communication. Rosie was one such child.

Rosie

Rosie was four years old when I met her and her family on the ward. She was born with a complex congenital heart disorder. The heart problem had been detected in utero so the family had always been prepared for the fact Rosie might need several operations and in later adolescence perhaps a heart transplant.

Rosie was a bright and friendly child. She had a healthy attachment to both her parents and a fond relationship with her younger sister, Ella, who was two at the time of Rosie's admission. They were an ordinary family plunged into extraordi-nary circumstances that disrupted much of their family life.

Not long before the start of therapy, Rosie had undergone cardiac surgery. This involved a three-month stay on the paediatric intensive-care unit (PICU). I had been on leave during this time, but on my return, both the school team and the psychology team identified Rosie as a child they felt would benefit from art therapy. There was desperation in the school staffs' request for me to see this child, which gave me a sense of a need not only with Rosie and her family but also with the professional team around her.

Initial sessions

I first met Rosie with her mum and dad on the ward awaiting another cardiac operation. She was in a bay of four beds and sitting up in bed with an alertness and vigilance that I've seen many times in children familiar with medical wards and procedures. Both parents sat by the bed with palpable anxiety. I approached the bed space with my red trolley full of art materials and introduced art therapy to Rosie. She listened while looking around, her eyes darting in lots of directions. I said that art therapy was to help with her feelings while she was on the ward and that she could use the materials in any way she wanted. Rosie agreed to the session and chose to have both her parents stay by the bed. I drew the curtains around the bed space, and wrote a note to ask not to be disturbed unless necessary, which I stuck on the curtain. I showed Rosie the red cardboard folder I had made with her name on it and explained this was her folder for the things she made in art therapy while she was in hospital.

Rosie's initial image was of 'the world'. This was somewhat prompted by Mum, and I was aware of my presence in their world, which had now become so small as they were confined to the hospital. Rosie, Mum and Dad spoke of the world outside the ward and the sky that could just be seen from the window; I sensed a great deal of hope and a need to know that the world out there still existed.

Rosie's next image was a picture of Christmas. She used glitter for the snow and very faintly in red drew a picture of Santa on his sleigh. Rosie explained that the last time she was in hospital she had to stay in over Christmas and she stayed a long time. Rosie was very worried she would have to stay a long time again. Her parents hurriedly reassured her and spoke of returning home to all the Christmas presents she had missed. I felt the pain and anxiety of staying with these difficult feelings, especially as the family awaited more surgery and all the uncertainty that this might bring. I was aware of maintaining my capacity to bear these difficult feelings with Rosie. When looking at Rosie's artwork I was struck by the faint red figure, which looked as though it was someone lying down connected to machines. I was reminded of the children I see on PICU and what Rosie had endured and what she may have to endure next.

The following week Rosie was back on PICU and lying on her bed, unable to move much due to all the medical equipment attached to her tiny body. A huge scar the length of her torso was covered with a protective bandage. The atmosphere on PICU can be notably different to the main ward. There is a necessary seriousness amongst the staff as they speak in hushed tones and go about their nursing with vigilance and precision, checking machines and monitors, administering medication to tiny babies and children while parents anxiously look on. Machines beep all around and breathing machines can be heard puffing and moving. I understand the perfunctory nature of the nursing I observe on PICU as a defence against the intense feelings that are aroused in the task of nursing such sick and vulnerable babies and children. Menzies' (1959, 1988) seminal studies talk of the personal and institutional defences that guard against extreme feelings and stress in nursing – defences that put emotional distance between patients and nurses. Cohn (1994), Dartington (1994), Skogstand (2000), Hall (2008) and Henry (2008) further elaborate on the complexities of working with physical illness in their observational interactions with nursing teams on medical wards.

As I sat with the family I was aware of my own anxiety and an experience of struggling to be present. Henry (2008, pp. 138–139) speaks of the 'real fear and pain' that overwhelmed her in her work with a very sick young boy, when similarly faced with an 'environment where life and death are so close'. Fear overwhelmed me and I felt I had to fight to continue thinking, perhaps much like Rosie's need to fight to stay alive in her body.

In this meeting Rosie's art making was more tentative because her movement was limited. I was aware of the pain and strain in her and the family. Rosie wanted to make a car out of play dough, but struggled to hold the material. I gently pressed the dough into a car shape and, together with Mum, pretended the cars were moving on a road.

Rosie kept the small car by her bed throughout her stay on PICU. This play and movement felt important for Rosie and Mum, as if symbolically holding something of the longed-for movement of Rosie out of PICU and, on a deeper level, the longed-for movement of blood through Rosie's heart. My active engagement in the art making served the purpose of allowing me to feel I was concretely doing something when faced with the feelings of being 'useless' in helping Rosie. In hindsight I wonder how Rosie received this: was I adding to her potential feelings of inadequacy as I played with Mum? I feel I was somewhat colluding with the organisational defences in guarding against feeling helpless and useless. This feeling was important to understand as something that Rosie was maybe feeling, as she lay passive in her bed, unable to engage with the materials.

The following week Rosie was out of PICU and back on the main ward. The procedure had gone to plan and she seemed brighter as the family prepared for discharge. Rosie was able to come off the ward and attend her session in a small, multi-use room belonging to the hospital school without her parents present. Rosie's image (Plate 4) depicted a shark-infested sea with a bridge made of scrunched-up paper. She was very clear that the water was not safe and she had to get from one side of the bridge to another using the paper lines and not the gaps between. This dangerous journey symbolised something of what Rosie was going through and the scrunched-up paper took on a heart-like quality, with veins dangling. She said the only safe places were right at the top of the bridge or at home under the covers, far away from the sharks/hospital, where dangerous and frightening things happen. She was discharged later that week.

A return to the ward

Several months passed before Rosie was readmitted. In morning handover, the news was given that her operation had not been successful after all; the only choice was a heart transplant. There was a heavy sadness in the team as this was reported.

Art therapy continued but had to take place by her bedside on the ward, as Rosie needed constant monitoring. Rosie engaged with the art making but the excited, playful feeling had gone. She drew a train track with a black pen, scribbly and messy. I was reminded of the scrunched paper bridge/heart in her previous artwork, but this time there was no way across – it was a tangled, colourless loop. The failure of her journey home hung heavily in the air.

Rosie went on to make play dough snakes, rolling and squeezing the play dough into thin sausage shapes. Having seen these snakes, Mum later relayed a dream she had of a snake getting a 'Hickman line' put in. As the doctors and nurses tried to catch this snake, it was backed into a corner, rearing up and spitting venom. Mum spoke of her own anger at the situation they were in with so little control. I thought of the ferocity of a mother protecting her daughter from the dangerous intrusions piercing her little body. I imagined she wanted to be that snake, fending off the intrusions, but, like Rosie, she simply had no choice but to bear it; she herself was backed into a corner. Hall (2008, p. 161) speaks of the parents' impossible task of having to allow 'torturous treatment' to take place, caught in a dilemma between knowing that the treatment is needed and a desperation to protect their child from the intrusive procedures. In my countertransference I felt a despairing, painful, heavy feeling as I worked on the ward with Rosie. It was important for me to recognise these feelings as opposed to defending against them, as I had done on the PICU, and, in so doing, contain some of the distress and disappointment Rosie and Mum felt at being back on the ward with an uncertain future.

In the weeks that followed, Rosie had to attend several appointments and undergo tests at another children's hospital to assess her suitability for the transplant. This was understandably unsettling for Rosie. Mum explained to Rosie that the heart transplant was a bit like when the batteries ran out on one of Rosie's toys – they need replacing.

Understanding the countertransference

As Rosie's condition stabilised, her art therapy sessions returned to the small room off the ward. Rosie was increasingly aware of the need for a heart transplant. The toy that Mum had referred to when explaining the need for a transplant would often feature. A baddie would try to destroy this toy and attack it again and again. It was in the midst of one such attack that Rosie said, 'I'm on the urgent list to have a new heart.' What followed was a feeling of numbness in me. This countertransference was so powerful – sadness filled my body and the room and momentarily stopped my thinking. I felt paralysed with an anxiety I could feel in my stomach. I found it too hard to think about the reality and urgency of the situation as I struggled to respond to Rosie. The paralysis of my mind was reflected in Rosie's art making as she tried to make a person, but the body was 'not good enough' and was quickly abandoned. This further added to the pain in the room.

O'Shaughnessy (1988) refers to the importance of momentarily identifying with the child's projections, to contain and think what these are and reflect back an understanding of what is felt. My somatic countertransference of feeling numb momentarily stopped me making sense of Rosie's projections. Margarian notes, 'Somatic countertransference is positioned as embodied, physical manifestations in the therapist's body' (Margarian, 2014, p. 137). Sibbett (2005) talks of feeling 'fear in the pit of the stomach' and quotes Schaverien, who suggests that 'bodily countertransference is particularly difficult when working with a life-threatening illness' (Schaverien, 2002 in Sibbett, 2005, p. 238). Ross (2000, p. 453) refers to the 'physical responses aroused in the therapist'. My bodily countertransference was perhaps itself a communication from Rosie in giving me a sense of her shock and terror at the reality of the situation. Feeling this in such a real, bodily way, while initially paralysing, was important in 'bearing the unbearable' (Emanuel et al., 1990) and containing something for Rosie.

The anxiety was further heightened in the session before the Christmas break, when uncertainty prevailed. Rosie wished for the break to be over quickly and to get through it safely and survive. This anxiety was manifest in Rosie looking and checking the intravenous pump she was attached to through her Hickman line (which was pumping drugs into her and keeping her heart beating), something she had never done much of before. Rosie spoke of the transplant, saying they were 'waiting for one to be available', perhaps also communicating something of her own waiting for me to 'become available again' when I returned after Christmas. Again I felt helpless and overwhelmed with the enormity of the critical situation and guilt for making Rosie wait for my return. The urgency of the need for the transplant felt unbearable, and I overcompensated by bringing this to the session and asking about concrete events, such as whether she had been to the other hospital that week. I struggled to stay with the feelings that Rosie was bringing. In the transference I was perhaps the well sibling that was envied and allowed to go home; my guilt was also perhaps Rosie's unconscious guilt at tearing the family apart over another Christmas holiday because of her ill health.

It was at this time that supervision became a critical lifeline for me in understanding the countertransference; I needed someone to hold some of the helpless feelings. The unthinkable reality that a suitable heart might not become available in time was acknowledged. The fact that Rosie's journey might end in death (and that I had no control over this) was voiced and understood and in turn 'the movement of the unconscious within me was renewed' (Erel-Brodsky, 2014, p. 99). This movement was further enhanced by my own physical movement in the running I did as a way of processing the work and which enabled me to start thinking and feeling again. As my body moved so did my mind, and the 'un-nameable meaningless elements' projected into me (Caccia, 1984, p. 57) were somatically processed as I pounded the streets.

The clay family

In the session after the break, Rosie picked up a plastic heart-shaped cutter and said, 'We can make a person.' She decided that clay would be the best thing to use. The previous 3D objects that she had made were in play dough, and Rosie had seen how they dried and fell apart. The importance of making a strong figure seemed to occupy Rosie – she wanted this to be real. Rosie asked for my help as she was not keen on getting her hands dirty with the clay. I wonder also how much Rosie was avoiding messy, hard-to-control feelings as she felt unable to use the clay but wanted to tell me what to make. Instructing me what to make also allowed for some assertion of control, something so very lacking for Rosie at the time. I of course could have chosen not to help Rosie as I did and in so doing perhaps some of Rosie's frustrations and negative feelings could have come into the session. Skaife (1993, pp. 27–28) discusses the therapist's avoidance of an envious attack in work with people with physical health problems by trying to please the patient. Indeed Rosie's potential envy of my health and my own guilt at having abandoned Rosie in the break perhaps made me protect her from further painful and potentially useful feelings being brought into the session.

These clay figures (Figure 3.1) were important to Rosie. They featured frequently in the sessions at times when they needed repair and strengthening or to be wrapped up and put to bed safe and warm. They served as a concrete reminder of the therapeutic relationship and as a symbolic family held together in Rosie's box. One of the figures was a girl who was also four and was in hospital with lungs that did not work. The clay girl was able to miss her sister and think about the uncertainty of not knowing what would happen, unlike Rosie, who defended against sad feelings. In reality the family were split and separated most of the time, except in these figures. Here in therapy there was a fantasy that the family were together.

FIGURE 3.1   Clay family.

Goodies and baddies

Through Rosie's painting and play, it was possible to glimpse something of her inner world: her processing of the fight in which she was embroiled, her own powerlessness and anger at the tests and appointments and ultimately her failing heart, about which she had little control or understanding. This was most evident in Rosie's 'goodie' and 'baddie' play.

At times the baddies couldn't be stopped until something more powerful came along. Often only the 'goodies' got to go home. Rosie created a giraffe family out of plastic animals. This more robust family could be thrown around and put in muddy water – they would not break like the clay. The 'baddie giraffe' in the family would attack without notice, aggressively hitting out. I got a sense of what it felt like to wait without knowing when something would happen. Suddenly the giraffe would leap, enraged, onto my hand or throw a 'baddie' into the muddy water (Figure 3.2); Rosie was showing me her anger and frustration. This play was perhaps a safe way to attack me in the transference. I could represent the 'baddie' doctor or nurse and/ or the abandoning father or mother who had to go home or to work. Perhaps, at times, Rosie felt like the 'baddie giraffe' in the family and wanted to get rid of these feelings by throwing them in the muddy water to sink forever.

Intermittently she would ask, 'When do you think a heart will be available?' I had no answer. I could only think about her communications and name her frustrated feelings, allowing them to be symbolised and contained in the therapy.

Breaks once more became fraught with anxiety. Rosie would seem profoundly sad before a break, and the family struggled with the loss of routine. I thought of

FIGURE 3.2 Muddy water.

myself as the bad, abandoning therapist and worried about Rosie's survival. It was after one such break that Rosie made a 'baddie bath'. This was a small, clear plastic tub with a lid, inside which the baddie was submerged in thick brown paint/mud. I felt an immediate emotional response to this, as it seemed like a small coffin filled with mud. The 'baddie' was killed off. My initial thinking was for Rosie's own mortality and her sense of this in the break. However, I later reflected on the possible unconscious desire for Rosie to kill off her own bad feelings and ill body and become a 'goodie' with a 'good' heart so she could go home. The frustration of this situation was reflected by Rosie: 'It's funny, as the baddie changes the only way to stop him is to turn him into a goodie, but that's hard because every time you nearly get him, things change.' I wondered about Rosie's sense of persecution at her failing health and her wish for a magical solution that could stop the baddie changing.

The tray of brown liquid (Figure 3.2) remained a focus in the fight between the baddies and goodies. In this concrete container, Rosie began to tolerate mess more and took great pleasure in mixing the brown paint mixture. Rosie began to talk about her 'cheerful' and 'not cheerful' feelings towards colours, labelling the different coloured sand as 'cheerful' and 'not cheerful'. She would allow only the 'cheerful' coloured sand to go in the tray; the 'not cheerful' colours were not permitted. It was at this time that Rosie looked through her folder and separated her images into two folders. The small red cardboard folder had been used when she began therapy and, as the admission wore on, a larger plastic one was used. Rosie chose to put her initial images into the red folder and kept the rest in the large plastic folder she now had. The art therapy folder holds particular significance as a containing object in which patients can store their artwork confidentially (Seth-Smith, 1997). In making use of both her folders Rosie was able to split her experiences and get rid of her initial 'failed' admission and all that held. Importantly around this time Rosie was also able to bring her more negative feelings of not being cheerful in hospital to her art therapy.

Preparing for a journey

As the admission wore on Rosie began to draw trucks and vehicles. She had done this outside of therapy too; these trucks were filled with sandwiches and teddies in preparation for a long journey. In a parallel process, Mum would speak to me about preparing for when the transplant came and the journey they would take. She said she could think about the practicalities of the journey and packing up the things round their bed. She never mentioned what she couldn't think about, but I knew without words that it was the unthinkable pain of Rosie dying, the transplant not coming in time or failing, the dreadful loss for the other family who donated the heart and all that this entailed. Rosie and Mum would talk about what teddies she could bring and what would happen to the other things left behind. This was how they managed the enormity of what was happening. In therapy, Rosie continued to draw her trucks and each week they became more mobile (Figure 3.3).

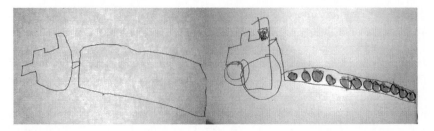

FIGURE 3.3   Rosie's trucks.

Mum and the wider hospital team reported that Rosie's mood was becoming low. She was more tearful in the hospital school and around procedures. I noticed her physical health was deteriorating – she was slower in her walking, her breathing seemed more laboured and the blue tinge to her lips and fingertips was more evident. I suggested offering Rosie an additional session of art therapy to help contain some of the difficult feelings and Rosie was eager to accept. The strain on the family and nursing team was evident, and the palpable fear of a heart not becoming available in time was growing with every week and was discussed with heightened anxiety by the team in morning meetings.

In the first additional session the following week, Rosie made a solid clay truck (Plate 5). Unlike Rosie's other trucks, this one had wheels and a full trailer. It looked like it was ready to go. She filled up the back with all the colours of the sand she had identified as 'cheerful' and 'not cheerful' all together in the trailer. Rosie touched and moulded the clay and used the cutter independently – no longer holding back from getting her hands messy as she had done at the start of therapy.

As we said goodbye, we spoke of how different it felt being able to say, 'See you Friday' instead of 'See you next week.' That evening, Rosie was called for her transplant. She was transferred to the other hospital and the new heart was transplanted in a lengthy operation.

The end of the journey

When Friday came, instead of having a session with Rosie, I (along with the rest of the team) waited anxiously to hear news. Feelings of elation and a slight sadness were present on the ward as we walked past the empty bed that Rosie had occupied for six months. We finally heard that the operation had been a success. Rosie was well enough to see me at the new hospital the week after her surgery.

I did not know what to expect. I rarely see children post-transplant, and I imagined a child similar to those I see on PICU, with wires and machines everywhere. When I turned up at the hospital, I was very surprised to see Rosie sitting up, bright with colour in her cheeks. The blue tinge of her lips had gone and she smiled at me in recognition.

Mum and Dad left the room and allowed Rosie her usual time with me. Rosie and I made a truck together out of play dough and we talked about journeys: the journey she had been on to the new hospital and the journey home, which Rosie thought would be 'weird and exciting'. It was a comfortable session. I held all that Rosie had been through and held it silently and thoughtfully, without the need to acknowledge anything of the enormity of what had happened.

Rosie spoke of the medication she was on 'because her new heart needed to be friends with her body'. I knew this would have come from Mum, but it made me think of the 'baddies' and the 'goodies' fighting in art therapy. This was now taking place inside Rosie.

Conclusion

This case illustrates how art therapy formed a crucial part of containing distress in a young hospitalised child. The extraordinary circumstances of waiting to find out if she could live filled Rosie with confusion, fear and anger. At times this was projected into me so strongly that I struggled to think past this life–and–death situation. As I was increasingly able to understand and process my countertransference, a containing mind was more available to Rosie and as the 'parents' protective containment' was continually pierced (Hall, 2008, p. 161), the containment and thinking in the therapeutic space were ever more important.

Rosie never returned to the ward to collect any of her artwork. I understood this as symbolic of her leaving behind part of the process and her bad, intolerable feelings. Klein describes the 'splitting off of aspects of the self which were feared as bad, usually through projective invasion into the object' (Klein, 1946, cited in Hinshelwood, 1989, p. 434). Rosie splitting off the bad, intolerable feelings into me and the art she made was a necessary defence in order for her to survive the critical situation. My role, as Judd says, was 'to bear the irreconcilable tension between the destructiveness of a serious illness in a child (or adolescent) and a need to understand the child's whole situation, even though our own feelings may shake us to the core' (Judd, 2010, p. 174). Art therapy provided containment for Rosie's intolerable thoughts and gave the 'not cheerful' feelings a space to be felt, understood and contained.

Acknowledgements

With thanks to Rosie and her family for kindly giving permission for me to use the images and clinical material for this chapter, and to Laura and Julia for proofreading in the early stages.

References

Bion, W.R. (1962) *Learning from experience*. London: William Heinemann, Medical Books.
Bion, W.R. (1963) *Elements of psycho-analysis*. London: Karnac Books.
Bissonnet, J. (2015) 'Intimations of mortality: Art therapy with children and young people with life-threatening and life-limiting illnesses', in Liebmann, M. and Weston, S. (eds.) *Art therapy with physical conditions*. London: Jessica Kingsley, pp. 240–255.

Caccia, O. (1984) 'Container and contained: Analysis of two ten-year-old boys'. *Journal of Child Psychotherapy*, 10, pp. 57–69.

Clifton, J. (2015) 'Receiving the dragon: A diabetic boy's experience of damage and repair in art therapy', in Liebmann, M. and Weston, S. (eds.) *Art therapy with physical conditions.* London: Jessica Kingsley, pp. 227–239.

Cohn, N. (1994) 'Attending to emotional issues on a special care baby unit', in Obholzer, A. and Roberts, V.Z. (eds.) *The unconscious at work: Individual and organisational stress in the human services.* London: Brunner-Routledge, pp. 60–66.

Dalley, T. (2000) 'Back to the future: Thinking about theoretical developments in art therapy', in Gilroy, A. and McNeilly, G. (eds.) *The changing shape of art therapy: New developments in theory and practice.* London: Jessica Kingsley, pp. 84–98.

Dartington, A. (1994) 'Where angels fear to tread: Idealism, despondency and inhibition of thought in hospital nursing', in Obholzer, A. and Roberts, V.Z. (eds.) *The unconscious at work: Individual and organisational stress in the human services.* London: Brunner-Routledge, pp. 101–109.

Emanuel, R., Colloms, A., Mendelsohn, A., Muller, H. and Testa, R. (1990) 'Psychotherapy with hospitalised children with leukaemia: Is it possible?' *Journal of Child Psychotherapy*, 16 (1), pp. 21–37.

Erel-Brodsky, H. (2014) 'Ghosts in the nursery: The secret thoughts of a sick child's parents'. *American Journal of Psychotherapy*, 68 (1), pp. 81–102.

Fischer, M. (2015) 'War zones: Art therapy with an eleven-year-old boy with Crohn's Disease', in Liebmann, M. and Weston, S. (eds.) *Art therapy with physical conditions.* Jessica London: Kingsley, pp. 210–226.

Hall, A. (2008) 'Trauma and containment in children's cancer treatment', in Rustin, M. and Bradley, J. (eds.) *Work discussion: Learning from reflective practice in work with children and families.* London: Karnac, pp. 148–164.

Henry, C. (2008) 'Working with sick children in a hospital setting', in Rustin, M. and Bradley, J. (eds.) *Work discussion: Learning from reflective practice in work with children and families.* London: Karnac, pp. 135–147.

Hill, J. (1986) 'A case on the paediatric ward'. *Inscape*, Winter, pp. 25–27.

Hinshelwood, R.D. (1989) *A dictionary of Kleinian thought.* London: Free Association Books.

Judd, D. (2010) 'Clinical commentary'. *Journal of Child Psychotherapy*, 36 (2), pp. 171–174.

Klein, M. (1946) 'Notes on some schizoid mechanisms'. *International Journal of Psychoanalysis*, 27, pp. 99–110; republished in Klein, M., Heinmann, S., Isaacs, S. and Riviere, J. (eds.) *Developments in psycho-analysis.* London: Hogarth, pp. 292–320.

Lillitos, A. (1990) 'Control, uncontrol, order and chaos: Working with children with intestinal motility problems', in Case, C. and Dalley, T (eds.) *Working with children in art therapy.* London: Routledge, pp. 72–88.

Malchiodi, C. (1999) *Medical art therapy with children.* London: Jessica Kingsley.

Margarian, A. (2014) 'A cross-cultural study of somatic countertransference: A brief overview'. *Asia Pacific Journal of Counselling and Psychotherapy*, 5 (2), pp. 137–145.

Menzies, I. (1959) 'The functioning of social systems as a defence against anxiety: A report on a study of the nursing service in a general hospital'. *Human Relations*, 13, pp. 95–121.

Menzies Lyth, I. (1988) *Containing anxiety in institutions: Selected essays, vol. 1.* London: Free Association Books.

Meyerowitz-Katz, J. (2003) 'Art materials and process – A place of meeting: Art psychotherapy with a four-year-old boy'. *Inscape*, 8 (2) pp. 60–69.

O'Shaughnessy, E. (1988) 'W. R. Bion's thinking and new techniques in child analysis', in Bott Spillius (ed.) *Melanie Klein today: New developments in theory and practice, volume 2: Mainly practice*, London: Brunner-Routledge, pp. 177–190 [originally published in *Journal of Child Psychotherapy* (1981) 7 (2), pp. 181–189, under the title 'A commemorative essay on W. R. Bion's theory on thinking'].

Ross, M. (2000) 'Body talk: Somatic countertransference'. *Psychodynamic Counselling*, November 6 (4), pp. 451–467.

Schaverien, J. (2002) *The dying patient in psychotherapy.* Basingstoke: Palgrave Macmillan.

Segal, B. (2010) 'Clinical commentary'. *Journal of Child Psychotherapy*, 36 (2), pp. 175–179.

Seth-Smith, F. (1997) 'Four views of the image', in Killick, K. and Schaverien, J. (eds.) *Art psychotherapy and psychosis.* London: Routledge, pp. 84–105.

Sibbett, C. (2005) 'An art therapist's experience of having cancer: Living and dying with the tiger', in Waller, D. and Sibbett, C. (eds.) *Art therapy and cancer care*, Maidenhead, UK: Open University Press, pp. 221–247.

Skaife, S. (1993) 'Sickness, health and the therapeutic relationship: Thoughts arising from the literature on art therapy and physical illness'. *Inscape*, Summer, pp. 24–29.

Skogstand, W. (2000) 'Working in a world of bodies: A medical ward', in Hinshelwood, R.D. and Skogstand, W. (eds.) *Observing organisations: Anxiety, defence and culture in health care.* London: Routledge, pp. 101–121.

4

'I DO DOTS . . .'

Art therapy with an Australian Aboriginal preschool child

Celia Conolly and Judy King

> *As she daubed the dots she said, 'I'm Aboriginal' (stumbling over the word Aboriginal). I replied, 'Yes, you're Aboriginal.' 'I do dots,' she told me. 'You do dots when you're Aboriginal.' She continued: 'You don't do dots when you're not Aboriginal.' She repeated this a number of times to make sure that I got it.*

Kara was a three-and-a-half-year-old Aboriginal girl who lived in inner-city Sydney. She attended a preschool situated in the midst of a Department of Housing complex, in which approximately 50 per cent of the children were Aboriginal. She was selected by the teachers to be part of a short-term art therapy project because of the instability and chaos in her home situation. The art therapist came to the preschool for weekly sessions that were held in a converted storeroom at the back of the preschool. Sessions were taped and transcribed and form the clinical material quoted in this chapter. The art therapy project was part of a research pilot study conducted by Gunawirra, a charity working with Aboriginal families in inner-city Sydney and rural New South Wales. Due to the nature of the wider research project, the therapists did not have any knowledge of the family history of the children involved.

Kara's opening sessions show clearly the key issues of identity, connection and 'otherness', and her ambivalence about her neediness, which arose in her therapy. While they are the issues of a particular little girl, living in Sydney in the early twenty-first century, they occur in a context of a long history of indigenous culture, and the trauma of colonisation. In order to understand her issues, it is necessary to know more about her context. The guiding principles of the National Strategic Framework for Aboriginal and Torres Strait Islander People's Mental Health and Social and Emotional Well-Being (2004–2009) were formulated to guide workers in this area, and two of them are particularly relevant to this chapter:

> (3) Culturally valid understandings must shape the provision of services and must guide assessment, care and management of Aboriginal and

Torres Strait Islander people's health problems generally, and mental health problems in particular.

(4)   It must be recognised that the experiences of trauma and loss, present since European invasion, are a direct outcome of the disruption to cultural wellbeing. Trauma and loss of this magnitude continue to have intergenerational effects.

(Dept. of Health and Ageing, 2004, p. 6)

A discussion will follow the opening two sessions of Kara's art therapy, demonstrating her issues, how she used the art therapy to explore these concerns, and the ways in which the art therapist responded to them. It will also examine these issues in their cultural context, according to the foregoing guidelines, so their full meaning can be understood and appreciated.

Coming together

As I entered the playroom to collect Kara the lights were down and all the other children were settling down for their 'quiet time'. The care worker encouraged her to get up, as 'it was time for her art.' Kara looked a little bemused. I felt she was unsure what this 'time' meant. I knelt down to be at her level while she got up, and her teacher put her long hair up into a ponytail. As Kara was led away from her bed with me, 'the stranger', I felt I was 'robbing her' of her quiet time. I also felt that the teacher tying up her hair as 'preparation' for her time seemed a little incongruous. It seemed to elevate the contrast with the cuddling, snoozing children surrounding her. She seemed so small and frail.

Kara was hesitant to begin therapy with a person she had not met before. She was initially quiet and restrained.

She walked slightly behind me as I led her into the room. I pointed out that we had felt tip pens and crayons as well as paints. I felt her hesitation as I welcomed her to the space and materials.

She immediately saw the paints and wanted some purple paint, naming it. I sat her down on the little chair by the little table and sat next to her. I noticed that she hadn't pulled herself closer to the table, so that there was initially 'an awkwardness' to her art making as she was so far from the table. I also experienced a sense of hesitancy — not wanting to step in too quickly, allowing her choice and control. She picked up a paintbrush, holding it awkwardly, and tentatively painted with the dry brush laden with purple paint in the corner of the piece of paper.

Kara was initially very unsure about what to make of this unfamiliar situation with this new person. She was right to be unsure about whether the therapist would be a safe person for her, and whether they could connect. Sitting away from the desk showed her reluctance to come close, holding her distance, as it were. The gap between Kara and the table seemed consistent with the therapists' countertransference responses – the gap between the 'big' white therapist and the 'small' Aboriginal girl.

Brightly she asked me to 'put some pink in here', nodding towards a section of the palette. I replied that we did not have pink but we could make pink paint together. (It was at this point that I felt she started to become a little more relaxed.) I asked if she wanted to pour out the paint or whether she wanted me to. She nodded for me to, so I poured the white paint and then the red into the same portion of the palette under her direction. She took a fresh brush to mix the two together. She appeared to enjoy the swirl of the red and white as she mixed it together, smiling up at me and giving a little giggle. 'We're making pink,' she said (Plate 6).

As she rinsed her brush in the water she excitedly said, 'See, I made pink,' and looking up, 'I made pink in here.' She seemed proud that she had made her own pink. I agreed with her, repeating back what she had said. She then said, 'I don't need red anymore because I made pink.'

Kara was so excited to have mixed the paints successfully. The therapist noted how she enjoyed the swirling and mixing, smiling and giggling at the activity. Together she and her therapist had 'mixed' together, successfully. She no longer needed to be separate, like the red paint, because they had come together, like the colours. This is a little girl for whom 'being together' is very important, despite her initial hesitation. The therapist had a strong maternal countertransference reaction, making her consider Winnicott's (1958) concept of 'primary maternal preoccupation' – as if this little girl was drawing her in, needing the therapist to be deeply focused on her and her mind.

'Otherness' and difference

She then asked, 'Can I do pink now?' on the paper, and she used her pink-laden brush to paint just above the purple she had painted earlier. She then started daubing dots across the page, working out from the two patches she had started in one corner. I felt that this was almost a visual representation of her settling into this new situation with this stranger, as the art making ventured from its initial first 'safe corner' (Figure 4.1).

At this point I commented on how far her chair was from the table, offering to move her closer in. So I asked her to stand and together we moved the chair closer. Once she was settled back down she started painting her dots again, totally engrossed with the process.

Coming together also brought with it a strong sense of difference and 'otherness'. Recognising that Kara was now relaxing into the therapy situation, the therapist felt able to encourage her to move closer to the table, symbolically encouraging her to come closer to her and the therapy. However, the therapist was simultaneously aware of her role as a 'white' worker, 'helping' an Aboriginal person, with all the connotations of colonialism, paternalism and misguided aid that have historically

FIGURE 4.1   Exploring the art materials and space.

accompanied 'helping' Aboriginal people (Jenkins, 2015). The therapist brought these feelings of 'difference' with her to the sessions:

Interestingly, even before the art therapy sessions began I had many thoughts and feelings that I had not had with other client groups. I was acutely aware of being a white, middle-class, educated 'helper', and accordingly I sought out an Aboriginal elder to inform my cultural awareness prior to beginning the therapy. I also investigated different courses to educate myself about Aboriginal customs and historical context. The thought of working with this client group evoked my awareness of losses within my own personal situation. With reflection this may have been because of my awareness of the widespread losses within the Aboriginal community. I lived in the same suburb, and so this was my community too, yet the differences between my little terrace house and the tower blocks where I was working with Kara also crystallised my feelings of difference.

The themes of 'otherness' and difference were present throughout the therapy. Kara herself had pointed out, 'You don't do dots when you're not Aboriginal,' no doubt acutely aware of the therapist's otherness. The 'gap' at the table was a gap between their worlds. And yet the therapist was also very aware of Kara's need for connection with her, and they shared a strong sense of togetherness. Kara had a curiosity, almost despite herself, to explore not just her inner world but also their shared world.

Identity and belonging

After some time, as she ventured across the page, she looked up and told me, 'My Mummy's name is Roberta.' 'Ah, Roberta, that's a lovely name, isn't it?' She nodded in agreement and then there was a pause. Wanting to follow this lead of a more personal introduction I then said, 'and your name is Kara, and my name is Judy.' Almost over the top of me she said excitedly, 'My sister's name is Josie.' She wanted me to know about her family. This was important to her.

This kind of introduction is a vital part of Aboriginal identity, which is embedded in relationship to family, community and land. It is about identifying where each person belongs. 'Demonstrating where one is from, what "country" and group/ people they belong to, is critical to any Indigenous person in their self-identity and when introducing oneself to other Indigenous people' (Dudgeon, Wright, Paradies, Garvey, and Walker, 2014, p. 5). Hence, Kara is telling her therapist where she belongs – her mother's and her sister's names are part of *her* identity. While individuals in Western culture will often introduce themselves in relation to their family and home, this is different to the sense of identity in Aboriginal 'belonging' culture.

Kara continued doing her dots, while mixing various colours (as described earlier):

As she daubed the dots she said, 'I'm Aboriginal' (stumbling over the word Aboriginal). I replied, 'Yes, you're Aboriginal.' 'I do dots,' she told me, and 'You do dots when you're Aboriginal.' She continued: 'You don't do dots when you're not Aboriginal.' She repeated this a number of times to make sure I got it.

Kara was making very sure that the therapist knew her Aboriginal identity. She was proudly locating herself within her community and her heritage. She understood that this was an important distinction between her and her therapist, discussed earlier as the 'gap'.

Understanding concepts like these is a vital component of working therapeutically with Aboriginal children, as discussed in the beginning of this chapter (Department of Health and Ageing, 2004). Therapists from Western cultures have to suspend their concept of individualised identity, and think in terms of a communal identity, or an 'identity of belonging'. Attitudes to the concept of boundaries and connection are modified: I am not 'me' in a Western sense – I am me as part of something bigger. The art therapist was acutely aware of this profound difference in thinking about relating and relationships. She felt that she had so much to learn, not just about this little girl but about her whole culture. The experience engendered both curiosity and a strong sense of 'otherness' and difference.

The other way in which Kara was expressing and exploring her identity was through her dot painting. There is much controversy over the role of dots within

Aboriginal art. This centres on the way in which, over the past forty-five years, a traditional form of expression for ceremonies in a particular region of the Northern Territory has become commercialised 'art' (Golvan, 1992). Now, Aboriginal designs on Western materials are used across the country; Geczy explains how, despite the controversy, dot painting 'has come to have talismanic significance for Aboriginal art and artists well beyond the boundaries of the Papunya region' (Geczy, 2013, p. 164). Coleman argues that Aboriginal art performs a function similar to an 'insignia', describing how, in contemporary culture, 'what appears to be important to many Aboriginal people is the way in which their art functions to provide them with a sense of identity' (Coleman, 2004, p. 28). While this is a complex and sensitive issue within Aboriginal communities, what matters here is that this little girl identifies dot painting as a defining feature of *her* Aboriginal identity, and an important way to differentiate between herself and non-Aboriginals, including her non-Aboriginal art therapist.

From her initial squiggles in the corner of the page, she was, as the art therapist felt, becoming braver as she moved across the page, expressing her identity in her artwork. She is an Aboriginal girl, and she could move across the page, towards her art therapist, as a proud Aboriginal person. She could locate herself in her culture, and hence feel stronger about who she is and where she belongs, at least in this therapy room.

She asked for more colours and we spent some time 'mixing colours'. At one point she asked me to mix 'as her arms were tired'. She then discovered the crayons, taking some for herself and giving me two: 'This is a couple for you.' I kept them in my hand for the duration of the rest of the session.

It is significant that this section follows directly from her expression of identity. When she was able to state clearly who she was, and where she belonged, then she could properly begin to 'mix' with her therapist. It appeared that she was feeling 'held' by the therapist (Conolly and King, 2015), and she gave her the 'couple' of crayons to hold — as if she was communicating her understanding that her art therapist was holding the two of them as a 'couple' in her mind. They had already had one experience of 'mixing' towards the beginning of the session, but now that the 'proper' introductions had been made, she could let herself be together with this person who was here to think about her and her mind. Given her culture of identity being part of something bigger, rather than an individual, the request could be thought of as asking the therapist to 'be her arms', as if they were actually one person.

Separation

Kara's response to separation highlighted how fragile her sense of togetherness could be, and how overwhelmed she felt by the prospect of being left:

I reminded her that we would have to be finishing in a little while. Straight away she said, 'I live across the road, at number 2,' gesturing with her arm to the building we could see through the glass door. I replied, 'Oh, you live across the road there.' 'No,' she said, 'on Sykes Street.' 'Ah,' I said, 'you live at number 2, Sykes Street.' 'That's where I live,' she replied. 'Yes. I live there with my mum and Josie,' she continued. 'Ah, you live with your mum and your sister?' 'Yes, she's my sister.' This was the second time she had wanted to share this with me.

Interestingly her response to separation was immediately to locate herself again, and to remind her therapist (and herself) where she lived, with whom, and where she belonged. It seemed that this important aspect of Aboriginal culture was giving her a sense of security, reassuring her that she did belong. Her worries about being separated could be managed by reminding herself and others that although she and her therapist were separating, she belonged, and had a place (at number 2, Sykes Street, with her mum and sister).

Again I reminded her that we had only five minutes left. As the session was drawing to a close, she continued pouring paint into the spaces in the palette. She no longer needed me to pour for her. She turned her shoulder away from me so that she had her back to me as she slowly poured the black paint into every well. I understood that her body language and her actions were telling me that she did not want the session to finish.

I then suggested we clean her hands 'now that we are finished'. After we had washed her hands in the soapy bucket and dried with the towel she asked, 'Are we finished now?' I replied, 'Yes, we have finished. I will come back again next week and we can spend some time together again.' She then immediately grabbed the green paint and slowly poured into each of the wells in the palette, on top of the black dollops she had just poured (Figure 4.2).

FIGURE 4.2 'Overfilling palette, overflowing feelings'.

The separation was so obviously difficult for Kara. She had to turn her back on the therapist, as she probably felt the therapist was doing to her by finishing their time together, where they had 'mixed' and connected. And then she had so much pouring to do – just like a person who starts talking rapidly and voluminously when it is time to leave. The paint came pouring out as if there was so much she needed to say and do and show. Similarly, the empty bottles showed how worried she was that she would feel empty when they were no longer connected. Whilst not unhappy at the end of the session, she could not, however, say goodbye to her therapist. Even though this was only a first session, she had communicated to her therapist that separation was painful.

Context

The themes of Kara's first session were clearly related to identity, connection, and 'otherness'. They are, of course, part of her own personal story, but they are also relevant to the story of her people. History shows us that, so often, trauma experienced by individuals of one generation can be passed on to the next generation, as adults struggle with their own trauma while still doing their best to bring up their children (Fonagy and Target, 2008, Sachs, 2013). For the Aboriginal people, this is exacerbated, as the damage was done not just to individuals but also to communities. Whole communities were forced to leave their own land (to which they had a deep spiritual attachment), to live on government reserves or religious missions, which were in essence detention centres aimed to remove their culture and heritage. This was followed by government policies of 'assimilation', in which Aboriginal children were forcibly removed from their families, especially if they had lighter-coloured skin (the 'Stolen Generations'), and frequently put into institutions without any family or personal caregivers, so that they lost connection with their personal and cultural histories and traditions. The underlying assumption was that Aboriginal people were inferior to white people, and could join white society only if they became 'white', which meant losing their people, culture, way of life, and spirituality (Human Rights and Equal Opportunity Commission, 1997).

Generations were traumatised as family and cultural ties were broken, in what was a 'belonging' culture, where who you belong to and the land you belong to are a vital part of your identity (as can be seen for Kara in her repeated introductions of her family and home); 'land was not owned; one belonged to the land' (Dudgeon et al., 2014, p. 4). Aboriginal people have a *relationship* with their land (country), in a deeply spiritual sense, which is fundamentally connected to the sense of self. Colonisation forcibly removed Aboriginal people from their country with no concern for the deep spiritual and psychological damage that dispossession caused. It is in this context that the National Frameworks guidelines (described earlier) become relevant for all mental health workers, including art therapists. The intergenerational effects of two centuries of trauma to a people must be considered when thinking about one little girl's art therapy. The themes of her sessions make sense in the light of generations whose very identity was under attack, while their connections were broken, their families torn apart, and they were forced to live as 'outsiders'.

'It's a lot': Will my neediness overwhelm you?

Kara's second session reflected the overwhelming nature of her neediness, and her ambivalence about it. She spent time filling up the wells on the palette with paint and made them overflow, often emptying the bottles of paint all onto the palette, even though it was already very full and/or overflowing. This was in contrast to her attempts at times to keep things clean – wiping paint when it went onto her hand, or carefully cleaning her brush in between colours. It seemed that she was compensating for her worries about overwhelming the therapist by occasionally holding back and trying to keep things under control.

She then poured paint into the next well, again almost to the top. I asked, 'Is it going to go over the edge?' 'No,' she simply replied. The paint then slurped over the edge and she said, 'Uh oh,' and we both watched together. As she got to the end of the jar, I said, 'And that's the end of the blue.' She then picked up the white jar, which was filled right up, and as she opened it she said, 'It's a lot.'

Perhaps it was her feelings that were 'a lot', and in particular her needy feelings, consistent with the end of the previous session. Perhaps the overflowing paint was her overflowing neediness that she became aware of when she had someone to sit and be present with her, and her thoughts and feelings. The therapist's focused concentration provides a space for the child to feel known, both psychically and emotionally, as the child is 'contained by (my) attentive attunement to his experience' (Meyerowitz-Katz, 2003, p. 66).

After pouring glue ('gue') on her painting,

She then asked if we could make 'gue' water, so she poured glue from the tin into the blue water. The glue solidified in the water and made 'flower' shapes as we squirted together. It made patterns in the water and then sank to the bottom. We sat together, watching these patterns wonderingly.

In this moving encounter, the two sat there wonderingly, joined by the common experience of curiosity and thinking. Isserow (2008) describes the importance of 'looking together' in the development of the therapeutic relationship. In this case, it was as if the therapist's capacity to sit with Kara's overflowing neediness opened up a new possibility for 'looking together': then they could look together at the 'gue' and wonder and think. Looking and thinking together represented a 'third' that had been allowed into the relationship and the therapeutic space. It made the therapist reflect upon the necessity of sharing 'thinking', in bringing together Aboriginal and White people (San Roque, 2006).

An interesting segment illustrates Kara's ambivalence about her neediness during this session. She began her work by painting a figure, which she then systematically covered up (Plate 7).

She started to paint a face quite quickly as I sat beside her and watched. A couple of times I said, 'Ah' wonderingly as I could see the face appear. She pointed out 'that's the eyes' and then 'I made the man,' which I simply reflected back to her.

She did not refer to the work again, but instead began to cover it, layer by layer.

She got up and picked out the big jar of glue. I pointed out that this was glue for sticking things and she continued: 'Can I use the gue?' She then picked out a large piece of pink tissue paper; she again delightedly informed me, 'It's pink,' and laid it on top of the other sheet. I said, 'You're putting it on top of your blue man,' and she pressed the tissue on top of the wet paint, deliberately pressing over the small image on the big page. She pasted the glue on the same spot.

(And soon after . . .)

She asked for a spoon. She then used the back of the spoon to spread the glue over the same spot on the tissue paper. There were then different coloured paints spooned onto this same spot, layer upon layer, on top of where the man had been. Each layer was smoothed over from one side to the other. She was quite particular about cleaning the spoon in between each colour.
She then started to use the spoon to ladle water onto the paper. Again she spread over the same spot with the back of the spoon, so that part of the page got wetter and wetter. There was something soothing about her movements, which had an almost meditative quality.

She was quite deliberately covering the artwork, and using a repetitive, soothing action, reminiscent of a baby self-soothing or a parent patting a baby. It seems as though she was soothing her own deep feelings, as if part of herself that had been acknowledged in the picture then had to be covered over, layer by layer, lovingly put to rest for the moment. However, when she came to add water to the activity, she was moving into different territory, from soothing to destroying. The glue and paint were less impactful, but the water added a new dimension of damaging the layers, different to her soothing.

She then took the wet cloth she had used for cleaning the wall, cut it, and lay half of it on top of the layers.
It was awkward for her to lay it on top as the edges sagged down. 'I can't put it on top of it,' she said. I supported the weight and together we placed it down. She patted on top of the cloth and exclaimed, 'Look it's coming through!' as the glue and paint seeped through the perforations in the cloth. This pleased her.
She then took one end and slowly rolled it up, seemingly delighted as it picked up white glue and blue paint. As she rolled it back I said, 'There's the man' as he appeared from under the sodden tissue paper. She replied, 'That's a ripped one now,' as the paper had torn a little (Figure 4.3).

FIGURE 4.3 'The man' revealed, and exposed.

She had worked hard to cover her work, but also been compelled to work hard to uncover it, especially as she added water and a cloth to the process. Her response showed that she didn't want to see it; she didn't want to expose that vulnerable part of herself. The aim was not to uncover; rather the point of the exercise was the process of pushing the limits of the paper to see how far it could hold out, and then to damage it. We can surmise that she was very aware of her own neediness, and was unsure that her carer would be able to withstand her demands (comparable to the rubbing). We could wonder if she feared that she would damage her carers if she revealed just how needy she felt. So instead she cleaned, in order to control her neediness, which felt so big and messy and dangerous.

Separation – a painful feeling

The ending of Session 2 aroused her feelings of neediness again, and a lot of pouring and overflowing followed.

I informed her that we had ten minutes left. She replied, 'I'm nearly done.' At this point she started pouring red paint from the 'almost empty jar' into the blue jar. More purple was poured into the palette as it was almost overflowing. It seemed more feelings needed to emerge.

Following this her art therapist cleaned her hands for her, but Kara was compelled again to keep them dirty, to show that her feelings about the ending were
overflowing:

*She immediately hovered her hands on top of the paint-filled palette and looked up at
me expectantly and giggled. I could see she wanted to put her hands into the paint and,
after that brief moment of checking in, she did and giggled again. She then plonked her
hands on the paper to the side of 'the man' and swirled from side to side. I reminded her
that we were 'finishing soon' – 'finishing nearly', she repeated back. We washed her hands
again in the bucket and dried them. I got up, as if to leave, and again she put her hands
in the paint.*

Kara did not want to separate when she had been so well 'mixed' with her therapist. Her 'messy' feelings came out when faced with separation and loss.

Conclusion

Kara knew about belonging and identity, because she had the benefit of her culture to offer her these valuable experiences. Her responses to the art materials
can be understood in the context of her 'belonging culture', which she so clearly
demonstrated to the therapist, painting dots and telling her, 'I do dots . . . you
don't do dots when you're not Aboriginal.' For her, the mixing of the paints was
a source of great pleasure, as the paints ceased being their individual selves, and
came together to belong to something 'better'. Her pleasure in mixing mirrored
the connection she developed with her therapist, as they came to 'mix together'
in their therapy time.

Despite this, however, she still suffered from intense neediness and separation anxiety. She demonstrated that she had so many overwhelming needs, as she
poured paint into a full palette time after time, emptying bottle after bottle of paint,
especially as the session was ending. She showed how much she had inside her that
needed to come out, and how empty she would feel when she lost her connection
with the therapist. By working so hard to cover up her 'man' painting, she showed
how much she needed her defences to smooth things over, to clean up the messy
feelings, and to cover them over, layer upon layer. But she was also compelled to
rub at the layers, and work upon them so hard that they were destroyed – exposing both her intense needs and, simultaneously, her guilt and fear that she might
damage her carers with the intensity of her neediness. This has to be considered in
the context of the needs of a people who have experienced so much dislocation
and generations of broken attachments. It would not be unreasonable to surmise
that unresolved issues of intense neediness, with fear of overwhelming an already
burdened and traumatised parent, could be passed down from one generation to
the next.

This would be a possible explanation for Kara's response to separation. She struggled to let go at the end of the sessions, and when she did it had to be by turning away and denying connection. We can only wonder about the trauma suffered by her family, and their unmet needs and the lack of support for them as a family. In traditional Aboriginal communities, there was always an attachment 'safety net' for children – if the parent could not look after a child, another adult relative ('aunties and uncles') would always be available. But the breakup of communities and families that has been part of the trauma of colonisation has led to families and caregivers being isolated from their relatives, as well as their culture and land. The safety net for children and families has been removed. In the context of all the other trauma suffered by Aboriginal people, losing contact with relatives who would help to support children (while the adults struggle with their own trauma) would be yet an extra source of trauma (Dudgeon et al., 2014).

Kara's art therapist had approached these sessions with a sense of her own lack of cultural knowledge and an awareness of her own 'otherness'. She was intensely aware of this little girl's need to assert her Aboriginal identity, and the huge gap that lay between them, and their worlds and cultures. However, by remaining present to both her own personal responses and her countertransference experiences in the sessions with Kara, the therapist could connect with her, and was not daunted by the little girl's need to overwhelm everything with pouring and emptying. She withstood it all through all their sessions, allowing space for thinking and for feelings to be 'played with' and named.

At the conclusion of her short number of sessions the staff at her preschool said that Kara had shown noticeable improvement with her speech, confidence, and expression of emotions, and they confirmed a year later that the results had been long-lasting. Like the two crayons which Kara gave the therapist to hold in her hand for almost a whole session, this little girl needed the art therapist to hold in mind both their togetherness and their otherness. From this space, she could begin to emerge with a stronger sense of her identity as Kara, an Aboriginal girl.

Notes

The art therapist was Judy King, and her work was presented to Celia Conolly at weekly supervision sessions.
All identifying material has been changed to preserve confidentiality.

References

Coleman, E.B. (2004) 'Aboriginal art and identity: Crossing the border of law's imagination', *Journal of Political Philosophy*, 12 (1), pp. 20–40.

Conolly, C. and King, J. (2015) 'The importance of being contained: Kylie, for whom nothing could be held', in Tracey, N. (ed.) *Transgenerational trauma and the Aboriginal preschool child: Healing through intervention*. Lanham, MD: Rowman and Littlefield, pp. 153–172.

Department of Health and Ageing (2004). *Social and emotional well-being framework, a national strategic framework for Aboriginal and Torres Strait Islander mental health and social and emotional well-being (2004–2009)*. Canberra: Australian Government Publishing Service.

Dudgeon, P., Wright, M., Paradies, Y., Garvey, D. and Walker, I. (2014) 'Aboriginal social, cultural and historical contexts', in Dudgeon, P., Milroy, H. and Walker, R. (eds.) *Working together: Aboriginal and Torres Strait Islander mental health and wellbeing principles and practice.* (2nd ed.). Canberra: Australian Government, pp. 25–42.

Fonagy, P. and Target, M. (2008) 'Attachment, trauma and psychoanalysis', in Jurist, E., Slade, A. and Bergner, S. (eds.) *Mind to mind: Infant research, neuroscience, and psychoanalysis.* New York, NY: Other Press, pp. 15–49.

Geczy, A. (2013) 'Who owns dots? or spirituality for the highest bidder, or can you buy an aura?' *Contemporary Visual Art+Culture Broadsheet*, 42 (3), pp. 163–165.

Golvan, C. (1992) 'Aboriginal art and the protection of indigenous cultural rights'. *European Intellectual Property Review*, 7, pp. 227–232.

Human Rights and Equal Opportunity Commission (1997). *Report of the National Inquiry into the separation of Aboriginal and Torres Strait Islander children from their families.* Retrieved from: https://www.humanrights.gov.au/publications/bringing-them-home-report-1997

Isserow, J. (2008) 'Looking together: Joint attention in art therapy'. *International Journal of Art Therapy: Formerly Inscape*, 13 (1), pp. 34–42.

Jenkins, S. (2015) 'Rehabilitating psychology in Australia: The journey from colonising agent to cultural broker'. *Psychotherapy and Politics International*, 13 (2), pp. 115–128.

Meyerowitz-Katz, J. (2003) 'Art material and processes – A place of meeting: Art psycho-therapy with a four-year-old boy'. *International Journal of Art Therapy: Formerly Inscape*, 8 (2), pp. 60–69.

Sachs, A. (2013) 'Intergenerational transmission of massive trauma: The Holocaust', in Yellin, J. and Epstein, O. (eds.) *Terror within and without: Attachment and disintegration: Clinical work on the edge.* London: Karnac Books, pp. 21–38.

San Roque, C. (2006) 'On Tjukurrpa, painting up, and building thought'. *Social Analysis*, 50 (2), pp. 148–172.

Winnicott, D.W. (1958) 'Primary maternal preoccupation', in *Through paediatrics to psycho-analysis: Collected papers.* New York: Routledge, pp. 300–305.

PART 2

Family and dyad art therapy with infants, toddlers and their parents

5

TRANSITIONS

Moving from infancy to latency through symbolisation and the acquisition of language

Tessa Dalley and Jen Bromham

Oliver

Figure 5.1 was the first image that three-year-old Oliver made in art therapy (Figure 5.1). He was trying to communicate his thoughts and feelings but did not have the words to express them. The image shows his tentative steps in mark making and exploration made by dipping the feet of a toy lion into the blue paint that he had insisted his mother pour out for him. This felt like the beginning of his journey towards relational independence: he became excited by his actions and consequently found the courage to move the blue marks closer to himself.

Jointly written by an art therapist and her supervisor, this chapter describes how both visual and verbal symbolisation evolved in Oliver's therapeutic work and how his language development progressed. Through the process of supervision, both the child and the therapist were able to find their respective voices. Oliver's difficulty in express-ing himself was echoed in the therapist's experience of finding it difficult to find the language to express her thoughts in his sessions and in her supervision. Understand-ing her own struggle to find words through supervision supported the therapist's and Oliver's capacities to communicate new understandings with each other.

Referral

Oliver was referred by his health visitor to a specialist parent–infant project within an existing under-fives service in a Sure Start children's centre. The parent–infant project was established in 2010 by two art therapists. The original focus of the art therapy service was to provide emotional support to mothers and babies up to two years old. This remit was subsequently extended to working with children under five years old due to demand from referrers, who included health visitors, other health and social care professionals and children centre staff (Bromham and

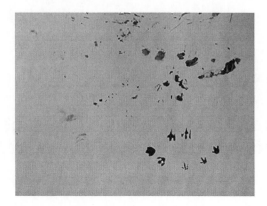

FIGURE 5.1 Dipping! Blue!

Jasieniecka, 2013). By placing art making as a focus for the development of the relationship between mother and child, the art therapy intervention was an adaptation of the Parent Infant Project (PIP) model at the Anna Freud Centre, London (Baradon et al., 2005).

Oliver lived with both his parents and was the younger of two surviving children. The first baby born into the family died five years prior to Oliver's birth; his seven-year-old brother was functioning well. Oliver's health visitor was concerned about his significant speech and language difficulties, poor eye contact, prolonged tantrums and feeding problems, with an unconfirmed diagnosis of autistic spectrum disorder (ASD). Oliver's mother was resistant to the possibility of ASD and had secured speech and language therapy for him. In addition Oliver presented with separation difficulties as his struggle to progress developmentally – in particular, in language acquisition – had adversely affected his attempts to master his world and take steps to move away from his mother. This process was fraught as attempts to communicate frustrations, distress and anxiety were channelled through a repertoire of regressive behaviour, sounds and bodily gestures.

Over the course of his therapy, Oliver was diagnosed with oral dyspraxia. Although he knew what he wanted to say, he had problems saying sounds, syllables and words due to difficulty coordinating the necessary muscular movements. This helped to explain why his efforts to make sounds often sounded back to front and why he focused on part sounds of words. The diagnosis meant that it was important to hold in mind that while encouraging Oliver to say things for himself, his mouth was part of the barrier to language. While he seemed to comprehend the therapist's words, his responses were hard to hear and make sense of.

Language development

Oliver's communication difficulties were complex, and were compounded by a variety of physiological, emotional and environmental factors, including the unspoken trauma of the death in the family. In order to develop language, as he attempted to move from preverbal to verbal levels of development, Oliver needed a dependable carer to receive and accept his signals and communication, and to provide psychological explanations and emotional labels for his experiences (Nelson, 1990). As Magagna (2012) explains, once the capacity for speech has developed, words create a bridge as a way of communicating states of mind. In what could be described as a 'broken bridge', certain interactions between mother and child can influence things to 'get better' or 'to become more difficult'. If the parents' own experiences impede sensitive understanding, the infant then relies on his own primitive mechanisms of defence, which constrain cognitive and emotional development. 'To be most effective, therapists and parents must not only provide opportunities for young children to express their understanding, but must draw inferences from non-verbal behaviour and translate it into verbal terms' (Gaensbaur, 2000, p. 383).

Assessment

An assessment, which included an initial meeting to which both parents were invited, and four mother-child dyad sessions were carried out by the art therapist. With the knowledge of the loss of their first child in mind, the therapist decided to offer the parents an initial appointment without Oliver. She felt that it was important to understand the impact of this significant event on the whole family history and to hear more about Oliver's presenting difficulties. Only his mother attended as his father worked abroad for many months each year. Mother presented as still grieving for her deceased child and struggled to put into words her experience of trauma and loss. She was anxious about Oliver because of his babyish behaviour and inability to speak like other three-year-olds.

Mother's grief and her inability to find words became the focus of attention in supervision. The 'ghosts in the nursery' (Fraiberg et al., 1980) seemed present in the room. We wondered if Oliver could not find his own words as so much in the family was not spoken about. As he was not present at the meeting, this seemed to be a repetition, albeit unconsciously, of talking about traumatic experiences without him, not giving him the opportunity to communicate his own sense of loss and trauma, and thus rendering him silent, the representation of a 'broken bridge'. The therapist's response to her own difficulty in articulating her feelings in this session suggested some early resonance with the communication difficulties within the family. It seemed that careful and considered dyad work would be helpful for mother and son to start to put the impact of loss, trauma and intergenerational silence into words rather than relying on incoherent sounds and gestures (Wajnryb, 2002). The absence of the father and how this may, in some way, have perpetuated the silence and lack of Oedipal resolution were also noted.

Dyad sessions

Oliver was an angelic-looking child, small for his age, with blonde hair and blue eyes. He had very poor eye contact, and the therapist's initial response was feeling somewhat at a loss about how to connect with him as he was so clingy with his mother. His only words were Mama, Dada and something similar to the sound of his brother's name. He made sounds and grunts to express his needs which his mother would mirror and interpret. This left them enmeshed together in a sym-biotic world, using a coded language to the exclusion of others. It was noticeable how Oliver relied on his mother to speak for him. Showing the therapist one of his scribbles he said, 'bahbah', which his mother translated as 'batman'.

At first, Oliver was carried into the children's centre building by his mother, but in subsequent sessions, he came along holding her hand, with his 'mamas' and a dummy in his mouth. Oliver made use of his comfort blankets ('mamas') as if they were toys, but he soon dropped them in order to play. He chose a family of toy lions and, sitting at the table with his mother, he painted them and some cars the colour blue, making indistinct vocal sounds. While the therapist felt confused and pushed out, his mother seemed to clearly understand his communication. She said that blue meant that Oliver was thinking about his father's car. The painting of the toys and subsequently the washing of them in the sink were a core element in Oliver's repeti-tive play as he insisted that his mother do it for him. His words 'do it!' made his demands clear, while the therapist commented on how much he wanted his mother to do things for him; how he wanted the colour blue to remember and be like his daddy and also wanted to rid himself of blue and have his mother all to himself.

Throughout the four-week assessment, it became clear how Oliver struggled with articulating his difficult emotions and predicament. However, hopeful signs of genuine progress emerged in his play and art making. This suggested that he was responding well to the therapist's interventions: mirroring his communications, naming his play with objects – thus extending their communication – and laying the foundation for a more affective language. It seemed that he experienced her as receiving his messages within the reciprocal relationship where words gave mean-ing to their shared experience. In this sense she became a developmental object who could transform his distress and facilitate shifts to this next stage of commu-nication and symbolisation (Hurry, 1998). As the process also involved collabora-tion with his mother, in which she could explore the relationship with her son, a tentative working alliance was established with the therapist and she agreed to the recommendation for further weekly dyad work.

Symbol formation

Segal (1957) describes how a baby will experience the transformation of bod-ily sensations and expressions of distress, crying, body gestures and psychosomatic responses into meaningful communications by a thoughtful parent (Bion, 1962, McDougall, 1989). With repeated experience of this process, the infant develops an understanding that he too has a space inside for containing and thinking thoughts, establishing a good internal object.

> As the good object is more securely established within the ego the fear of bad objects and anxieties around the loss or inaccessibility of good objects can

be displaced onto the external world and symbolic representations of these anxieties become possible (Segal, 1957).

(Magagna 2012: p. 288)

In the presence of the therapist as a good object, working together in this way permitted the start of difficult emotions, such as Oliver's frustrations with his mother, being communicated and thought about.

Alvarez (2010) points out that there is still a lot to learn about steps in the development of symbolic capacities. For example, there may be a tendency in traumatised children to create drawings that take the form not of symbolic representations but of representations that are not genuinely symbolic (Moore, 2004). Despairing children, such as Oliver, may arrive at this transitional phase marked by symbolic emptiness and desolation. When working with Oliver, the therapist held in mind that however negative or repetitive the content of his play, any use of his imagination, capacity to play or use of art materials implied some measure of hope.

> Enactment through play and action in therapy can bring back the story of the self overwhelmed by subjective states which were never given words or thoughts by the self, but were instead avoided by emotional numbing and avoidance through not thinking (i.e., dissociation and splitting off of this part).
>
> *(Alvarez, 2010, p. 101)*

Treatment

During their weekly dyad sessions Oliver continued to make good use of the therapist's interventions. Her close observations, attentiveness to small changes and countertransference-based responses enabled his confusion, worries and complex communication through his images to be thought about. Oliver's play began to change as repetitive patterns evolved to include the therapist in some interactive games. He brought a gun into one session, and referring to his brother became part of his verbal repertoire. He also brought some of his own toys with him and he began to use the paints more freely. He became less compliant or at times was actively defiant with his mother, walking away from her on arrival and refusing to take off his coat when she asked him to. On these occasions, however, what tended to follow was a conversation between Oliver and his mother that excluded the therapist in a way that made her feel de-skilled and without a voice as the therapist.

Oliver was increasingly exasperated when he could not make his mother understand. At these times, the therapist felt silenced and hopeless, and could identify with Oliver. His absent father was also in her mind and the extent to which she was carrying a sense of castration or impotence. However, it was as if, through her physical presence, Oliver had some experience of paternal function. He began to master the idea of being in not only a two-way but also a three-way relationship, as Oedipal issues began to surface (Britton et al., 1989, Urwin, 2002). In her discussion regarding language development, Irwin (2002), using ideas from Lacan (1966), suggested that language delay or disorder may reflect difficulties in negotiating the Oedipal situation or its precursors (Urwin, 2002, p. 88).

In supervision, the relationship between the threesome – therapist, mother and Oliver – and the complexities of the relationship with his father became the focus of reflection. The dilemma of how the therapist could meaningfully intervene between the mother–child couple was thought about. Oliver was becoming a more separate little boy who could decide for himself and know his own mind, but his mother's anxiety about his poor progress resulted in a parenting style that was full of anxiety, and this prevented forward movement. This powerful dynamic at times caused the therapist to feel at a loss and unable to find words for her experience, which on reflection seemed to maintain the unmourned loss. The therapist worked creatively with what she heard and positioned herself as a present, available object within the mother and child dyad with a view to creating the 'bridge' for thought and language necessary to make this conflict conscious. This effectively changed the dynamic between the therapist and her young patient.

Case (2005) describes how 'entangled' children are confused with their mother and lack a separate identity. She points out the technical difficulties of working with these children and how underlying loss and experiences of death affect the normal process of separation. 'The entangled child has some kind of awareness of relationship followed by fear of separation and a clinging on to the object as part of oneself' (Case, 2005, p. 115). Case also describes how the fathers of entangled children may lack a presence in the family, which may then contribute to the illusion of fusion with mother and difficulties in managing Oedipal conflicts and rivalries with father. Given the loss of the first baby, it was understandable that it was problematic for Oliver's mother to relinquish his dependency, particularly without the support of a parental couple that included his father to work together through some normal Oedipal aggression.

Vignette after two months of art therapy

Oliver continued to make his wishes felt by his actions. His mother announced some good news: 'His potty training was, at last, going very well.' The therapist made a link to his brother, asking Oliver, after congratulating him, did he want to be grown up, more like him? He replied with a loud and definite 'No – no, I am a baby.' The therapist thought about this with him and asked his mother whether she felt she had a baby or a little boy. Mother confirmed that she had a little boy, and the therapist spoke of Oliver's wish to still be a baby. Oliver threw himself into his mother's arms, saying, 'No, I am a baby.' When the therapist tried to engage Oliver in further thinking about why this might be, he began throwing bricks everywhere, creating chaos and muddle.

Oliver both wished and feared becoming a potent little boy and was communicating his confusion and conflict about remaining a messy, chaotic baby, thereby carrying his mother's unresolved grief. What was noticeable in his therapy were the developmental shifts that took place when aggressive, conflictual and defiant feelings in the relationship with the therapist were brought directly into the room through his actions and play. In these moments, words were found that created meaning for him in relation to his thought and actions, which led onto development of curiosity as Oliver began to explore the room, discard the old toys and find new patterns of behaviour.

Vignette after four months of art therapy

Oliver was standing on the sofa, building three small towers with the plastic building bricks on the windowsill. The small towers stood side by side. The therapist commented on this and wondered aloud if Oliver was thinking about the three of us being together. His mother asked, 'Do you want to look out of the window to see what is outside?' The therapist asked Oliver what he thought. Oliver climbed down and began to break up the three towers, throwing the bricks onto the floor towards the therapist. She said, 'I think you are showing us lots of cross throwing feelings.' Oliver picked up more toy bricks and threw them vigorously about the room. His mother became anxious and said, 'Stop it.' Things became scary as bricks were flying everywhere. The therapist spoke to both his mother and Oliver about having scary feelings and how he may just want to get rid of them. The therapist suggested that he could throw the bricks into a nearby empty basket. Oliver responded and began to pick up and throw the bricks in the direction of the basket. Oliver became excited by this new game and repeated it several times.

By throwing the bricks, Oliver showed his 'scary' internal conflict and perhaps a feeling of breaking apart at that moment. The therapist helped to contain these feelings by naming them and providing a safe container for them through the game of throwing the bricks into the basket. His aggressive feelings diminished as there was a sense of working through; by repeating the game he could 'practice' a process of containment and experience a safe outlet for his anger and a space for thinking.

Managing despair and the beginning of representational imagery

Barrows (2002) describes his work with a three-year-old boy who had no speech, with a number of marked autistic features in his presentation. The paper explores how playfulness facilitated the emergence and expression of aggressive feelings and phantasies which linked with the development of the capacity for speech. Barrows stressed the critical role of aggression and the need for the therapist to take an active role in initiating and engaging the child in play: 'claiming or reclaiming him' (Alvarez, 1992). In supervision, the therapist reflected on her countertransference. She realised she needed to manage her own feelings of despair and continue to 'claim' her relationship with Oliver in a reciprocal way by being in 'live company' (Alvarez, 2012). This awareness helped her to be more interactive in the art therapy sessions and so deepened the therapeutic relationship.

Subsequently, Oliver asked the therapist to join him as he began to paint rockets and other objects. His response suggested that this deepening relationship with the therapist reflected a stronger sense of self. He pointed to his paintings, wanting to experiment with different materials, doing things for himself and sort of vocalising a sentence. When he moved closer to the therapist, he did not seem to realise that he was, at times, leaning on her. He invited her to play tug of war with the pillow, even throwing bricks at her in a playful/aggressive way. He looked around the room as if searching for something, and when the therapist enquired about what he was looking for, he said, 'Imba' (his word for Simba the lion cub). He found the lions and when he began to play with them, it was clear he was making up a story and playing out something for himself. His imaginative play suggested both conflict and resolution.

Six months of art therapy: the first scribble painting

With more eye contact and purposeful playful interactions with the therapist Oliver was showing signs of slowly becoming separate from his mother and his 'tangle' with her. After six months, Oliver painted a picture which was his first scribble paint- ing (Figure 5.2). He poured out his own paint and, mixing the colours together with confidence, used the thick paint with strong circular movements. When it was finished he jumped up, looked directly at his therapist, smiled and initiated a game of soft ball play. This seemed a first attempt to paint something at a representa- tional level, a reproduction of himself and his world (Matthews, 1984, 1989, 1999). This may have been a first circle or an attempt to draw a face (Dubowski, 1990). Visual symbolisation seemed to be happening in parallel with language acquisition, imaginative play and interaction with the therapist as his play, image making and speech were evolving together. He was demonstrating a growing capacity to make links between thoughts, ideas and feelings, and it may be that his joined-up scrib- bles were an external representation of a more boundaried internal world and a developing sense of self.

FIGURE 5.2 Look at me! I can paint circles!

Oliver's mother was still uncertain about her son's progress and in a moment of despair booked his speech and language therapy at the same time as his sessions. This clash meant that his sessions became fortnightly as she was struggling to manage many things in her own life, such as her work schedule, collecting the older child from school and taking Oliver to his many appointments. Her response was unexpected but, on reflection, not surprising as Case suggests, 'One area is that the parents come, consciously wanting help for their child, but the powerful unconscious processes underlying this wish work against a successful outcome' (Case, 2005, p. 110). The latter part of the treatment was compromised for a while, but it was important to maintain the therapeutic frame and the therapist renegotiated for Oliver to attend his sessions on his own for the remaining three months.

Ending phase

During this phase, Oliver made a lot of progress. The ending process seemed to bring issues of loss and separation into focus for Oliver, which could be talked about. His speech improved considerably, and he relinquished his dummy and no longer brought his 'mamas'. In the penultimate session Oliver stood beside the therapist, looking out of the window and pointing his fingers to the sky. He looked at the therapist and with a sentence that started with babbling sounds ended with two words that were very clear, saying, 'see clouds'. He proceeded to paint his 'cloud' picture, mixing the colours and applying the paint with excitement (Plate 8). When it was finished he said, 'Clouds'. The cloud picture suggested more working through of ideas, thoughts and purposeful intention as, for the first time, he used words to explain his picture. The therapist wondered to herself if Oliver's recognition of the clouds was his way of showing his understanding of what he knew of his world, the actual clouds and the internal cloudy landscape that so far had prevented him from acquiring language. His thoughts suggested a capacity to make links, and verbalise his experience, separate and independent from his mother, and, sowing seeds for further development, consolidation of an early experience of 'what is inside me is me and what is outside me is not me' (Winnicott, 1953 p. 90).

By the end of his treatment, Oliver had made some, albeit precarious, progress, in becoming less enmeshed and more individuated from his mother. Improved speech meant he was more confident that others could understand his thoughts, feelings and words and he did not need to rely on his mother to translate. He had moved on to be able to work independently, painting on the floor and asking for paints and different materials. Some of the last words in his final session were 'I need.'

Supervisory relationship

The supervisor's role within this project was both managerial and clinical. Consultation to the art therapists involved thinking through systemic and institutional issues in relation to the children's centre and other health service providers. The evolution of the project within the centre required establishing clinical governance protocols with considerable liaison, negotiation and networking between the different professionals involved (Dalley, 2007).

Parent–infant psychotherapy promotes the relationship between parent and child in order to facilitate development. The project introduced a specialist component by placing art making as a focus for the development of this relationship. Clinical supervision attended to the details of these therapeutic encounters, and the art therapist brought the dilemmas and challenges of working on the entangled relationship between Oliver and his mother. It was, at times, a struggle for both therapist and supervisor to understand Oliver's complex communications and his struggle to articulate his experience through words: the therapist often had the same experience in supervision. It may have been that some entanglement occurred between therapist and supervisor.

By staying in the not-knowing and mulling over the various processes together, even steps towards 'thinkability' were elusive and transient. These steps were facilitated by exploring Oliver's images, artwork and the sequence of play, which were not yet thought processes but visual or dramatised images which contained powerful expressive and evocative elements. At those times when the therapist felt overwhelmed with despair and hopelessness, she may have been processing Oliver's despair but also that of his mother. Consideration of her own bodily sensations brought a deeper empathetic connection with them both and helped her to find her own words and, in this way, understand Oliver's predicament. She had to move beyond the symptom of not speaking to understanding Oliver's communication without coherent words.

> In each moment of the therapeutic encounter, a question is being asked of you. When the child is not speaking to you, *even more* is being asked of you. You are being asked to transform non-symbolised, inchoate experience into thought suitable for shared understanding to emerge.
>
> *(Magagna, 2012, p. 46)*

Da Rocha Barros (2002) introduced the idea of a 'continuum of working towards', as a precursor to working through, which can then lead onto symbolic function and verbal understanding. This seemed helpful when exploring what Oliver was trying to 'tell the therapist' through his images and actions, what he wanted her to receive and understand without words and what she, subsequently, brought to think about with her supervisor. At times she felt unable to find words, and this experience of not knowing which words to sound out had a profound effect. On reflection, it was experienced as a kind of dread of communication – of not knowing how her words would sound and whether they would be understood as trying to say something, important to her supervisor.

It became apparent that perhaps what she was experiencing within the supervision relationship was linked in some way with Oliver's early relationship with his mother, where communication had an internal intensity of connectedness. The therapist also imagined that her supervisor had some sense of what she was trying to say and, that while the therapist could hold this in mind, the supervisor was also struggling to hear in more depth what it was the therapist needed to say on behalf of the child.

When thinking about containment and understanding the fluctuating levels of both the mother's and the therapist's anxiety, Briggs (1997) outlines how different types of parental containment aid the child's psychological capacity to speak, naming these as 'convex', 'flat' and 'concave'. Heightened parental anxiety leads to convex containment with excessive parental control, intrusion and hostility. Flat containment occurs when parents are unavailable to receive the projections and communications of the child, whereas concave containment is marked by parent-child interactions which promote the child's capacity to think and to speak about his experiences. This model of parental containment was helpful when thinking about the therapist's response to the presence of Oliver's mother in the sessions in creating a 'bridge' for his communication and language.

For both therapist and supervisor, these different modes of containment could be reflected on when the therapist felt she had no thoughts or words to offer at that moment, that she may have become 'flat' in her containment. Through projective identification, she may have been embodying Oliver's experience of a 'flat mother', or even at times a 'convex' mother, which had become internalised but was slowly replaced by a more concave mother object. The supervisor was able to think about her role as container and the extent to which she could maintain concave containment to promote this thinking.

Concluding remarks

Developmental progress does not necessarily take place smoothly but often through leaps in physical, emotional and cognitive achievement. Both progressive and regressive pulls were in evidence in Oliver's precarious balancing act of continuous development (Stern, 1985). It was noticeable how progress contained a tension for him. It represented a gain but he also had to manage the loss of the previous stage.

During his progress in building object constancy, the ups and downs in the work were marked by periods of repetition and regression and at other times, progressive steps were evident from week to week. In forward moves towards independence, he used his 'mamas' or transitional object to manage the illusion of separation from his mother (Winnicott, 1953, p. 2). This linked to development of thought and a more secure internalised sense of a mother that he could move away from. Previously they had been bound together in unresolved loss. This enabled the start of the ability to play, explore his own marks through art making and move onto a capacity to symbolise. As the therapist created firm and consistent boundaries for Oliver, he felt safe enough without his mother to begin to experience for himself a reliable process which occurred in a third area in which his non-verbal primitive gestures, both visual and verbal, could be held, shared and transformed.

The supervisor had a parallel role in holding the consistent space in which the therapist's communications, anxiety and dilemmas were processed, contained and understood. Echoes of the impact of parallel processes operating in the relationships in the therapy, the supervision and within the family clarified certain aspects of how thoughts and speech were impeded, which helped to transform the capacity for language to develop. The gradual reorganising and recognising of the confusion and despair in Oliver's internal world, which was a fluid and changing process, resulted in some fluidity in the roles and experiences of both therapist and supervisor. For example, at times, supervisor and therapist shared the despair and confusion, and at other times, in the delight of hopeful moments, like the enlivening parents, when progress was being made. These moments could be understood as 'wow' moments (Alvarez, 2010) or, as Stern (1985) suggests, the 'vitality effects' of each child.

Alvarez describes these 'wow' moments as times when there can be 'repair in the deficits in the child's internal objects when the infant needs to feel proud and the mother is delighted by his cleverness' (Alvarez, 2010, p. 103). Notable examples were when Oliver put words to his 'cloud' picture, when he made his first circle and when the therapy model was renegotiated with a shift from parent-child therapy, where the relationship between the mother and child was the main focus, to individual child art therapy, when Oliver began to work independently and to manage without his mother in the room. It was as if the therapist had found a stronger voice to provide a separate space for Oliver and transform feelings of despair to hope for both of them.

On starting school Oliver had progressed into a speaking world. He could communicate through words and was understood by peers and adults around him. At first, through his images and his play, sounds and gestures progressed into language, promoting change in states of isolation, inhibition and anxiety to possibilities of a separate, independent sense of self and social interaction. The dyadic work with his mother laid some foundations for better communication between them. It was the acquisition of his own language that could be shared and understood by the social world into which he was growing, not the private idiosyncratic language between himself and his mother, which was essential for these developmental moves to take place. Throughout the work, the therapist was active in paying attention and naming each small change, bringing aggressive and frustrated feelings into the relationship, making a narrative of the shared experience and understandings. Oliver's pictures tell the story of these transformations into symbol formation and thought. Stern (1985) gives credence to the vital presence of the therapist as an instrument in the child's therapy. The presence rather than the absence of the object and the importance of the role of 'proto-positive feelings' provided a central therapeutic focus (Alvarez, 2012). This helped facilitate the process for both Oliver and his mother by which Oliver could begin to think his own thoughts and sense his own agency. 'Something and someone have to matter. This is work at the very foundation of human relatedness' (Alvarez, 2012, p. 25).

References

Alvarez, A. (1992) *Live company.* London: Tavistock/Routledge.

Alvarez, A. (2010) 'Mourning and melancholia in childhood and adolescence: Some reflections on the role of the internal object', in McGinley, E. and Varchevker, A. (eds.) *Enduring loss: Mourning, depression and narcissism through the life cycle.* London: Karnac, pp. 3–18.

Alvarez, A. (2012) *The thinking heart: Three levels of psychoanalytic therapy with disturbed children.* London: Routledge.

Baradon, T., Broughton, C., Gibbs, I., James, J., Joyce, A. and Woodhead, J. (2005) *The practice of psychoanalytic parent-infant psychotherapy: Claiming the baby.* London: Routledge.

Barrows, P. (2002) 'Becoming verbal: Autism, trauma and playfulness'. *Journal of Child Psychotherapy*, 28 (1), April, pp. 51–70.

Bion, W.R. (1962) *Learning from experience.* London: William Heinemann (Reprinted Karnac 1984).

Briggs, S. (1997) *Patterns of containment: Relationship of mothers and infants where infants are at potential risk.* London: Tavistock.

Britton, R., Feldman, M. and O'Shaughnessy, E. (eds.) (1989) *The Oedipus complex today.* London: Karnac.

Bromham, J. and Jasieniecka, M. (2013) *The Loreto drawn together, parent-infant project.* UK: Harpenden Children's Centres. Unpublished Report.

Case, C. (2005) *Imagining animals: Art, psychotherapy and primitive states of mind.* London: Routledge.

Dalley, T. (2007) 'Piecing together the jigsaw puzzle: Thinking about the clinical supervision of art therapists working with children and young people', in Schaverien, J. and Case, C. (eds.) *Supervision of art psychotherapy: A theoretical and practical handbook.* London: Routledge, pp. 64–79.

Da Rocha Barros, E. (2002) 'An essay on dreaming, psychical working out and working through'. *International Journal of Psychoanalysis*, 83, pp. 1083–1093.

Dubowski, J. (1990) 'Art versus language (separate development during childhood)', in Case, C. and Dalley, T. (eds.) *Working with children in art therapy.* London: Routledge, pp. 7–22.

Fraiberg, S., Adelson, E. and Shapiro, V. (1980) 'Ghosts in the Nursery: A psychoanalytic approach to impaired infant-mother relationships', in Fraiberg, S. (ed.) *Clinical studies in infant mental health.* London: Tavistock, pp. 164–193.

Gaensbaur, T.J. (2000) 'Psychotherapeutic treatment of traumatised infants and toddlers: A case report'. *Clinical Child Psychology and Psychiatry*, 5 (3), pp. 373–385.

Hurry, A. (1998) (ed.) *Psychoanalysis and developmental therapy.* Psychoanalytic Monograph No. 3. London: Karnac Books.

Lacan, J. (1966) *Ecrits.* Paris: Seuil; Trans. A. Sheridan. London: Tavistock, 1977.

Magagna, J. (ed.) (2012) *The silent child: Communication without words.* London: Karnac.

Matthews, J. (1984) 'Children drawing: Are young children really scribbling?' *Early Child Development and Care*, 18 (1), pp. 39.

Matthews, J. (1989) 'How young children give meaning to drawing', in Gilroy, A. and Dalley, T. (eds.) *Pictures at an exhibition: Selected essays on art and art therapy.* London: Routledge, pp. 127–142.

Matthews, J. (1999) *The art of childhood and adolescence: The construction of meaning.* London: Falmer Press.

McDougall, J. (1989) *Theatres of the body: A psychoanalytical approach to psychosomatic illness.* London: Free Association.

Moore, M.S. (2004) *Differences between representational drawings and re-presentations in traumatized children.* Paper presented to Association of Child Psychotherapists' Annual Conference. London, June.

Nelson, K. (1990) 'Remembering, forgetting and childhood amnesia', in Fivush, R. and Hudson, J, A. (eds.) *Knowing and remembering in young children*. Cambridge: Cambridge University Press, pp. 301–306.

Segal, H. (1957) 'Notes on symbol formation', *International Journal of Psychoanalysis* 38, pp. 391–397, republished in *The work of Hanna Segal. A Kleinian approach to clinical practice*. London: Free Association Books, Maresfield Library, pp. 49–65.

Stern, D. (1985) *The interpersonal world of the child*. New York: Basic Books, pp. 49–64.

Urwin, C. (2002) 'A psychoanalytic approach to language delay: When autistic isn't necessarily autism'. *Journal of Child Psychotherapy*, 28 (1), pp. 73–79.

Wajnryb, R. (2002) *The silence: How tragedy shapes talk*. London: Allen and Unwin.

Winnicott, D.W. (1953) 'Transitional objects and transitional phenomena: A study of the first not-me possession'. *International Journal of Psychoanalysis*, 34, pp. 89–97.

6

THE IMPRINT OF ANOTHER LIFE

Assessment and dyadic parent-child art psychotherapy with an adoptive family

Anthea Hendry

The setting

This chapter describes work in a UK child and adolescent mental health service (CAMHS). The multidisciplinary team included the professions of child and adolescent psychiatry, clinical psychology, child psychotherapy, art psychotherapy, nursing and social work. The wide range of services offered included prioritising children separated from their birth families and living in the care of social services, and a specialist service for adopted children and their families (Hendry and Vincent, 2002).

The chapter focuses on an attachment theory and adoption research-based assessment modelled on specialist therapeutic post-adoption services (Burnell and Vaughan, 2003, Brenninkmeyer, 2007), and a dyadic parent-child art therapy intervention with an adoptive mother and her recently placed daughter. This is a time when there is a high risk of placement disruption because of the complex interplay between the past lives of both the child being placed for adoption and the prospective adoptive parents (Smith, 1994, Selwyn et al., 2014).

The family

Natasha (aged four) and her birth brother Tom (aged two and a half) were referred through social services. Although placed for adoption three months previously the social services department were responsible for reviewing the children's progress until an adoption order was made. The siblings had been removed from their White British birth parents when Natasha was aged two years and Tom was six months old. They had had two fostering placements before this placement for adoption.

Robert and Diane, the new parents, were in their early forties, had been together for twelve years and were White British-born. They had both worked in the public sector before Diane gave up her job when the children were placed. She had been diagnosed with polycystic ovarian syndrome, which can affect fertility. They had hoped that she would still conceive but this did not happen. They did not consider in vitro fertilisation, deciding to make a family through adoption. Three months into the placement they were struggling in their parenting of Natasha and Tom and had explained at a social services review that they did not feel Natasha was attaching to them and they had concerns about Tom's development. They wanted this assessed.

The family art-making session

The adoption clinic assessment for this family had involved myself and a colleague in three meetings with Diane and Robert, a visit by a trainee clinical psychologist to observe the children in nursery, another member of the clinic team speaking with Natasha and Tom's social worker, social services reports on the children's background and the adoption approval report on Diane and Robert. A family art-making session that I facilitated was the last stage of the assessment process.

I had previously explained to the parents that the purpose of the family session was for me to meet the children and observe how the family interacted together. I also explained that they could engage with the art materials with their children in whatever way felt right for them.

The introductory minutes of my first meeting with Natasha and Tom for the family art-making session were memorable. I held the door open and Natasha walked in with a critical glance at me, hesitated momentarily as she took in what she could of the room and then purposefully crossed the carpeted floor to a chair facing the door. She appeared older than I had expected. She sat on her hands on the edge of the chair so that her feet reached the floor. Following her into the room was Tom, hand in hand with Robert, the prospective adoptive dad. Tom was making gurgling noises and burst into the room, dragging Robert across to one of the two settees in the room. He disengaged his hand and more or less pushed Robert onto the settee and leapt with a delighted yelp on to his lap and turned to face him. Tom took hold of Robert's hands and they started a playful game, moving their arms together up and down and then in a circle. A little behind was Diane, who I knew was relieved to be finally bringing the two children into a service that she hoped could help them all.

These first moments set the scene for the remainder of the session. I observed a boisterous boy immersed in play with a dad who gave him his full attention. I saw a preschool girl who took control of where to sit in this new, strange room and appeared to be independent and separate, and an uncertain mum with a gentle, kind face.

For most of the family session Tom played noisily, mainly with Robert. He was a completely disinhibited boy who flailed his limbs around and communicated his needs and feelings through his exaggerated actions. Neither parent showed any sign of putting any boundaries round his behaviour, even when he tipped a box of toys over and started kicking them wildly round the room. Natasha was attracted to the play dough on the low table near her, repeatedly rolling out small lumps of it, and then cutting shapes before lumping it back together and rolling it out again. She was dexterous with her fingers and seemed to enjoy the soft texture and rhythmic movements of her play. Diane moved to the table and knelt on the floor near to her. Natasha gave no sign of wanting to share what she was doing, and Diane seemed reluctant to invade her space and so she did not join her play.

Formulation following the assessment

The adoption clinic team felt that there was potential for these parents to provide a permanent home for these two children. This was based on the degree of commitment to the children that they showed and their willingness to reflect with us on what had been going on since the children were placed. However, they were struggling and changes were needed quickly if they were going to survive as a family. Adoptive families often need packages of support from different sources (Argent, 2003), and there are limits to what any family can manage at any one time. We had to be aware both of the limitations of our service and how best to prioritise the support package. The four main areas we felt needed addressing immediately were:

- Helping Diane and Robert with appropriate parenting strategies to manage Tom's behaviour
- Practical home help to relieve the stress that we understood Diane to be under
- More reflective time for Diane to understand why the first few months of parenting had been so difficult for her
- Facilitating the start of Natasha's attachment to her new parents

A colleague and I met with Diane and Robert to discuss our formulation and proposals. We had observed their natural laissez-faire style of parenting and explained this was unlikely to work with Tom or Natasha. Tom needed firm boundaries. They had responded to him claiming them because of his disinhibited attachment style but now needed help to contain his behaviour. We proposed that a member of the CAMHS team would meet with them regularly over the next two months to advise them on parenting strategies for Tom.

It was not just physical tiredness from caring for two young children that Diane was suffering from. A few weeks after the children arrived she began to experience a level of anxiety, exhaustion, tearfulness and loss of initiative that was new to her and that persisted. We suggested she was suffering from 'post-adoption depression' (Foli and Thompson, 2004). In my clinical experience this is not uncommon for adoptive mothers. It has some similarities, in terms of symptoms, to postnatal depression but there is little research and it has no medical diagnosis. Loss of control, the reality of the complexity of the task and the reawakening of grief relating to infertility may all be factors in triggering this response to adoptive parenting. Diane had not expected, after all the anticipation and excitement of finally becoming a mother, that she would feel so confused and miserable.

Diane and Robert agreed to arrange for some home help to relieve an area of stress for Diane in relation to their home. She had struggled with the washing, cooking and cleaning up after two preschool children and wanted to reserve more energy and time for the children themselves. She also wanted time to reflect on her symptoms of 'post-adoption depression' with us.

Our fourth proposal involved Natasha, and we spent some time discussing with Diane and Robert our shared understanding of her.

Understanding Natasha's needs

Natasha had a difficult start in life. She had experienced seven moves with her birth mother in her first year and a half, with domestic violence and neglectful parenting the norm. Early trauma impacts on a child's developing brain (Schore, 1994, Perry, 2009), their attachment patterns (Ainsworth et al., 1978, Howe et al., 1999) and their physiology and self-regulation (van der Kolk, 1994, 2005). It is children with backgrounds like Natasha who are now being placed for adoption from the care system (Bingley Miller and Bentovim, 2007). Diane had not expected to feel so rejected by Natasha, who could dress and wash herself and positively rejected help brushing her teeth or hair. An attachment framework is one way of making some sense of this. The attachment drive has a biological function to seek proximity and protection from an attachment figure in time of need in order to survive (Bowlby, 1973). When Natasha was anxious or distressed as an infant it seems likely that her birth mother responded in an anxious, distressed or hostile way. 'It is the infant's need, emotional arousal and distress that seems to cause the parents of avoidant babies particular difficulty. The more emotionally needy and demanding is the baby, the more distressed or rejecting becomes the caregiver' (Howe et al., 1999, p. 62). If this was the case then Natasha had learnt to reduce her neediness and disconnect from her own feelings in order to maintain some closeness, but not intimacy, with the adults around her, developing a predominantly avoidant pattern of attachment (Ainsworth et al., 1978). Internal working models (IWM), internal representations of how we see ourselves, relate to others, and view the world, are formed from these early experiences (Bowlby, 1973).

Attachment behaviour is resistant to change and persists even when not needed (Bowlby, 1973). A new nurturing environment is not enough to redress the impact of early adverse care, particularly for over-four-year-olds (Hodges et al., 2003). Natasha had also experienced other sources of caregiving within the changing environment of her first four years. This is likely to have made her 'hyper-sensitive to the attachment-related states of mind of new attachment figure(s)' (Steele et al., 2003, p. 4). Natasha needed help to begin to feel safe with her new parents.

When relatively securely attached parents, like Diane and Robert, adopt children with insecure or disorganised attachment patterns, they need to understand why their children are not responding to them in ways they had anticipated and what to do to make them feel safe. They also need, over time, to acknowledge the significance of the child's birth family (Brodzinsky and Schechter, 1990) and the fact that there is loss for everyone connected with an adoption.

Our proposal was to offer Diane and Natasha dyadic parent–child art psychotherapy.

The rationale for dyadic parent-child work

Studies show 'the efficacy of interventions which focus on the caregiver-child interaction, in particular focusing on caregiver sensitivity and therefore behaviour towards the child, in improving the security of attachment of young children to their caregivers' (Prior and Glaser, 2006, p. 250). Including the adoptive parents in the therapy, providing their own issues are sufficiently resolved, allows the intervention to focus on 'real-life interactions between parent and child' (O'Connor and Zeanah, 2003, p. 234).

My own approach to working dyadically with adopted children was influenced by specialists in the field (Archer and Burnell, 2003, Hughes, 1997, 2004) using an attachment perspective to help attachment-disturbed children. I looked for models of dyadic art therapy with parents and children but found none. Research (Hendry, 2005) confirmed that experienced art therapists were not generally working dyadically with adopted children with attachment disturbances.

We had hypothesised that Diane was a relatively securely attached adult and that Natasha had a predominantly avoidant style of attachment. My experience is that a child with this attachment style will find it easier to start art making initially if there is some direction offered by the therapist. My approach was to encourage Diane and Natasha to jointly engage with the art materials so that any art product would be made collaboratively.

Prioritising interventions is essential. Moderating risky or inappropriate behaviour and making simple practical changes within a family to allow more space for thinking come first. My colleague arranged times to meet with both parents to work on boundary setting for Tom. Within a month this parenting work was going well. Robert was fully engaged with it and Diane was becoming a more confident and assertive parent.

Preparation for the dyadic work

In the first session with Diane in order to prepare her for the dyadic work we reflected on the progress made. She understood more about the fantasy of falling in love with two children she wanted so much versus the reality. She acknowledged the need for very different parenting styles for the two children. Despite Tom's loveable nature he needed structure and boundaries, while Natasha's assertive independence needed to be understood for what it was: not developmentally advanced behaviour but adaptive behaviour to early neglect.

In the second session I invited Diane to use the art materials that would be available for the dyadic sessions. These were age-appropriate for a preschool child. They included play dough, plastic tools and moulds, finger paints, poster paint, a box full of cardboard boxes, cartons, and rolls, felt-tipped pens, glue, sellotape, scissors and various sizes of paper. It is often underestimated how important the preparatory work with a parent is before dyadic work starts. In my experience this includes both observing and talking about how comfortable a caregiver is in using these materials. I hoped encouraging the use of these multisensory materials with this adoptive parent would assist developmentally appropriate interaction with Natasha and help Diane's understanding that their qualities can stir up unexpected feelings.

Diane loved the materials and sculpted a figure with the play dough. She became suddenly overwhelmed and tearful, describing feeling guilty that she was somehow responsible for taking Natasha away from her birth mother. It emerged that this was interfering with her ability to parent Natasha. She and Robert had met the birth mother. Diane felt deeply sorry for the young woman and wondered if she had really been given enough support to keep the children.

On the one hand Natasha desperately wanted intimacy but feared rejection. On the other hand, Diane desperately wanted to experience the warmth and intimacy of physical and emotional closeness to Natasha but was inhibited. These inhibitions seemed to be related partly to thoughts about the birth mother's loss, but also to the reality of grief regarding her own infertility, which had come to the surface since the children's placement. This trigger is common at the time of adoption placements (Tollemache, 1998). Unspoken, but also in my thoughts, was the devastating loss for Natasha of her birth mother.

I had three individual sessions with Diane. They confirmed that she was emotionally ready for the dyadic work.

The dyadic work

The early objectives of the dyadic sessions were to help Diane claim Natasha as her daughter and become more sensitive to her needs. Natasha needed a secure base to begin to understand and show difficult feelings without fear of rejection. They both needed help to begin to understand each other. I explained to Diane that I would give them some direction initially and that I wanted her to actively engage with the art materials, and proactively encourage making things together with Natasha. We would both take a reflective stance, focusing on the art-making process. The dyadic sessions were planned to be weekly, with a meeting for reflection between each session with Diane on her own.

Beginning phase: coming alive as a mother

After reintroducing myself to Natasha I invited them both to make something together using play dough. I knew they both seemed willing to use this material and wanted this first session to be as non-threatening as possible. I had asked Diane in the preparatory meetings to think of Natasha as younger than her four years and asked her to encourage eye contact as much as possible. Diane asked Natasha what colour play dough she wanted them to use, and Natasha pointed to the pink tub. Diane moulded a lump of pink dough briefly, saying she was warming it up to soften it. She then divided it into two, putting half of it in front of Natasha. Diane quickly moulded what turned out to be a cat, saying how soft and warm the dough was. Natasha watched initially and then started fingering and shaping the other lump of dough.

They initially worked independently but alongside each other. Diane talked quietly about what she was making at the same time as observing Natasha, who rolled out the play dough and used mould shapes, some of which were animals, to create objects. Diane put into words what she observed Natasha doing and commented on how well she used the moulds. After a while they had created a small group of animals. Looking at the animals I wondered aloud how they would get on together. Diane said, 'Well, I don't think they know each other very well because they haven't lived together for long.' Diane and I had a conversation about how difficult that might be and how it might mean that the small animals find it hard to say what they want or make themselves understood. Natasha was attentive but did not speak.

In our reflection meeting following the session, Diane described still finding Natasha's desire to be independent difficult. She needed reminding there was no miracle cure to Natasha's early life of neglect.

In the second session the task I suggested was to build something together, using things from a box of cardboard rolls and cartons. Diane asked Natasha which materials she would like them to use. Natasha picked out three small cardboard boxes. Diane suggested taping them together, which they did, and then wondered if it could be a house for their animals made in the previous session. Natasha nodded. The home for the animals was painted and the animals moved in. During the moving-in process Diane and I had a conversation about what is needed for young animals to feel safe and how important it is for them to have grownups to look after them.

This pattern of Natasha and Diane jointly engaging with the art materials and Diane and I co-constructing a narrative that might have some resonance for Natasha continued in the next few sessions. We were introducing her to the language of feelings in a calm, safe way and to the idea that difficult feelings could be talked about. Diane's natural maternal instincts and functioning were coming alive after the slow and painful beginning of her being a mother. She was potentially a very capable parent who was very unlikely to have needed this help had she had her own birth children.

Middle phase: developmental re-parenting outside the therapy room

The middle phase of this dyadic work took an unexpected course. Diane rang to cancel the sixth session because Tom had chicken pox. The following week she rang to say Natasha was very unwell and spots were just appearing.

I told her this might be the perfect opportunity for some developmental re-parenting (Archer, 1999) and described what I hoped she might be able to do. I suggested encouraging the natural regression due to the illness: 'Carry her, cuddle her, feed her, wash her, and allow her to be as dependent as possible for as long as possible.' Diane understood. During this phase of the therapy, which lasted three weeks, I did not see Natasha or Diane but had twice weekly phone calls with Diane. This therapeutic work happening outside the sessions was as important as anything that went on in the sessions. I was helping Diane use developmental re-parenting to support the attachment work going on in the sessions. Natasha was really poorly. She had no choice but to let Diane take over much of her physical care and with that the emotional bonding started. As Natasha began to recover we started talking about how to maintain the good parts of this intense experience.

Natasha had three months before she started full-time school. I suggested taking Natasha out of nursery altogether for these three months for them both to make up for some of the years of togetherness they had missed. After a week of thinking and talking about this Diane and Robert decided that is what they would do. Natasha was to be at home full-time until she started school to experience consistent and predictable care and establish the foundation of really trusting her new parents' capacity to nurture her.

Taking stock

I had first met this family in November. The preparation work for the dyadic parent-child art psychotherapy had started the following February. We had six dyadic sessions during March and April and then the chicken pox intervened, changing the course of the dyadic work and speeding up Diane's transformation to a fully functioning, competent full-time mother. I met with Diane at the beginning of June, after the chicken pox, for a review.

Diane wanted to continue the dyadic therapy but thought it was important for Natasha to start school in September free from the extra demands of appointments. I could see a more confident mother thinking carefully about what she wanted for her child. We arranged four further dyadic art psychotherapy sessions finishing in mid-July and planned to have a review, with just the parents, before their holiday in August.

Ending of the dyadic work: accepting a mummy

In the first session after her chicken pox Natasha walked in comfortably holding hands with Diane. This was so different from the first time I met her. She started spontaneously drawing with felt tips on A4 sheets of coloured paper and told me that she was drawing herself in bed. Another picture followed – a self-portrait with spots and then one with her wrapped up in a blanket. Diane asked if she would like her to write words underneath the pictures. Natasha quickly passed them to her and while watching said, 'Mummy writing words.' Natasha had never called Diane 'Mummy' in my presence and I learnt from Diane later that the very first time she had ever called her Mummy was in the second week of the chicken pox. More pictures were made and between them more of the story of the weeks with chicken pox was shared.

In the following session, clearly confident that Natasha could tolerate this level of touch and intimacy, Diane painted Natasha's hands and they made a large sheet of hand prints. They engaged in eye contact in a fun-loving way. Diane asked if the paint tickled. Natasha giggled slightly and nodded. This unexpectedly stirred something in Diane and she welled up. Making eye contact very deliberately with Natasha and holding one of her painted hands she told her how sad she was that she had not known her when she was a little baby. She squeezed Natasha's hand and they maintained a gaze. I was deeply moved while observing this poignant moment. Diane's ability to acknowledge to Natasha her sadness of the lost years between them showed me how much they had moved on from the uncertain and detached relationship I had observed seven months previously.

In the last session they decided that they wanted to take their artwork home. This seemed very important to them both. We spent the session looking at all the artwork. Natasha wanted to play with the animals in their cardboard box. With Diane's encouragement she told us a story about the animals. Diane reported that Natasha was playing imaginatively at home and often narrating stories involving her toys. It seemed that understanding the imprints of their earlier lives had enabled them to have a hopeful future together.

After the dyadic work

The dyadic work combined with the parenting strategies work achieved the goal of facilitating the parents' capacity to provide a secure base for Natasha and Tom. During a meeting to review all the work since their referral to CAMHS, spanning a period of nine months, Diane and Robert acknowledged that they felt much more secure in their parenting role. They were planning to celebrate the first anniversary of the placement as a special day. Tom and Natasha were adopted by Diane and Robert the following year. They had further therapeutic support at different stages of the children's development but always attributed their survival as a family to the package of support offered at this very early stage of the children's placement.

Conclusion

The convergence of thinking and research from psychoanalytic theory, developmental psychology, attachment, neuroscience and trauma over the last twenty years has led to a richness of understanding that lends itself to dyadic work. Art therapists can use this knowledge to develop art psychotherapy approaches to dyadic practice. Other dyadic parent-child models of therapy with older children focusing on increasing caregiver sensitivity and facilitating positive change in a child's attachment security are well established (Jernberg and Booth, 1999, Vanfleet and Guerney, 2003, Hughes, 1997). Art therapy with mothers and infants in the UK is a developing area (Hosea, 2006, Hall, 2008, Arroyo and Fowler, 2013). Research relating to dyadic parent-child art therapy with older children has begun (Taylor Buck, 2012) and wider sources of evidence for this approach are indicated (Taylor Buck et al.,

2012). This, together with training (Hendry and Taylor Buck, 2014/2015), will lead to more expertise and research.

There are many aspects of dyadic art therapy that will warrant further theoretical consideration and exploration. Three of them are described here: the significance of the sensory nature of the art materials, the role of the art therapist in dyadic work and the continuation of therapy outside the therapy sessions.

The significance of the sensory nature of art materials

Art therapists have explored the significance of the tactile nature of the art materials in individual work with traumatised children (Sagar, 1990, Murphy, 2001, O'Brien, 2004). The integration of body awareness and understanding the role of touch with specific materials such as clay in relation to trauma work is described by Dalley (2008, pp. 77–79) and Elbrecht and Antcliff (2014, pp. 19–30). Our understanding of sensory-based approaches to trauma and attachment work with children is developing (Malchiodi and Crenshaw, 2014, Malchiodi, 2015) and will be significant in some dyadic parent-child art psychotherapy.

I chose tactile materials such as play dough with Natasha and Diane in order to provide sensory-rich experiences. These sensory-stimulating experiences and the importance of touch are part of the normal parenting of infants and toddlers and contribute to the development of secure attachments which develop at this age between the caregiver and the child. Recreating in dyadic art psychotherapy some of the elements that build a healthy attachment can contribute to reconstructing an insecure or disorganised pattern of attachment (Proulx, 2003, pp. 59–67).

The role of the art therapist in dyadic work

In dyadic parent-child work the art therapist 'is not the parent's therapist, nor the child's therapist, but the dyad's therapist' (Proulx, 2003, p. 162). There are different approaches to dyadic art psychotherapy and this will influence the role of the therapist. I used a 'joint engagement' approach. This involves the child and parent jointly engaging in the process of art making. This was the most appropriate approach given the attachment style of the child, the stage of their relationship and the identified goal of facilitating the start of a more secure relationship. I combined a directive and non-directive stance. Two other approaches to dyadic art psychotherapy, though not previously described in the art therapy literature or researched, have been developed from clinical experience and outlined in the dyadic training (Hendry and Taylor Buck, 2014/2015).

A 'child-led approach' invites the child to work with the art materials in the first part of a session while the caregiver is invited to 'watch, wait and wonder' (Cohen et al., 2003). This approach was not suitable for Natasha and Diane because it would have put too much focus on Natasha. A 'co-construction of narrative approach' (Saltzman et al., 2013) is used to help a dyad share a perspective on an event or experience of trauma from their own lives. It was too early in their relationship for this approach, although I used the idea of co-construction of narratives in my dialogues with Diane to introduce the language of feelings and relationships to Natasha.

Dyadic work will often involve separate sessions with the parent (Vanfleet and Guerney, 2003). In these sessions the art therapist may be offering psycho-educational sessions with the caregiver based on his or her knowledge of the dyad and observations made in sessions or exploring the nature of what is known of the child's early life experiences. Understanding what Natasha had missed in infancy helped Diane know what gaps she had to fill and how important it was for Natasha to have a safe environment and new experiences of attuned and nurturing caregiving.

Diane was to become Natasha's permanent caregiver. My role was not to develop a special trusting relationship with Natasha. This would have interfered with Diane's developing role as a mother. My task was to facilitate the dyad's attachment by modelling attunement and nurturing in my relationship to the dyad.

Natasha needed encouragement to express her feelings. My dialogues with Diane and our co-constructing narratives were a way of introducing difficult feelings in a safe, indirect way, at a time when it would have raised Natasha's anxieties if we had focused more directly on her feelings. We were modelling normal maternal functioning, and it involved a degree of understanding between myself and Diane, which was partly developed outside the sessions with Natasha.

Therapy continues outside the therapy room

The middle phase of the dyadic work described here was fortuitous. The timing and severity of Natasha's chickenpox were extremely helpful to the process of facilitating a healthier attachment relationship between Diane and Natasha. Maybe this was coincidence or perhaps it was Natasha unconsciously feeling safe enough to become vulnerable, needy and able to allow the virus to take over. Whatever the cause it enabled Diane to start the physical process of developmental re-parenting at a time when she was growing in confidence as a mother, and Natasha was able to accept it. Continuing my therapeutic relationship with Diane through our phone conversations provided a way in which to maximise the therapeutic opportunities inherent in Natasha's regression to a more needy, dependent child.

Parent-child dyadic work with children beyond infancy frequently actively continues the therapy into the home as a part of the dyadic work (Jernberg and Booth, 1999, Vanfleet and Guerney, 2003). These models will be useful for art therapists to consider in dyadic work.

References

Ainsworth, M., Blehar, M., Waters, E., and Wall, S. (1978) *Patterns of attachment: A psychological study of the stranger situation.* Hillsdale, NJ: Erlbaum.

Archer, C. (1999) 'Reparenting the traumatised child: A developmental process.' *Young Minds Magazine*, 42, pp. 19–20.

Archer, C., and Burnell, A. (2003) *Trauma, attachment and family permanence*. London: Jessica Kingsley.

Argent, H. (ed.) (2003) *Models of adoption support: What works and what doesn't*. London: BAAF.

Arroyo, C., and Fowler, N. (2013) 'Before and after: A mother and infant painting group.' *International Journal of Art Therapy*, 18 (3), pp. 98–112.

Bingley Miller, L., and Bentovim, A. (2007) *Assessing the support needs of adopted children and their families*. London: Routledge.

Bowlby, J. (1973) *Attachment and loss. Vol. 1, Separation: anxiety and anger*. London: Hogarth Press.

Brenninkmeyer, F. (2007) *Family work at PAC: Overview of the theoretical frameworks and practice principles*. London: Post Adoption Centre.

Brodzinsky, D.M., and Schechter, M.D. (eds.) (1990) *The psychology of adoption*. Oxford: Oxford University Press.

Burnell, A., and Vaughan, J. (2003) 'A model of post placement therapy and support for adoptive families,' in Argent, H. (ed.) *Models of adoption support: What works and what doesn't*. London: British Association for Adoption and Fostering (BAAF), pp. 241–252.

Case, C. and Dalley, T. (eds.) (1990) *Working with children in art therapy*. London: Routledge.

Case, C., and Dalley, T. (eds.) (2008) *Art therapy with children: From infancy to adolescence*. London: Routledge.

Cohen, N.J., Lojkasek, M., and Muir, E. (2003) 'Watch, wait and wonder: An infant-led approach to infant-parent psychotherapy.' *IMPrint*, 35, pp. 17–19.

Dalley, T. (2008) 'The use of clay as a medium for working through loss and separation in the case of two latency Boys,' in Case, C. and Dalley, T. (eds.) *Art therapy with children: From infancy to adolescence*. London: Routledge, pp. 69–85.

Elbrecht, C., and Antcliff, L.R. (2014) 'Being touched through touch. Trauma treatment through haptic perception at the clay field: A sensorimotor art therapy.' *International Journal of Art Therapy: Inscape*, 19 (1), pp. 19–30.

Foli, K.J., and Thompson, J. (2004) *The post-adoption blues: Overcoming the unforeseen challenges of adoption*. New York: Rochdale Press.

Hall, P. (2008) 'Painting together: An art therapy approach to mother-infant relationships,' in Case, C. and Dalley, T. (ed.) *Art therapy with children: From infancy to adolescence*. London: Routledge, pp. 20–35.

Hendry, A. (2005) *After the break: An investigation into art psychotherapists' work with adopted children and their parents*. Unpublished MA thesis. Goldsmiths College University of London.

Hendry, A., and Taylor Buck, L. (2014, 2015) *British Association of Art Therapists professional development training programme*. March and July.

Hendry, A., and Vincent, J. (2002) 'Supporting adoptive families: An interagency response.' *Representing Children*, 8 (2), pp. 104–118.

Hodges, J., Steele, M., Hillman, S., Henderson, K.S., and Kaniuk, J. (2003) 'Changes in attachment representations over the first year of an adoptive placement: Narratives of maltreated children.' *Clinical Child Psychology and Psychiatry*, 8, pp. 351–367.

Hosea, H. (2006) 'The brush's footmarks: Parents and infants paint together in a small community art therapy group.' *The International Journal of Art Therapy: Inscape*, 11 (2), pp. 69–79.

Howe, D., Brandon, M., Hinings, D., and Schofield, G. (1999) *Attachment theory, child maltreatment and family support*. London: Macmillan Press.

Hughes, D. (1997) *Facilitating developmental attachment: The road to emotional recovery and behavioural change in foster and adopted children*. Northvale, NJ: Jason Aronson.

Hughes, D. (2004) 'An attachment-based treatment of maltreated children and young people.' *Attachment and Human Development*, 6 (3), pp. 263–278.

Jernberg, A., and Booth, P. (1999) *Theraplay: Helping parents and children build better relationships through attachment-based play* (2nd edition). San Francisco: Jossey-Bass.

Malchiodi, C.A. (ed.) (2015) *Creative interventions with traumatised children*. New York: Guilford Press.

Malchiodi, C.A., and Crenshaw, D.A. (eds.) (2014) *Creative arts and play therapy for attachment problems.* New York: Guilford press.

Murphy, J. (ed.) (2001) *Art therapy with young survivors of sexual abuse: Lost for words.* Hove, UK: Brunner-Routledge.

O'Brien, F. (2004) 'The making of mess in art therapy: Attachment, trauma and the brain.' *Inscape: The Journal of the British Association of Art Therapists*, 9 (1), pp. 2–13.

O'Connor, T.G., and Zeanah, C.H. (2003) 'Attachment disorders: Assessment strategies and treatment approaches.' *Attachment and Human Development*, 5 (3), pp. 223–244.

Perry, B. (2009) 'Examining child maltreatment through a neurodevelopmental lens: Clinical application of the neurosequential model of therapeutics.' *Journal of Loss and Trauma*, 14, pp. 240–255.

Prior, V., and Glaser, D. (2006) *Understanding attachment and attachment disorders.* London: Jessica Kingsley.

Proulx, L. (2003) *Strengthening emotional ties through parent-child dyad art therapy.* London: Jessica Kingsley.

Sagar, C. (1990) 'Working with cases of child sexual abuse.' In Case, C., and Dalley, T. (eds.) *Working with children in art therapy*. London: Routledge, pp. 89–114.

Saltzman, W.R., Pynoos, R.S., Lester, P., Layne, C.M., and Beardslee, W.R. (2013) 'Enhancing family resilience through family narrative co-construction.' *Clinical Child and Family Psychological Review*, 16, pp. 294–310.

Schore, A. (1994) *Affect regulation and the origin of self: The neurobiology of emotional development.* Hillsdale, NJ: Laurence Erlbaum.

Selwyn, J., Wijedasa, D., and Meakings, S. (2014) *Beyond the adoption order: Challenges, interventions and adoption disruption.* Bristol: University of Bristol/UK Government Department for Education.

Smith, S. (1994) *Learning from disruption.* London: British Association for Adoption and Fostering (BAAF).

Steele, M., Hodges, J., Kaniuk, J., Hillman, S., Kaniuk, J., and Henderson, K. (2003) 'Attachment representations and adoption: Associations between maternal states of mind and emotional narratives in previously maltreated children.' *Journal of Child Psychotherapy*, 29, pp. 187–205.

Taylor Buck, E. (2012) 'Dyadic parent-child art psychotherapy.' *The British Association of Art Therapists Newsbriefing*, November, pp. 14–16.

Taylor Buck, E., Dent Brown, K., Parry, G., and Boote, J. (2012) 'Dyadic art psychotherapy: Key principles, practices and competencies.' *The Arts in Psychotherapy*, 39 (1) pp. 163–173.

Tollemache, L. (1998) 'The perspective of adoptive parents.' *Journal of Social Work Practice*, 12, pp. 27–30.

van der Kolk, B. (1994) 'The body keeps the score: Memory and the evolving psychobiology of post-traumatic stress.' *Harvard Review of Psychiatry*, January–February, pp. 253–256.

van der Kolk, B. (2005) 'Developmental trauma disorder: Towards a rational diagnosis for children with complex trauma histories.' *Psychiatric Annals*, 35, pp. 401–408.

Vanfleet, R., and Guerney, L.F. (eds.) (2003) *Casebook of filial therapy.* Boiling Springs, PA: Play Therapy.

7

AMAZING MESS

Mothers get in touch with their infants through the vitality of painting together

Hilary Hosea

Introduction

The UK government began to roll out a nationwide programme of Sure Start centres in 2001 with the aim of supporting the lives of children and their families, particularly in the most deprived communities. Child development and 'school readiness' were key aims, alongside building parenting skills and aspirations. The hope was that the children would go on to access education, training and employment, preventing poor children from growing up to become poor adults.

The painting group described in this chapter was set up in partnership with Sure Start and a child and adolescent mental health service (CAMHS) to support families where additional needs had been identified to strengthen mother-infant relationships. A pilot painting group started in 2004. In 2007 we began to use the Solihull approach (Douglas, 2007) as a theoretical underpinning. This brings together established psychodynamic theories of containment (Bion, 1962) and reciprocity (Brazelton, 1974) in an integrated therapeutic model for work with families. This model embraces two decades of neurobiological research and emphasises the need for early intervention (Figure 7.1).

The painting group

The painting group takes place in an overcrowded and deprived area where nearly half of its largely White British population have low levels of education, skills and training. Families referred to the group receive home visits prior to attending, and parents and children are supported in accessing the weekly sessions. There is time for evaluation, planning and supervision from the art therapist, who co-facilitates the group with experienced Sure Start workers, a nursery nurse and a family support worker.

FIGURE 7.1   A young child focuses on his experience of paint.

Parents referred to the group need a holding framework in order to find their innate skills and successfully build up containment and reciprocity (Douglas, 2007) with their child. This involves co-operation between mother and infant in order to support potency and responsiveness. Ideas from parent-infant psychotherapy that stress the importance of working with both the parents and their young children together are used to strengthen the bond between parent and infant (Lieberman and Pawl, 1993, Acquarone, 2004). The group does not aim to directly address negative factors (Barlow and Svanberg, 2009, Woods and Arget, 2009). Fathers are invited and welcomed to the group. Fathers are valuable nurturing figures, providing support for the infant or for both mother and child (Hosea, 2006). Father's attentive care of their babies can help their emotional regulation, particularly with their sons (Feldman, 2003). In practice fathers usually attend only when they become the main carer for their young child, often after a painful dissolution of their partnership.

The painting group is non-directive and offers a contained, non-judgemental space for parents and infants (Hosea, 2006). The art therapist and co-facilitators work in the present, in circumstances that are to some extent unpredictable and messy, echoing the nature of the ordinary mother-infant relationship that is full of rupture and repair (Beebe and Lachmann, 2005, Douglas, 2007). This is an optimistic approach which focuses on positive interactions and is similar to the ideas of video interaction guidance (Biemans, 1990, McDonough, 1993).

Group processes are not worked with directly, but the group sustains a sense of being in something together, fostering a dynamic of mutual support. A central concern is to bring the 'mentalising' (Music, 2011) and reflective capacities of parents into play; the art is a large part of this. We respect unconscious themes as they arise from the images and the verbal exchanges. The paintings are important and in the room where the group takes place they are central, hanging on a washing line that crosses the room (Figure 7.2). The older children peg their paintings up themselves when it is lowered. The paintings are looked at as they dangle in a lively, colourful line and commented on by the group. When the parents return to the first section of the room, with its chairs and sofas, we turn the paintings round so everyone can see them while the changing of the children is managed. The pictures are dried carefully and handed back at the end of the next session, symbolically showing respect for people of all ages and their inner worlds (Hall, 2008).

Parents are often guarded or defensive and trust is built up slowly. Facilitators may at times be perceived as critical and withholding mother/grandmother figures. When a new mother joins, feelings of rivalry and competition for attention can be evoked. We aim to remain empathic and containing figures who do not retaliate or reject in the face of fear, anger and confusion. Mess and anger

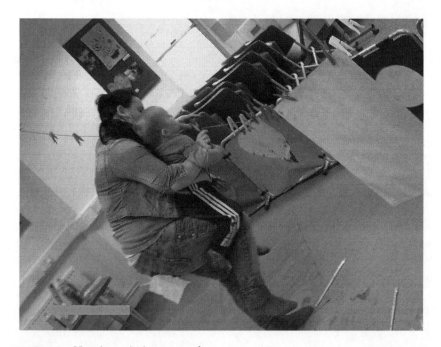

FIGURE 7.2 Hanging paintings up to dry.

can emerge in the images and get commented on safely, often in metaphorical terms. Our aim is for the group to provide a space where the young child is more able to use his or her carer as a 'safe haven' (Powell et al., 2013) or a 'secure base' (Bowlby, 1988).

Our experience is that when dyads use the group fully it becomes a safe space in which relationships can be freed of some of the distortions that are evoked in the caregiver in connection to the infant in everyday life. Distortions arise when the caregiver developed strategies as a child or infant in order to get his or her own attachment needs met. These distortions potentially prevent the caregiver recognising or correctly interpreting the needs of his or her own child. These distortions in attachment behaviour are akin to Fraiberg's 'ghosts' (Fraiberg et al., 1975) in that they are transmitted across generations.

Boundaries are important in this group. The group happens in the same place and at the same time each week. We provide a boundaried and containing response to the messy art making of the children. For example when a mother sees only 'a terrible mess' as her son spreads paint across the paper and walks through it across the floor, the facilitators and other parents may turn the event into a creative opportunity and capture the unique footprints and show the child's exhilaration in the moment. The painting can become an alive act in a deadening place (Plate 9). The mother might fear that she cannot contain her child physically and emotionally and that she does not have enough resources. Through the group's containment this mother can begin to relax and find her own containing resources, communicated to her child through her posture, gaze, touch, voice and inventiveness. She is able to remove her projections from her child.

After about forty-five minutes we wheel out a tray of warm, bubbly water so the children can wash the brushes, be soothed and wind down. We look at the paintings and at photos of the parents and children painting together as the children are dressed. The welcoming and ending rituals are important in providing containment and include supporting children to paint, wash, dress and get ready to zoom off in their buggies. This does not mean pre-empting the mother's initiative, but it might mean hunting for shoes and singing songs to ease the process of getting ready for the off.

Amplifying maternal sensitivity in the context of painting

The photo frame

At the end of the group, while the babies and young children are being bathed, cleaned up and changed with towels and bowls of water, we play back images on the digital photo frame. These are pictures taken by us during the group – a reflective function if you like. The children are usually thoroughly engaged by this screen. The images capture, in effect, moments of parental attunement: mum and child painting together; finding a rhythm; a mother stimulating her child and together dabbing her brush into the purple paint and stroking it across the mustard paper;

containing a tired, frustrated infant who may have had enough; restoring equilibrium and responding to children's feelings. McDonough (1993) in her 'interaction guidance approach' refers to this as a focus on pre-existing aspects of quality caregiver-infant interaction. Moments of meeting and connection are singled out where it can be seen that parent and child are responding to each other and, in Daniel Stern's words, 'sharing vitality' (Stern, 1985). Trevarthen (2001) and Stern (1985, 2010) both stress the importance of the 'sharing of vitality' between infant and adult partner through their creation of reciprocal behaviour. Vitality affects underpin the attunement of parent and child and underlie the process of feeling alive. It seems to me that in the painting group, the mothers, young children and the facilitators, Clara, Liza and I, give out vitality affects as we use the paint, clay and glitter and respond to each other.

The group facilitators are seeking to enlarge maternal sensitivity. This involves alertness to infant signals, appropriate and prompt responses and the capacity to negotiate conflicting goals: the infant may want to paint Mum's arms and Mum may not want this exploration, so she needs to find an alternative, intimate use of the paint, perhaps taking up the brush and painting the child's feet and together printing her feet.

This kind of attentiveness tends to promote a secure relationship in which the child can use the mother as a base for protection and nurturance and for exploring the environment. Beebe and Lachmann's (2013) research contributes to the knowledge of the complexity and sophistication of the dyadic exchange from birth. Their studies of early patterns of relating reveal the moment by moment negotiation of attention, emotion, orientation and touch and the subtle missteps in the dance between the mother and baby's communications.

The grandmother transference

Stern (1995) believes that the therapeutic setting in infant-parent psychotherapy is about the holding that allows mothers to develop their abilities. He believes that the transference from the therapist in this context works best as that of a benign mother/grandmother, who holds the new mother positively so she can find her innate repertoire of techniques. He writes, 'The therapist can be more active, less abstinent emotionally . . . more focused on assets, capacities and strengths than on pathology and conflicts' (Stern, 1995, p. 187).

We can also give a mother time for herself to explore her new identity. This is with an awareness of Stern's concept of the 'motherhood constellation', which he says is a response to a woman getting pregnant and having a baby in the context of western industrial society. He sees it as a type of basic psychic organisation that displaces the Oedipus complex (Stern, 1995, p. 184). He claims that the mother, with the birth of her child, 'experiences a profound realignment . . . her interests and concerns now are more with her own mother . . . more with her mother-as-mother . . . more with women in general and less with men' (Stern, 1995, p. 172). She is interested in caregiving and the survival of her baby.

Mentalising as enabled through the painting group

The ability to understand the child's state of mind is central in forming secure attachments. A great deal of research has been undertaken in recent decades to understand the processes by which parents and infants interact successfully with each other from the very early, preverbal stages onwards (Tronick, 1989, 2002, Stern et al., 1998).

Mentalising enables parents to see their child as an intentional being and focus on what the child is feeling, thinking and experiencing rather than on physical needs or external behaviour (Music, 2011). The concept of mind-mindedness was developed by Elizabeth Miens (Meins et al., 2001). It has much in common with the concept of 'mentalisation', already referred to, and developed by Fonagy (1998).

In Arroyo and Fowler's (2013) case study of a mother-infant painting group they suggest that the mentalising process was strengthened between mothers and infants as they created shared imagery. Shai and Belsky (2011) introduce the importance of 'parental embodied mentalising', the parents' capacity to implicitly understand the whole body movement of their infant and adjust their own kinaesthetic patterns accordingly.

Art materials, mess, chaos and sensory experience

Art materials seem ideal for expanding mother-infant reciprocity (Douglas, 2007). Robbins (1987) sees art materials as an extension of the holding environment that links clients to the 'primary creativity' that Winnicott (1971) delineates. Meyerowitz-Katz (2008) describes the containment that art materials can provide for young children. The infant drumming with her paint brush may not immediately draw a response from her mum, but when the nursery nurse replies with movement, her mum may invent a further expression with her voice, 'dum-de dum', and, sitting opposite, may extend her child's finger-tip printing when she drops the brush and thrusts her hands into the palette. We physically contain the mess of the art materials and clear them up. This gives mothers and children the freedom to experiment on the edge of mess and chaos and to create something joyful and meaningful without the fear of being overwhelmed. Parents develop their communication skills and explanations . . . 'That's enough paint for now, Nathan. Let's peg your picture on the line and get that car and drive it on the road I've painted.'

In the painting group mothers have the chance to see their child in a new way. Through the activity of painting together feelings of being alive, of being seen, received and held in the moment, are experienced by the infant.

Our sense of aliveness and reality is mediated by our body (Redfearn, 1998), with which we literally make sense of the world. Tactile contact is the first mode of communication that we learn at the mother's breast (Orbach, 2009). The use of primary tactile art materials explored freely without a directed goal puts us in touch with ourselves; sensory motor contact with substances such as paint, clay and sand gives us an awareness of our feelings (Hosea, 2002). Powerful and aggressive emotions can be channelled and absorbed by them, affection and vitality expressed. As Elbrecht and Antcliff write about clay, 'it provokes basic needs such as to touch and find the other, to grasp and grab, to have for oneself, to find and know one's own rhythm with movement, to discover one's sense of unity and wholeness through balance' (Elbrecht and Antcliff, 2014, p. 23).

Mess is a reality here. Paper is ripped as a young child crawls across it, glitter is tipped out in sparkling trails across the floor and paint oozes out over the edges of the coloured cartridge paper. Infants often explore their own skin by painting their hands, arms, legs and faces, continuing to find out about their uniqueness and identity through this primary sensory material and boundary of their body.

Vignettes from the painting group

Vignette 1. Janey and Sara: a depressed mum

Sara had been struggling with depression after the birth of her second baby, Joe. Her health visitor referred the young family to painting group as a place where Janey, aged two years and ten months, and her mother, Sara, could share some playful time together and strengthen their attachment. At the same time Sara could look after six-month-old baby Joe's needs in a nurturing, holding environment. This would allow Sara to see that she is doing a 'good enough job' as a mum. Her baby would be responded to and admired, and she could see the creativity and resourcefulness Janey has in her mum's presence. Sara's own mother died two years ago and her partner had moved out of the household.

They have been coming for eight weeks and are at ease in the group. Joe, asleep in his buggy, is now waking up. Mum takes him out, unwraps him from his winter coat and shows him where he is.

I help Janey help herself to paint. She picks up the bottles one by one and squeezes her chosen colours into the palette, pausing to think which ones she wants: purple, red, orange, viridian, white and yellow. She takes a piece of mauve paper back to her mum. Sara says, 'That's a nice colour, can you get a blue piece for me?' Janey trots back and gets a sheet of paper and a brush for her mother in preparation for them working side by side on the floor with the paint between them. The expression on Janey's face is rapt and concentrated. Her marks are bold and purposeful. She puts on broad areas of colour vertically with a thick brush: orange next to green and overlapping so that a bronze stripe appears and then sweeps of yellow are applied horizontally. She looks at Joe, who Mum has placed on the floor on his tummy. He watches the activity, raising his head with his hands and arms. 'You'll be painting soon,' Sara says, in a sing-song croon that makes him smile and bounce in response.

Janey looks at Joe and then slightly anxiously at Mum, who notices her disengagement and slight tensing of her posture and says soothingly, 'That's lovely Janey.' Her daughter smiles with pleasure and says, 'You paint too.' Sara begins to paint, understanding her daughter's desire to share this activity with her, something special for the two of them that Joey is not yet doing. Sara gives Janey attention and praise, and Janey visibly relaxes as she dabs paint onto her paper in a version of what seems to be a 'rock-a-bye baby in the treetops', a potent choice of nursery rhyme.

Comment

Sara said at the end of the session, 'Janey would like to live here in this room, painting all day.' She is aware that Janey has 'come out of herself' in this environment and with her mother's attention focused on her. Clara, the nursery nurse and co-facilitator, responds, 'She's made a lovely series of paintings. She loved it that you were noticing her colours and painting alongside. Shall we hang them up, Janey, so everyone can see and Joe can see his big sister's paintings on the line?' Clara responds to the mum's feeling of not being able to provide enough of what Janey needs by showing her through the paintings how close they can be and how well they can communicate.

Vignette 2. Freddy and Gina: a traumatic birth and a new baby on the way

Freddy's birth was traumatic for Gina. Her baby was small and delivered with forceps and the experience felt like an assault to her. As the weeks went by she felt panic and anxiety and did not have much sense of pleasure in him. There was a lack of ready support from Gina's family and her husband worked long hours. She felt low and her GP started her on antidepressants.

Gina has had support from her health visitor and a CAMHS psychologist, and she has been coming to painting group for several months. She felt that she needed to be better at play-ing with and understanding her child. Gina was born with a mild form of spina bifida and was hospitalised as a baby. Her own sense of infant vulnerability seemed to come back with the birth of Freddy, whose high-pitched wails had put her in touch with her own distress as a baby. It seemed that her own attachment needs were not fully met. She struggled with feelings of abandonment and of not being good enough.

In the group she was angry with me as a potentially harsh, judging parent and with Freddy as an insatiably demanding infant. Gina wanted to be understood, to understand Freddy and herself and to improve their relationship.

Freddy is now two, and Gina is expecting a second baby and is feeling uncomfortable and sick some of the time. Freddy is sitting on his mum's lap and Gina has arranged paint and paper in front of them. She has mixed a lilac colour in their palette and lays it on the paper. She tries to help Freddy reach the paper with his long-handled brush. However, the *paper buckles awkwardly as he draws the palette towards him. Nevertheless, Freddy puts his brush into the brown and dabs this on top of her lilac marks. She is not sure how to receive his marks but rallies and encourages him to lay on more paint that rather obliterates her lilac and green pattern.*

Freddy is easily distracted by what is going on around him and his brush drops from his hand. Gina reassures him and they make eye contact for the first time since this painting group began. She pats and strokes his hand, his anxious face lights up and he returns to painting, echoing Mum's latest blue marks with his own. She manages to retain his interest by offering him a second brush so he paints with both hands. Not long after, he has had enough and wanders away, but their engagement, struggle and closeness with the paint are clearly portrayed in the painting as it hangs on the line. The art therapist is able to comment on the smile of delight that Freddy gave his mum and his enjoyment of her encouraging him to make his marks on the image although it effaced what she had begun.

Comment

In this vignette we see the developing attunement between the mother and toddler. Gina is able to contain Freddy's aggression as he obliterates her original painting, which leads to an interesting connection between them. The art therapist comments (like a grandmother) on the smile of delight that Freddy gave his mum and draws attention to how Freddy enjoyed his mother encouraging him to make his marks despite the obliteration of her own painting.

Vignette 3. Laura, Dan and Jack: Mum's struggle to engage with her boys

Laura is sitting on a plastic mat with Dan (age three) and Jack (age two) with one palette and the two boys opposite. They have just sat down and are eager to paint. Laura gets paper for both her sons but Dan has his eye on a box. Laura feels a bit watched and wary. Jan, co-facilitating the group, has a good rapport with Laura, but she has been to a child protection meeting this week to give feedback on the family's progress. Laura feels criticised by the professionals, although things are going better for the family since her partner left and the boys seem happier. They are beginning to look around and explore.

Dan gets a box for himself with Jan's encouragement and starts to paint the inside black and blue with a large brush, looking as if he is getting to understand about inside. Laura looks up and suggests he can do the outside. She is printing Jack's hands and she suggests they put handprints on Dan's box. He looks uncertain so she coaxes him with a new liveliness in her manner and he suggests they do it in yellow. For several minutes there is a scene of animation with Laura painting Jack and Dan's hands yellow and carefully printing them on the box. She then adds hers, building up a pattern and commenting on where the yellow meets the blue and creates a lovely fresh green. For a brief moment Dan smiles, and then he leaves the box and wants to paint with Mum, who has turned to her papier-mâché 'dragon's egg', riven with carefully painted cracks. She relinquishes this and turns back to paint with the boys.

PLATE 1

PLATE 2

PLATE 3

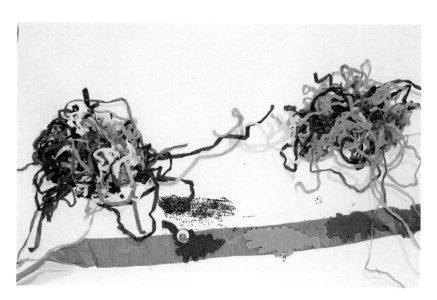

PLATE 4

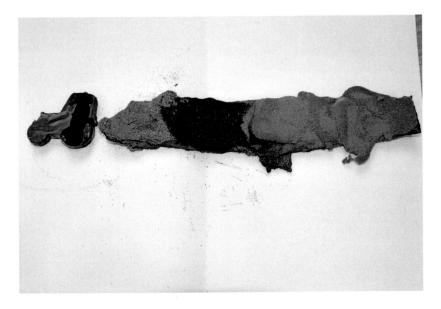

PLATE 5

PLATE 6

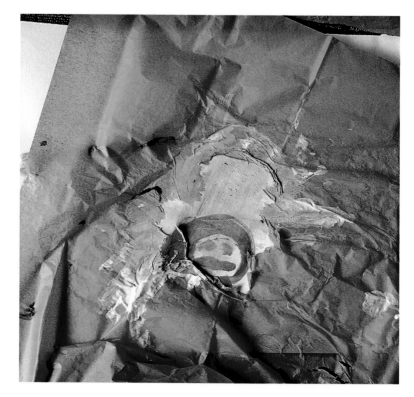

PLATE 7

PLATE 8

PLATE 9

PLATE 10

PLATE 11

PLATE 12

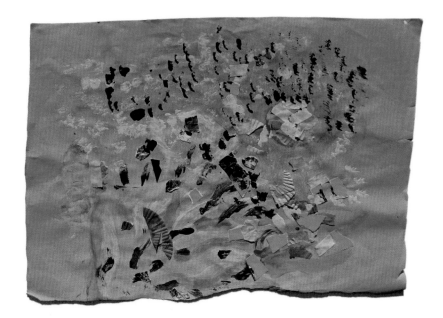

PLATE 13

Laura is beginning to reflect on her own difficult experiences as a child and her desire to provide a better environment for her children, free of the threat and tension of domestic violence.

Comment

In this vignette we get a sense of Laura's struggle to attend to both her children as they all try to be together. There are moments, such as with the hand printing, when all three are engaged in a single painting activity. This togetherness is fragile, and we can see how Laura's need to represent something of her own infantile fragility gets in the way of maintaining a containing relationship with her two boys, as the three of them seem to drift apart. We then see how Dan re-engages his mum so that the three can get back to painting together.

This is an example of the way a carer may be intrusive, unresponsive or inconsistent. Laura is sometimes unresponsive towards her boys and sometimes inconsistent in the way she responds, but she is becoming more aware of their need for her attention, help and containment.

Vignette 4. Support from another mum helps Kate and Marie to connect; John and his son, Ben, get into squishy clay

Kate watches Marie, her lively two-year-old, cross the room, play dough hanging from her mouth, bent on mischief with her baby brother, Tom, six months old, who is on Mum's knee.

'Leave him alone,' Kate snaps.

'Let me hold him,' offers Tara, whose little boy, Ben (three), is using clay with his dad, John. Dad has introduced water and laughs to see his son squeezing and squashing the clay through his fingers. Long ago John remembers using clay in primary school when he made a lion with a big ruff of a mane. Tara is at ease with baby Tom, but wary of the clay, which probably equates with mud, dirt and shit. She's been watching from the sidelines.

This is Marie's chance — she's been trying to attract Kate's attention for some time. She picks up a discarded brush as Kate dictates: 'Paint Daddy. Start with a circle, put in the eyes, where's his nose?' There is a pause and Marie makes some fluent, untutored, wavy strokes, clearly representing hair.

'Isn't she clever,' says Tara. Kate visibly relaxes and begins to offer her own praise.

Comment

Kate and Marie appear to increase their confidence in themselves and get to know each other better as individuals without too much conflict. Tara has provided a safe space so mother and daughter can share and co-operate in the meaning of things. There is a sense of overlapping containment present, with Dad containing Ben, so Tara can hold Tom, so that Kate can engage with Marie — a sense of a group as a community or family. Tara has given support and empathy, and this has probably increased her own self-esteem and given her a sense of belonging. She can also watch Ben's messy adventures with the clay from a safe distance and share in the fun he is having.

The art materials are being used creatively and in a bodily, tactile way as mothers, fathers and children interact together. Feelings of hope, anxiety, creative energy, rivalry, defensiveness, sadness and cheerful communality ebb and flow through the session. There are unconscious feelings present as the young children constantly evoke in their parents memories of their own childhood – new meanings and connections emerge and warm, vital, ephemeral moments can be recognised and held onto.

Conclusion

Concentric circles of containment

The Sure Start painting group is embedded in a community that grew up around a new housing project started in the 1970s. The Sure Start children's centres provide a vital focus for the families of local communities, with particular responsibility for vulnerable families and children under five. The painting group exists within concentric circles of holding and containment: this is a systemic conceptualisation with the parent-child dyad at its core. Embodying a grandmotherly role, the art therapist functions as a containing elder for the mothers, fathers and babies and for the Sure Start workers. The Sure Start workers function as a community who contain and support each other and who are skilled at containing their clients.

The painting group has been running for ten years, providing hard-to-reach parents and their children with opportunities to see each other in new ways. Trowell and Huffington write that 'Perseverance, hard work and mutual support from a multidisciplinary group has [sic] enabled an idea to become a working reality' (Trowell and Huffington, 1992, p. 114), and they stress how important it is 'to hold onto hope and creativity in the face of diminishing resources' (Trowell and Huffington, 1992, p. 114). The painting group provides a space for powerful feelings to emerge through adult and infant art making, and I believe this creativity is effective in its own right. The paintings are central, authentic, smeared and dabbed, carrying aliveness and new ways of understanding children and enabling their feelings to emerge. My experience is that the tactile and visual nature of the images lends them more readily to playfulness, invention and understanding of emotion than conventional play and purely verbal interaction.

Therapeutic groups that run for many years develop their own culture and sense of community, which is itself of great value when families find themselves in unstable situations – for example with regards to benefits, housing and broken relationships.

Within the group, facilitators' comments often take the form of mentalising about the mark making and explorations of the children. This provides a circle of containment that gives the parents space to reflect on their child and his or her emotional state and to become curious about this. In this way the infants are held in mind and thought about, and through this and their sensual, tactile investigations they develop a burgeoning sense of themselves.

Group members themselves have a containing function, commenting on the children's sensory experience, excitement or distress and making sense of the feelings, and sometimes physically holding a fellow member's baby. Being with a small group of people and sharing difficulties creates another level of containment, instilling hope, breaking down isolation and finding a sense of one's own value. Here we have a representation of the group as a community, with members acting like helpful neighbours or maybe aunties, uncles or cousins.

The painting group creates a holding environment, not predominantly dependent on words, through which the parent-infant relationship can be strengthened. It provides a containing space where 'The caregiver's understanding of the child's mind encourages secure attachment' (Fonagy, 2001, p. 167). The parents have opportunities to reflect on their child's inner experience: the fright of falling over; the excitement of putting their hands into the squishy paint; the joy of making marks on the paper; the tentative exploring of the room and crawling back fast to Mum. If they can let go of some of their defences and respond sensitively to the shock, the excitement, the joy, the ambivalence of their child, they are building up the child's secure sense of self.

The photo frame offers another layer of containment, revealing the uniqueness of mother and child as they paint, including their posture and gaze – concrete evidence of the growth of their relationship and positive interactions. The photo frame provides an expressive use of technology in art therapy.

> In painting group there is no expectation of the parents. They don't have to know how to play. They learn through using the materials. Paint is basic and neutral and they can watch until they feel comfortable. They don't have to participate verbally unless they want to. Sometimes the parents need people who will give them time and thoughtfulness. You are the keeper of that safe space. You hold them in mind. And the rest happens as they interact with their child and the materials . . . It is very powerful doing painting.
>
> *(Joanna, an experienced family support worker,*
> *who co-facilitated the group)*

References

Acquarone, S. (2004) *Infant-parent psychotherapy: A handbook*. London: Karnac.

Arroyo, C. and Fowler, N. (2013) 'Before and after: A mother and infant painting group.' *International Journal of Art Therapy*, 18 (3), pp. 98–112.

Barlow, J. and Svanberg, P.O. (eds.) (2009) *Keeping the baby in mind*. London: Routledge.

Beebe, B. and Lachmann, F.M. (2005) *Infant research and adult treatment: Co-constructing interactions*. Hillsdale: Taylor and Francis.

Beebe, B. and Lachmann, F.M. (2013) *The origins of attachment: Infant research and adult treatment*. New York: Routledge.

Biemans, H. (1990) 'Video home training: Theory method and organisation of SPIN', in Kool, J. (ed.) *International seminar for innovative institutions*. Ryswijk, The Netherlands: Ministry of Welfare and Culture, pp. 177–179.

Bion, W.R. (1962) *Learning from experience*. London: Heinemann.

Bowlby, J. (1988) *A secure base: Clinical applications of attachment theory*. London: Routledge.

Brazelton, T.B., Koslowski, B. and Main, M. (1974) 'The origins of reciprocity: The early mother–infant interaction', in Lewis, M. and Rosenblum, L.A. (eds.) *The effect of the infant on its caregiver*. London: Wiley, pp. 49–76.

Douglas, H. (2007) *Containment and reciprocity*. Abingdon: Routledge.

Elbrecht, C. and Antcliff, L.R. (2014) 'Being touched through touch.' *International Journal of Art Therapy*, 19 (1), pp. 19–30.

Feldman, R. (2003) 'Infant-mother and infant-father synchrony: The co-regulation of positive arousal.' *Infant Mental Health Journal*, 24 (1), pp. 1–23.

Fonagy, P. (1998) 'Prevention, the appropriate target of infant psychotherapy.' *Infant Mental Health Journal*, 19 (2), pp. 124–150.

Fonagy, P. (2001) *Attachment theory and psychoanalysis*. New York: Other Press.

Fraiberg, S., Adelson, E. and Shapiro, V. (1975) 'Ghosts in the nursery. A psychoanalytic approach to the problems of impaired infant–mother relationships.' *Journal of the American Academy of Child and Adolescent Psychiatry*, 14 (3), pp. 387–421.

Hall, P. (2008) 'Painting together: An art therapy approach to mother-infant relationships', in Case, C. and Dalley, T. (eds.) *Art therapy with children*. London: Routledge, pp. 20–35.

Hosea, H. (2002) 'Art materials and art therapy.' Literature review as part of MA in Art Psychotherapy, Goldsmiths College, University of London. Unpublished.

Hosea, H. (2006) 'The brush's footmarks: Parents and infants paint together in a small community art therapy group.' *International Journal of Art Therapy: Inscape*, 11, pp. 69–78.

Lieberman, A.F. and Pawl, J.H. (1993) 'Infant-parent psychotherapy', in Zeanah, C. (ed.) *The handbook of infant mental health*. New York: Guilford Press, pp. 472–484.

McDonough, S.C. (1993) 'Interaction guidance: Understanding and treating early infant caregiver relationship disorders', in Zeanah, C. (ed.) *The handbook of infant mental health*. New York: Guilford Press, pp. 414–426.

Meins, E., Fernyhough, C. and Fradley, E. (2001) 'Rethinking maternal sensitivity: Mothers' comments on infants' mental processes predicts security of attachment at 12 months.' *Journal of Child Psychology and Psychiatry*, 42 (5), pp. 637–648.

Meyerowitz-Katz, J. (2008) 'Art materials and processes, a place of meeting: Art psychotherapy with a four-year-old boy.' *Inscape: Journal of British Association of Art Therapists*, 8 (2003), pp. 60–69.

Music, G. (2011) *Nurturing natures*. Hove, NY: Psychology Press.

Orbach, S. (2009) *Bodies*. London: Profile Books.

Powell, B., Cooper, G., Hoffman, K. and Marvin, R.S. (2013) *The Circle of Security intervention*. New York: Guilford Press.

Redfearn, J. (1998) 'The body-self relationship', in Alister, I. and Hauke, G. (eds.) *Contemporary Jungian analysis*. London: Routledge, pp. 29–43.

Robbins, A. (1987) *The artist as therapist*. New York: Human Science Press.

Shai, D. and Belsky, J. (2011) 'When words just won't do: Introducing parental embodied mentalizing.' *Child Development Perspectives*, 5 (3), pp. 173–180.

Stern, D.N. (1985) *The interpersonal world of the infant*. London: Karnac Books.

Stern, D.N. (1995) *The motherhood constellation: A unified view of parent-infant psychotherapy*. New York: Basic Books.

Stern, D.N. (2010) *Forms of vitality: Exploring dynamic experience in psychology, the arts, psycho-therapy and development.* Oxford: Oxford University Press.

Stern, D.N., Bruschweiler-Stern, N., Harrison, A.M., Lyons-Ruth, K., Morgan, A.C., Nahum, J.P., Sander, L. and Tronick, E.Z. (1998) 'The process of therapeutic change involving implicit knowledge: Some implications of developmental observations for adult psycho-therapy.' *Infant Mental Health Journal*, 19 (3), pp. 300–308.

Trevarthen, C. (2001) 'Intrinsic motives for companionship in understanding: Their origin, development and significance for infant mental health.' *Infant Mental Health Journal*, 22 (1–2), pp. 95–31.

Tronick, E.Z. (1989) 'Dyadically expanded states of consciousness and the process of thera-peutic change.' *Infant Mental Health Journal*, 19 (3), pp. 300–307.

Tronick, E.Z. (2002) 'New thoughts on mutual regulation: Co-creation and uniqueness', in Raphael-Leff, J. (ed.) (2003) *Parent-infant psychodynamics: Wild things, mirrors and ghosts.* London: Whurr, pp. 35–53.

Trowell, J. and Huffington, C. (1992) 'Daring to take a risk: Issues from the first year of the Monroe Young Family Centre.' *ACPP Newsletter*, 14 (3), pp. 114–118.

Winnicott, D.W. (1971) *Playing and reality.* Harmondsworth, UK: Penguin.

Woods, J. and Arget, K. (2009) 'Group psychotherapy: The role of the therapist', in Lan-yado, M. and Horne, A. (eds.) *Child and adolescent psychotherapy.* London: Routledge, pp. 235–246.

8

THE CRISIS OF THE CREAM CAKES

An infant's food refusal as a representation of intergenerational trauma

Julia Meyerowitz-Katz

Here I am

On the threshold of discharge from a therapeutic playgroup (TPG) within a child and adolescent mental health service (CAMHS), two-year-old Jamil sat with me at a low table on which there were drawing materials. He picked up a marker and intently drew an image that had an enclosed shape, with some lines emerging from it, roughly corresponding to where a head, arms and legs might be. He was deeply engrossed in his image, in identification with it (Schaverien, 1992). I felt the depth of his engagement in my reverie despite my awareness of the other children and adults in the room. When he had completed this drawing, he looked up at me, emphatically saying, 'Boy.' I replied, 'You drew a boy. You showed us you know you are a boy.' He smiled happily at me, and then looked at his mother, Jayti, who was sitting nearby. She beamed back at him with a proud smile and said how much she liked his drawing of a boy.

This was a poignant 'Here I am' moment (Winnicott, 1971, p. 153) for Jamil and Jayti, which was shared by the four members of staff, the three other mothers and their three toddlers in the playroom. Jamil had come a long way in approximately six months since being referred for treatment due to his refusal to eat. This had been affecting his physical, emotional, psychological and social development, and his consequent weight loss had become life-threatening; it seemed he was choosing to starve himself to death.

Jamil's drawing represented a significant and multilayered achievement. It demonstrated that he had a vocabulary of marks, a capacity to create a symbolic image and his understanding that making art was a communication that other people could understand (Matthews, 1989, 1994). The drawing signalled that he had a developing sense of inside and outside (Winnicott, 1971, Meyerowitz-Katz, 1998, 2003), a sense of who he was: a boy with a sense of himself as a separate person in relation to other people. After he had completed it he looked to his therapist for affirmation, conveying an understanding of her role in sharing and witnessing his experience, before looking at his mother in order to share this moment with her too. She responded in an appropriately maternal and loving way. He then looked around the room, aware that there was a group there that he was part of and with whom he had shared a journey, to check whether they too had shared this moment with him.

In the account that follows, I will describe how Jamil's attainment of health was inextricably intertwined with the way in which art making within the TPG supported the healing of the wounded unconscious dynamics between him and Jayti. This was because their art making enabled the expression of psychosomatically held pre-symbolic material to be communicated, received, contained and transformed.

History and referral

Jamil was the only child born to Jayti and her husband, Gopan. They were traditional, Gujerati-speaking Hindus who had a shared traumatic history. Their families were among the ninety thousand Indian and Pakistani minority who were ethnically cleansed, expelled from Uganda in 1972 and given ninety days to leave the country (Wikipedia, Rajani, 2012). Their families became part of a group that fled firstly to Kenya, and then subsequently to Britain, where they settled in London. After their marriage, they lived with Gopan's parents. Jayti was expected to assume the traditional role of a helpful daughter-in-law and to provide grandchildren.

Ten years of multiple miscarriages and failed in vitro fertilisation (IVF) treatments preceded Jamil's birth. Repeated experiences of failure had been traumatic and painful for both Jayti and Gopan. As a couple they had had to adapt to their shared experiences of hope, loss and despair. Jayti had resigned herself to her role as her mother-in-law's companion and to her disparaged status as a childless, married woman within a traditional family and community. In spite of all these difficulties, they presented as a united parental couple, and they both attended all the reviews.

At a party to celebrate Jamil's first birthday, the whole extended family experienced a trauma. Jamil had an extreme allergic reaction after eating dairy products for the first time and had to be rushed to hospital by ambulance, with his parents fearing that he may not survive. The family had bought cream cakes, symbolic of the host culture, in order to celebrate his birthday and he had had a few mouthfuls. His food refusal began at this point and had intensified over several months. This was in marked contrast to his compliance in other areas, including having been fully toilet-trained when about fifteen months old. At the time of referral he was twenty months old and was existing on sips of soya milk. He had been referred to the CAMHS by his paediatrician, who, after having carried out exhaustive tests, was confident that his food refusal was a psychological and not a medical matter.

However, we know from the burgeoning evidence in contemporary research in neuroscience that 'mind' has an organic basis and it emerges through relationship (Knox, 2003, 2004, Gerhardt, 2004, Siegel, 2012). We know too that 'mind' is inextricably connected to the processing of emotions and feelings (Damasio, 1999, 2003, 2012). We are feeling selves before we are thinking selves, and our experience of our feeling selves depends on how our emotional experience is mediated by carers.

Writing originally in 1947, Jung presciently wrote, 'It is extremely difficult, if not impossible, to think of a psychic function as independent of its organ, although in actual fact we experience the psychic process apart from its relation to the organic substrate' (Jung, 1960/1969, para. 368). Winnicott considered that mind is 'no more than a special case of the functioning of the psyche-soma' (Winnicott, 1949, p. 244). Siegel (2012) considers that mind is not only 'enskulled' but also 'embodied'.

The context of the therapy

Patients were referred to the CAMHS from a variety of sources that included GPs, health visitors and nurseries. Patients referred to the TPG were drawn from the multicultural community that the CAMHS served. Staff too reflected the multicultural nature of the city. At the time that Jamil attended the TPG, most of the adults, including the staff, were migrants from different countries, while all the children had been born in the UK.

Children were referred to the TPG following an assessment by a multidisciplinary team that included a consultant paediatric psychiatrist who was also a psychoanalyst, child psychotherapists, an art therapist, psychodynamically trained psychiatric social workers, a group psychotherapist and family therapists. The TPG had four members of staff: an art therapist, a child psychotherapist, a group psychotherapist and a psychotherapy or art therapy trainee. The TPG was restricted to four families, each with a child under the age of five, who was the identified patient. Fathers were invited and encouraged to attend, although in practice, they rarely did. However, many fathers joined the mothers in attending regular family reviews with team members from the TPG. Referred children had a range of difficulties, including developmental delay, autistic spectrum disorders, failure to thrive and behaviour problems; some children had been affected by parents with mental health problems or environments impacted by neglect or domestic violence.

The TPG was intended to provide a holding and containing environment which supported parents and children as individuals and as parent–child dyads within a multi-family group process (Asen, 2002, Dalley, 2008). Interventions aimed to support the children's psychosomatic development within the context of their relationships with their parents. The TPG took place weekly and each weekly session had three parts.

Each weekly tripartite session began with a shared meal. This took place in a group room. Staff and families would sit around low tables arranged as one and covered with a tablecloth. Families and staff all brought their own packed lunches, sitting together around the table to eat lunch and catch up on the week's news. The shared lunch offered families opportunities to bring their traditional foods – which in Jayti and Jamil's case were Hindu vegetarian – and in this way introduce their different cultures and values. It also offered opportunities for the staff to role model behaviours around food and eating: some of this was social, inviting sharing and tasting, discussing flavours and textures, and some was more subtly educational, aimed at supporting parenting. Staff modelled how to encourage reluctant eaters to eat, and how to encourage children to participate in a shared social activity. Although discussions focused on eating real food, staff worked with the understanding that food had to do with projective and introjective processes. It was understood that taking in and digesting food also signalled taking in and digesting emotional and psychological experience.

After lunch, the families and staff crossed the passage to the playroom, which was laid out with art materials and toys, to engage in a joint mother-and-child therapy group (Plate 10). Following this, mothers would leave the playroom with the group psychotherapist and return to the group room, where the furniture had been rearranged so that they could sit in a circle and have a shared discussion. With the departure of their parents from the playroom, the focus of the children's activity changed. This part of the session offered them the opportunity of engaging in a different kind of play – as separate children within a group, with each other as a children's group and with the three remaining staff.

Ordinary psychotherapeutic boundaries were upheld, so that the different parts of the overall weekly session began and ended clearly and on time. All three parts were facilitated on psychodynamic lines, with close attention being paid to the conscious as well as the unconscious communications present in the group. The four members of staff met weekly following each tripartite session for psychodynamic supervision with the consultant paediatric psychiatrist.

Art materials and processes played a central role in the playroom for both mothers and children. A range of art materials were consistently provided. There was always a two-sided easel with paper, bottles of paints and brushes, a table with clay and a drawing table. A sand tray was always available as were a range of age-appropriate toys, including Duplo, toy cars, soft toys and a soft ball. For the duration of the therapy, the families' artworks were kept in folders and boxes and were available in each session. On discharge, families could decide what to do with their artworks – some were taken away, some were disposed of and others were left in the care of the staff.

Jayti and Jamil presented as a tense, vigilant and anxious mother-child dyad. Their capacities to play together as a dyad were impaired, with Jayti's participation being confined to 'teaching' Jamil how to draw shapes, and Jamil trying to please her (Figure 8.1).

Jamil seemed drawn to painting from the first day, and his art making seemed to represent a kernel of healthy curiosity in, and engagement with, the world that lay alongside his extreme regression from it (Figure 8.2). He easily immersed himself in the process and was proud of the finished images. His actions, when choosing colours and then deciding where they were going to go, were very considered. It was quite obvious that he found the experience meaningful (Smith, 1993, Matthews, 1994).

FIGURE 8.1   Jamil and Jayti's first co-created drawing.

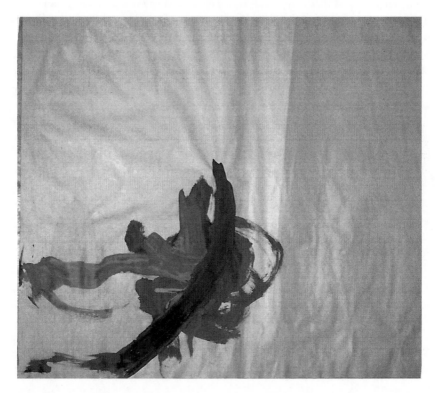

FIGURE 8.2   Jamil's first painting.

To begin with, Jayti needed a lot of encouragement and support to use the materials. However, she soon became confident. She created this painting, which she said represented her hopes for Jamil and herself – to have a home and a garden and for him to have a friend to play with (Figure 8.3). She painted a black sun, then a house, a car, a cat, a garden and two children in an enclosed space playing

FIGURE 8.3   My hopes for the future.

with a ball, and rain. She wanted to portray a happy domestic setting, but looking at it I found it a sad painting – the sun is black, there is a lot of empty space and it is raining. My countertransference while she was painting and then looking at the completed image was one of emptiness and depression. Given her history of expulsion and migration I was interested that the car, as a symbol of transportation and relocation, had such a strong presence in the image.

Jamil's return to health involved achieving a 'satisfactory psychosomatic partnership' in which psyche and soma engage in a mutually interrelated developmental process (Winnicott, 1949). In order to develop a language for thinking about psychosomatic experience and communications, I will consider relevant theory that addresses psychosomatic processes.

The crisis of the cream cakes: a catastrophe for the 'psychosomatic partnership'

The cream cakes were consumed as a cultural symbol intended to be celebratory. Instead of this, Jamil's psychosomatic partnership was severely disrupted, creating a crisis that was shared by the whole family. His response to this crisis involved a psychosomatic regression in which he eventually stopped eating.

Winnicott writes that this psychosomatic partnership is a process that goes on over time and leads to the development of a 'live body, with its limits and with an inside and outside, (and which) is felt by the individual to form the core for the imaginative self' (Winnicott, 1949, p. 244). It depends on the experience of undisturbed '*continuity of being*' (Winnicott, 1949, p. 245, italics original), which in turn is a consequence of the environment being actively adaptive to the infant. Failures of adaption by the environment are experienced as impingements which cause the infant to withdraw from external reality. The infant relies instead on 'confusional mental states' in which use of the mother/environment is foreclosed and the desired 'satisfactory psychosomatic partnership' is not achieved. The cream cakes crisis could be understood as a catastrophic impingement on continuity of being for Jamil and for the whole family – a catastrophic failure of containment.

Jamil's fear of impingement was demonstrated when he was attracted to the clay for the first time. His sense of his body as being vulnerable to catastrophic impingements, of not having a sense that the clay was outside his body, was acute. He began tentatively touching the clay, but as soon as he noticed that his hands were becoming covered in wet, mucky clay he screamed in terror and stretched out his hands as far away from his body as possible while desperately trying to remove the clay. He became hysterical but began to calm down while we washed his hands together and I showed him how the clay was outside his body.

Orbach writes,

> the body is not so much the truth but it's a relational outcome of the intersubjective field of the carer and the baby just as much as the mind is. Winnicott frequently tells us that 'there is no such thing as a baby. Whenever you see a baby you see a mother and baby pair' (Winnicott, 1971). I would like to extend this idea to say there is no such thing as a body. Whenever you see a body, you see a body that has been internalised in the context of a relationship with another body.
>
> *(Orbach, 2006, pp. 68–69)*

One can only imagine what was going on in the bodyminds of Jayti and Gopal, who had experienced so much trauma and loss in their lives, as they sat with their only living infant in the ambulance. Whatever was happening for the three of them would have been laid on top of earlier bodymind experiences, including experiences of impingements and the trauma of ethnic cleansing and forced geographic relocation as children (Akhtar, 1999). Grinberg and Grinberg (1989) describe migration as a trauma that extends over time. They suggest that the effects of migration, which involves complex and ongoing losses, may be buried beneath primitive defences. Migration is described as a rupture, 'an upheaval which shakes the entire psychic structure' (Grinberg and Grinberg, 1989, p. 26), causing internal disorganisation. It can affect symbolic and creative capacities. This is because without sufficient capacity for mourning and working through, these experiences can remain unrepresented (Freud, 1914) and therefore not part of symbolic functioning.

In addition, Jayti and Gopan had experienced the psychological and emotional stress of infertility and failed IVF (Harvard Mental Health Letter, 2009). Experiences of miscarriage can become a secret, disenfranchised trauma and grief (Seftel, 2001, 2006). Unrepresented trauma can affect parents' capacity to provide the necessary containment that will enable thinking and symbolising in their infants. The foetal environment may be impacted so that the foetus develops in an environment impinged on by the mother's trauma (Meyerowitz-Katz, 2011, 2016).

In this context, Orbach's idea of body being an entity that has been internalised in the context of a relationship with another body raises many questions. These are to do with what kind of mother/father/parental body relationship Jamil may have experienced and internalised in early infancy, what experiences of continuity of being, and therefore internal robustness, may have been brought to the cream cakes crisis – both individual and shared; how Jamil had experienced and internalised the 'family bodymind' during and after this crisis, and how he had reacted to this experience of trauma, as an expression of his own and the family's bodymind. In other words, I am approaching thinking about the 'psychosomatic partnership' as representing an embodied experience of intergenerational transmission, including trauma (Fraiberg et al., 1980, Faimberg, 2005, Frosh, 2013) that exists in and between individuals.

That an aspect of Jamil's reaction to the crisis had to do with regression was obvious through his food refusal. I was given a clue as to the extent of his regression in the following experience.

The experience of something not-yet-born

As their therapy progressed, and Jamil and Jayti became more aware of themselves as separate people, the separation between them when the mothers left the room for their mothers' group became more difficult for them to manage, as this vignette shows:

Jamil is extremely distressed. Jayti has left the room in order to join the mothers' group. I am holding him in my arms in order to support him in his distress at the separation from Jayti. He is very small and light and seems so much younger than he is. I feel that I am cradling a baby only a few weeks old. I hear his cries, which sound so young, and observe how he screws up his face as he howls, his eyes tightly shut. I notice how he clenches and unclenches his fists and waves tiny fingers in the air. I feel his distressed body pressing hotly against mine. He is curled up, rather like a neonate, who has not yet stretched out, and I understand that part of what I am holding is very young and unformed. I have a growing sense that makes absolutely no sense: I feel as if I am holding a creature, part of whom is not yet born. That is curious as he is over one year old; he can walk, verbalise and, precociously: he is toilet-trained.

There are four aspects of this experience that I wish to consider: the degree of Jamil's regression into something that I experienced countertransferentially as 'not-yet-born'; the intensity of the interrelational psychosomatic deposit into me of the quality of this regression, which signalled that the projection was real; how this deposit remained in my bodymind for an unusually long time and how it became transformed into a thought and then a curiosity.

In an ordinary way, through projective processes like projective identification (Klein, 1946, Bion, 1962), or *participation mystique* (Jung, 1971), our patients leave traces of themselves with us. Mostly we are aware of these in our thoughts and memories. However, this experience with Jamil left me with a profoundly embodied experience which did not leave me for a long time – not until I had an insight over a decade later. During a seminar when trying to grapple with Jung's (1960/1969) paper where he introduces his concept of psychoid experience, my viscerally embodied memory of holding Jamil emerged. And then, as I began to speak about it, the experience of holding something in my body that felt as if it was 'not-yet-born', and the visceral embodied feeling that had been with me for so long, dissipated, never to return. Instead, I was left with a deep curiosity about what this all could possibly mean.

Psychoid processes and participation mystique: a psychosomatic partnership

Drawing on the biological research of his time, Jung (1960/1969) proposed a deeply unconscious mind-body structure and process that he called psychoid experience, which he considered to be the fundamental source of all psychic experience. Clark (2010) describes psychoid experiences as unconscious, unrealised and unborn mind-body potential and potency that exist even in regression. He suggests that they are emergent and vital organic forces, containing DNA-like seeds of their own form. They are designed to emerge and develop in both a 'species-typical and an idiosyncratic way' (Clark, 2010, p. 90). They depend on interactions with the conscious and unconscious environment in order to come into existence and develop to their full potential. In this way psychoid experiences and processes are our being and becoming (Meyerowitz-Katz, 2013).

In addition, resonant with Jung's proposition that 'Emotions are contagious because they are rooted in the sympathetic nervous system. . . . Any process of an emotional kind immediately arouses a similar process in others' (Jung, 1935/1968, para. 319), Clark (1996) proposes that psychoid processes are unavoidably interpersonal. He suggests that they operate in an unconscious, embodied way and are signalled and communicated via projective processes intra-psychically as well as through somatic sensations. They are psychosomatic evacuations of primitive, undigested experience which form a 'psychoid substance' in which both participants are affected and changed (Clark, 1996). In this way psychoid processes are the unconsciously embodied psychoid substance of the complex projective processes that Jung referred to as '*participation mystique*' (Meyerowitz-Katz, 2016).

Participation mystique, a term that Jung borrowed from Levy Bruhl (Jung, 1971), operates through projection and identification. Both parties become swept up in a dynamic 'shared reality' that must ultimately be metabolised by both (Winborn, 2014). Experiences of *participation mystique* involve unconscious identifications where the boundaries between self and other are blurred. They are 'a feature of early infancy in which infants identify with aspects of their parents' unconscious experience' (Jung, 1971, para. 741). As Knox (2003) says, children have a very tangible experience of their parents' unconscious life.

Laplanche (1999, cited in Hinton, 2009) suggests that the infant, as well as negotiating his or her own developmental stages, endeavours to make sense of and take in aspects of the mother which are incomprehensible and therefore enigmatic. Hinton suggests that experiencing such enigmas may create dread and anxiety, and the danger of psychic collapse in the infant (Hinton, 2009, p. 642). This implies that the mother/early environment is not just a support for projections (Klein, 1946) nor only a provider of holding (Winnicott, 1971), containment and alpha function (Bion, 1962), but that mother has experiences of her own, including unconscious experiences, of which the infant is aware, that he or she responds to and identifies with.

Bearing in mind that there was an unconsciously shared psychosomatic partnership in the form of the psychoid substance of participation mystique between Jamil and Jayti, and that it contained pockets of dread and anxiety, I turn now to describing a pivotal moment in their therapy. This occurred at a time when a considerable amount of psychotherapeutic work had already been done. Jamil had begun to enjoy food and was putting on weight. He and Jayti were relaxed and confident in the TPG. Jayti was enjoying her status as a mother with a recovering child.

A shared psychosomatic partnership made visible

After witnessing another mother and her child creating a life-size portrait of the child together, Jayti decided that she and Jamil would make one too.

Under her instruction, Jamil willingly lay down on his back on a large piece of paper on the floor, enjoying the attention that he was getting from his mother and me. When the outline was complete, Jayti told him to get up and to go away. He walked a little way away and watched while she began painting in the legs. After a while, he approached her, picked up a brush and painted a small black shape just touching one foot. Jayti angrily banished him to the other side of the room because she didn't want him to 'mess up' her painting. She then sat with her back to everyone in the room and carefully completed the image. Jamil did not attempt to approach the painting again.

When the image was completed we picked it up off the floor and hung it on the wall. There it was visible to everyone in the room. Strongly identified with her image, Jayti was very pleased with it and very proud of her efforts. Jamil reacted with terror, calling it a 'monster' and running to the far corner of the room, where he cowered in fear. Jayti reacted to his response by laughing. Everyone else in the room was shocked into silence.

Jayti's portrait of Jamil (Plate 11) has green trousers and a yellow shirt, bearing no relationship to what he was wearing that day. The feet are not distinguished from the legs nor are hands and fingers distinguished from the arms. The facial details are painted in black, the surrounding flesh in a greyish white and the hair radiates out from the scalp in short, darting black lines. The overall effect is quite strange and disturbing, especially considering that it is a portrait of a small, dark-skinned boy with tidy brown hair. Whilst an amount of distortion can be expected in portraits of this nature – children wriggle, the silhouette is inevitably slightly distorted and mothers are not usually trained artists – in the context of the TPG, the amount of distortion in this painting was extremely shocking. It seemed to have nothing to do with what Jamil really was, even on a superficial level. The clothes he was wearing that day did not resemble those depicted in the image. The greyish-white-painted face had a deathly pallor and the black line underneath the head seemed to convey a wound, separating the head from the rest of the body. The face seemed more like a death mask than a portrait of a living child.

This was a pivotal moment because the art-making process enabled the expression of a deeply unconscious, previously unrepresented, shared trauma. It was as if in Jayti's turning her back on the room, telling Jamil to go away, and his compliance with that (another child may have protested and stubbornly, tearfully or defiantly returned), the two of them were unconsciously agreeing to communicate a fundamental predicament. This was in the unconscious hope that their predicament would be contained and transformed, and was something along the lines of: 'See, this is what is happening to us. When we try and co-create something, in spite of our love for each other, a terrifying, deathly dread interferes. It separates us and it leaves us in fragmented, frightened and slightly mad bits.' This was represented by the two of them at opposite ends of the room, one laughing and the other cowering in terror at the presence of this ghostly 'monster'.

This communication was contained by the therapeutic processes in the playroom, so that both Jamil and Jayti were supported, and it was discussed in the mothers' group. This segued into Jayti being enabled to engage in a process of mourning and working through, which supported her in developing her symbolic capacities. Jamil was freed from a life-destroying psychoid entanglement with his mother, which was to do with unmourned, disenfranchised aspects of trauma and grief, so that his 'kernel of healthy curiosity in and engagement with the world' could grow and he could begin to thrive.

Their individual and joint healthier psychosomatic partnership was made apparent in Jamil's subsequent engagement with clay. There was evidence too in their joint play of their individual and shared evolving symbolic capacities.

For instance, in a session, Jamil joined me at the clay table, where I was absent-mindedly fiddling with clay. He began touching small pieces. I began to mirror his actions and then when I felt we were engaged in a communicating activity, I showed him how to roll clay into balls. He began making big lumps of clay and then took some of my clay balls, saying they were 'McDonald's' – alluding to what had become his favourite food. He began stacking the clay shapes and created a sculpture. While making his sculpture he smiled and chatted to me and thoroughly

FIGURE 8.4 'McDonald's'.

enjoyed himself. The following week, he and Jayti enjoyed painting the sculpture together, while talking about 'McDonald's' and pretending to 'eat' the clay 'food' (Figure 8.4).

Conclusion

Art psychotherapy has long understood that 'Often the hands know how to solve a riddle with which the intellect has wrestled in vain' (Jung, 1960/1969, para. 180), and that making art is a matter of 'the living effect upon the patient himself', which enables patients to 'give form, however crude and childish, to the inexpressible' (Jung,1954/1982, para. 104). There is evidence from research in neuroscience that art making in the presence of a therapist can support the integration of left-right brain functioning, thereby improving the individual's quality of life and relationship with the environment (O'Brien, 2004, Hass–Cohen, 2008). But, as Siegel (2012) says, the mind is embodied and not only enskulled. Neurons do not stop at the border of the skull – they reach into the furthest and deepest parts of the body; neurological integration can then perhaps be considered a psychoid matter.

Consideration of the psychoid structures and processes that lie underneath and determine the psychosomatic partnership, both internally in individuals and intrapersonally within relationships, offers a way of understanding and naming how the hands *do* 'know' how to solve the riddle. They 'know' because there is a deeply unconscious, psychoid bodymind structure and process that operates internally as well as interpersonally. Psychoid experience can be usefully expressed through art making in the presence of an art therapist and so provides opportunities for an individual to have a living experience of his or her unconscious process received, understood, contained, recycled and so transformed.

References

Akhtar, S. (1999) *Immigration and identity: Turmoil, treatment and transformation.* London: Jason Aronson.

Asen, E. (2002) 'Multiple family therapy: An overview'. *Journal of Family Therapy*, 4, pp. 345–358.

Bion, W.R. (1962) *Learning from experience.* London: Maresfield Reprints.

Clark, G. (1996) 'The animating body: Psychoid substance as a mutual experience of psycho-somatic disorder'. *The Journal of Analytical Psychology*, 41, pp. 353–368.

Clark, G. (2010) 'The embodied countertransference and recycling the mad matter of symbolic equivalence', in: Heuer, G. (ed.) *Sacral revolutions: Reflecting on the work of Andrew Samuels – Cutting edges in psychoanalysis and Jungian analysis.* London: Routledge, Taylor and Francis, pp. 88–96.

Dalley, T. (2008) 'I wonder if I exist?': A multi-family approach to the treatment of anorexia in adolescence, in: Case, C. and Dalley, T. (2008) *Art therapy with children: From infancy to adolescence.* London: Routledge, pp. 215–231.

Damasio, A. (1999) *The feeling of what happens: Body, emotion and the making of consciousness.* London: Vintage Books.

Damasio, A. (2003) *Looking for Spinoza: Joy, sorrow and the feeling brain.* Orlando: Harcourt.

Damasio, A. (2012) *Self comes to mind: Constructing the conscious brain.* London: Vintage Books.

Faimberg, H. (2005) *The telescoping of generations: Listening to the narcissistic links between generations.* London: Routledge, Taylor and Francis, and the Institute of Psychoanalysis.

Fraiberg, S., Adelson, E. and Shapiro, V. (1980) 'Ghosts in the nursery: A psychoanalytic approach to the problems of impaired infant-mother relationships', in: S. Fraiberg (ed.) *Clinical studies in infant mental health.* New York: Basic Books, pp. 164–196.

Freud, S. (1914) 'Remembering, repeating, and working through', in: Strachey, J. (ed.) (2001) *The standard edition of the complete psychological works of Sigmund Freud.* Vol. 12: *The case of Schreber, papers on technique, and other works.* London: Vintage Books, pp. 145–156.

Frosh, S. (2013) *Hauntings: Psychoanalysis and ghostly transmissions.* New York: Palgrave Macmillan.

Gerhardt, S. (2004) *Why love matters: How affection shapes a baby's brain.* London: Routledge, Taylor and Francis.

Grinberg, L. and Grinberg, R. (1989) *Psychoanalytic perspectives on migration and exile.* New Haven: Yale University Press.

Harvard Mental Health Letter (2009) Available at: http://www.health.harvard.edu/newsletters/harvard_mental_health_letter/2009/may (Accessed 8 November 2015).

Hass-Cohen, N. (2008) Partnering of art therapy and clinical neuroscience, in: Hass-Cohen, N. and Carr, R. (eds.) *Art therapy and clinical neuroscience.* London: Jessica Kingsley, pp. 21–42.

Hinton, L. (2009) The enigmatic signifier and the decentred subject. *The Journal of Analytical Psychology*, 54, pp. 637–657.

Jung, C.G. (1935/1968) 'The Tavistock lectures, Lecture V', in: *The collected works.* Vol. 18. Bollingen Series 20. Princeton: Princeton University Press, pp. 135–167.

Jung, C.G. (1954/1982) *The collected works.* Vol. 16. *The practice of psychotherapy.* Second edition. Bollingen Series 20. Princeton: Princeton University Press.

Jung, C.G. (1960/1969) *The collected works.* Vol. 8. *The structure and dynamics of the psyche.* Second edition. Princeton: Bollingen Foundation.

Jung, C.G. (1971) *The collected works.* Vol. 6. *Psychological types.* Bollingen Series 20. Princeton: Princeton University Press.

Klein, M. (1946) 'Notes on some schizoid mechanisms'. *International Journal of Psychoanalysis*, 27, pp. 99–110.

Knox, J. (2003) *Archetype, attachment, analysis: Jungian psychology and the emergent mind.* London: Routledge, Taylor and Francis.

Knox, J. (2004) 'From archetypes to reflective function'. *The Journal of Analytical Psychology*, 49, pp. 1–19.

Matthews, J. (1989) 'How young children give meaning to drawing', in: Gilroy, A. and Dalley, T. (eds.) *Pictures at an exhibition: Selected essays on art and art therapy.* London: Tavistock/ Routledge, pp. 127–142.

Matthews, J. (1994) *Helping children to draw and paint in early childhood: Children and visual representation.* London: Hodder and Stoughton.

Meyerowitz-Katz, J. (1998) 'Working with a two-year-old boy and his mother in art therapy: 'The world outside and the world within are related things, but not the same as the self' – A case study'. Unpublished paper submitted as part of the MA in Art Psychotherapy at Goldsmiths College, London.

Meyerowitz-Katz, J. (2003) 'Art materials and processes – A place of meeting: Art psycho-therapy with a four-year-old boy'. *Inscape: The Journal of the British Association of Art Thera-pists*, 8 (2), pp. 60–69.

Meyerowitz-Katz, J. (2011) 'Putting the dis-ease of psychoid infection to good use: Support-ing individuation and developing an analytic bodymind'. Unpublished long case study. ANZSJA C.G. Jung Institute.

Meyerowitz-Katz, J. (2013) 'Consciously forgotten, unconsciously remembered relationships made visible: The therapist's use of art making to understand the embodied transference-countertransference relationship'. ANZATA Conference, Sydney, October.

Meyerowitz-Katz, J. (2016) 'Navigating ambivalent states of bodymind: Working with inter-generationally transmitted Holocaust trauma in couple therapy'. *Couple and Family Psy-choanalysis*, 6(1), pp. 25–43.

O'Brien, F. (2004) 'The making of mess in art therapy: Attachment, trauma and the brain'. *Inscape*, 9 (1), pp. 2–13.

Orbach, S. (2006) 'Contemporary approaches to the body in psychotherapy: Two psycho-therapists in dialogue', in: Corrigall, J., Payne, H. and Wilkinson, H. (eds.) *About a body: Working with the embodied mind in psychotherapy.* London: Routledge, Taylor and Francis, pp. 68–69.

Rajani, R. (6/8/2012) Ugandan Asians: Life 40 years on. Available at: http://www.bbc.com/ news/world-africa-19066465 (Accessed 29 June 2015).

Schaverien, J. (1992) *The revealing image: Analytical art psychotherapy in theory and practice.* Lon-don: Tavistock/Routledge.

Seftel, L. (2001) 'The secret club project: Exploring miscarriage through the visual arts'. *Art Therapy: Journal of the American Art Therapy Association*, 18 (2), pp. 96–99.

Seftel, L. (2006) *Grief unseen: Healing pregnancy loss through the arts.* London: Jessica Kingsley.

Siegel, D.J. (2012) *The developing mind: How relationships and the brain interact to shape who we are.* Second Edition. London: Guilford Press.

Smith, N. R. (1993) *Experience and art: Teaching children to paint.* Second edition. London: Teachers College, Columbia University.

Wikipedia: https://en.wikipedia.org/wiki/Expulsion_of_Asians_from_Uganda (Accessed 29 June 2015).

Winborn, M. (2014) 'Introduction: An overview of participation mystique', in: Winborn, M. (ed.) *Shared realities: Participation mystique and beyond*. Skiatook, OK: Fisher King Press, pp. 1–29.

Winnicott, D.W. (1949) 'Mind and its relation to the psyche–soma', in: *Through paediatrics to psycho-analysis* (1982). London: The Hogarth Press and the Institute of Psychoanalysis, pp. 243–254.

Winnicott, D.W. (1971) *Playing and reality*. Aylesbury: Penguin Books.

PART 3

Group art therapy with infants and toddlers

9

BUILDING A FORT

Art therapy with a group of toddlers going through the adoption process

Marcela Andrade del Corro

Introduction

This chapter describes the way in which art therapy supported a group of toddlers living in a residential care home (hereafter referred to as 'the Home') while awaiting adoption. The toddlers had all experienced complex trauma and had all been separated from their biological families after suffering some form of abuse. Overwhelmed by experiences that had caused them unbearable psychic pain or anxiety, they came to the Home traumatised and without recourse to the usual defensive mechanisms (O'Brien, 2004, p. 3).

The work took place in Barcelona (Catalonia) Spain. I begin with a description of the context. I then introduce the children, followed by the discussion of the effects of the trauma. I then describe the clinical material and the unfolding of the therapeutic process.

The context of the art therapy

In Catalonia, when it is determined by Social Services that children are in need due to emotional and/or physical abuse or deprivation, and where their well-being is endangered, they are removed from their families. Ideally when this happens, the Department of Childhood in Catalonia (DGAIA) tries to place them with a foster family. As there are not enough families on the list to cover the need, many children are placed in residential care homes. During this time, the children are the legal responsibility of DGAIA and are awaiting a resolution from the court regarding possible adoptions.

The Home had the capacity to host children from birth to twelve years. This chapter describes work with a group of five young children aged from one to three years old during their stay in the Home. In order to respect their background and protect their identities I have called them Lucas, Denise, Carmen, Jasmin and Jussef. I introduce them in the sequence of their arrival at the Home.

The children

Lucas

Lucas was fifteen months old and initially lacked speech. He presented as being confident and happy. He freely explored the Home, crawling from one area to another, seemingly un-intimidated by the unknown adults and unfamiliar environment. Lucas subsequently displayed challenging behaviour and self-harm, slapping his face or scratching his cheek. He self-soothed by rocking to calm himself or scratching his ear.

Lucas was born in Portugal to a Spanish mother and Portuguese father. Neighbours reported hearing Lucas crying for extended periods of time and physical violence between his parents to the police. His mother was found lost and drunk, walking on the street with him.

There were no medical explanations for why Lucas wasn't walking, but the neuro-psychologist diagnosed global developmental delay. In terms of attachment, his seemed to be a case of emotional deprivation. Gerhardt (2004) writes that when a mother is present but not available physically or emotionally, she won't understand or respond adequately to the baby's needs, leaving him unregulated and in a state of helplessness.

Denise

Living in a single-parent family, two-year-old Denise was neglected by her depressed mother, who frequently left her with neighbours for weeks. Denise was removed from her home by a squad of police officers. She was traumatised by this experience and lost her capacity to speak, arriving at the Home mute.

Carmen

Carmen was nearly two years old and came from a gypsy family, where she had suffered neglect. In Spain, the word gypsy makes reference to people who belong to a different cultural and ethnic background but hold a Spanish citizenship. The term is not derogatory, but is connected with marginalisation and poverty.

Her mother was unable to assume guardianship due to having a moderate learning disability, and her father was absent. Carmen and her mother were living with Carmen's grandparents and aunts, who assumed responsibility for her education. The whole family was dependant on state benefits. There was an intergenerational history of deprivation and a long-standing tension between the family and Social Services: Carmen's family had come to the attention of Social Services when her mother and aunts were young.

Carmen arrived at the Home distressed and did not stop crying for hours.

Jasmin

Jasmin arrived at the age of three after having experienced multiple separations, experiences of having been 'dropped and picked up' (Edwards, 2008). Her mother left her with her grandmother in Morocco, where she was born, and went to Catalonia to work. Her mother took her to Barcelona when she was about a year old, but after a few months she was left with another relative. Subsequently, her mother just dropped her into DGAIA. She came to the Home carrying a plastic bag with a spare pair of trousers and a t-shirt. Jasmine spoke Arabic.

Jasmin had terrible tantrums and also had difficulties during the night-time routine. Sometimes she would refuse to go to bed while displaying distress and self-harm, pulling her hair and slapping herself or biting her own hand, and sometimes just crying.

Jussef

Jussef was sixteen months old when he arrived. He was also from an Arabic background and had not yet developed speech. He was born in Catalonia but his parents were immigrants from Morocco. He came from hospital because his father, who was misusing alcohol and physically abusing his mother, had begun physically abusing him. Jussef was hospitalised and separated immediately from his parents. Jussef found being alone, even for short periods of time, unbearable.

Migration and poverty

Catalonia was a welcoming region from the 1990s onwards, receiving people from different nationalities (especially from the north of Africa, Pakistan and South America) who were motivated to migrate from poverty to pursue a better future. However, on arrival, migrants were often confronted with the reality of poverty, inequality and marginalisation, which left families vulnerable to mental breakdown and substance misuse. Vives (2008) describes how exile and migration are powerful and disorganising experiences, which mobilise intense anxieties. Bion (Symington and Symington, 1996) defined this as a catastrophic change. The individual leaves his country and is now in a place where identity, organisation and integration are not possible: 'the trans zone' (Sor, 1988).

The parents of the children at the Home could feel victimised by a state system which acts like an abuser through marginalisation, and society tends to demonise these parents. The tension between the love bonds in these families and the state's decision to intervene to protect the children was painful to contemplate.

Trauma

Trauma for Papadopoulos 'means "injury", or "wound", and metaphorically in psychology and psychiatry refers to a psychological injury, a deficit, a pathological state' (Papadopoulos, 2007, p. 304). 'The psychiatric definition of trauma includes any experience which threatens your life or your body, or any harm which is inflicted on your intentionally' (APA, 2013 in Gerhardt, 2004, p. 158).

All the children had experienced complex trauma, including their placement in the Home. Spitz (1999) studied the effects of separation for young infants who were separated from their mothers for more than three months. Effects included global developmental delay and disruption of perceptual-motor skills and language. Robertson and Robertson (1989) noticed a range of emotions, including sadness and aggression. Within this group there were clear patterns of intergenerational transmission of trauma, which led to disrupted attachments. Fraiberg et al. describe how 'The baby in these families is burdened by the oppressive past of his parents from the moment he enters the world. The parent it seems is condemned to repeat the tragedy of his childhood with his own baby in terrible and exacting detail' (Fraiberg et al., 1975, p. 388), enacting what Freud (1948) described as 'repetition compulsion'.

In terms of attachment, difficulties arise when the main caregiver is not able to attune, to identify the baby's states or to be emotionally available, but the most damaging experiences for the baby are abuse and abandonment (Comín, 2012). The work of Bowlby (1976) and Ainsworth (1978) has identified and documented the terrible damage that can occur as a result of these experiences (Dio Bleichmar, 2005).

We know from research that abuse causes damage to the right hemisphere of the brain (Schore in O'Brien, 2004, p. 3). 'The abused child may be hypervigilant or aggressive, the neglected child may be profoundly inhibited in their exploration and learning' (Wassel, 2008, p. 50). O'Brien (2004), Hass-Cohen (2006) and Shore (2014) conclude that the consequences of this damage are expressed in behavioural issues, dissociation, cognition, affect regulation, sense of togetherness and empathy.

The whole group of children described in this chapter somatised their anxieties: chronic bronchitis, atopic skin complaints or allergies were commonplace where there were none reported previously. The carers referred to all of them (except Jasmin) as 'fussy eaters'. The group faced difficulties with falling asleep, and the challenging behaviour of Lucas and Jasmin was displayed with more intensity, showing us their inability to cope and communicating discomfort on many levels. When this experience cannot be elaborated it becomes self-aggression, 'the attack of the own body' (Comín, 2012, p. 12).

Institutional care

The purpose of the Home is to protect the children. The experience of institutionalisation does not necessarily condemn a child to unsettledness and vulnerability. It can potentially be a safe and holding environment if all the professionals work together to provide a good level of support. Robertson and Robertson (1989) suggest that the provision of a positive caring environment can mitigate almost all adverse reactions to separation.

However, the length of time that the child spends in the institution matters. Waiting for a long period of time can cause a child to feel abandoned. The resources of the residence and the ratio of staff to children have an impact on the possibilities of offering an attachment figure for each child; otherwise the child is condemned to the 'stigmata of the child who has spent the better part of her life in a crib with little more than obligatory care' (Fraiberg et al., 1975, p. 31). At the time the DGAIA's ratio for children under four was one caregiver for three and a half children.

The children arrived with severe attachment disorders, unable to attach satisfactorily with objects as well as people, or even recognise a piece of clothing as a familiar one with significance and value. In order to provide a corrective experience for attachment disorders the child will need an attuned, coherent and constant attachment figure (Stern, 1999, 2011), who is willing to help the child to regulate feelings and physical states (Gerhardt, 2004). Comín states that in this kind of setting the caregivers embody the attachment figure and sometimes this is not a single figure but the sum of the caregivers and the place (Comín, 2012).

Adoption practices in Catalonia

The adoption system in Catalonia is open to all types of families, including single parents and gay couples. Social Services do not match children with a family of the same ethnical/cultural background. Returning a child to DGAIA is a possibility for a family who have adopted and are not coping, particularly if this situation could potentially cause more harm to the child. At 30 per cent, the statistics of children returned in Catalonia are very high (Amorós, 2008), and inside the Home there were two cases of children being adopted and later returned. This led to the staff feeling overwhelmed in order to ensure a successful adoption.

Adoption is a life process and the emotional implications for the child have to be taken into consideration.

> The complexity of children's needs, the lifelong implications of adoption and the three parties to adoption – child, birth parents and adoptive families – together with the evidence from research have all highlighted the fact that family making through adoption is a complex and challenging process.
>
> *(Hindle and Schulman, 2008, p. 3)*

Amorós (2008) recommends giving the child an active role in which his voice, feelings and experience are fundamental, describing how during the adoption process the child has to face and elaborate many griefs. This may include the loss of his or her birth culture, country and identity, and idealised 'mum and dad' family. The child, in his or her own time and rhythm, has to accept these strangers as parents and, symbolically speaking, adopt them.

The art therapy group

The art therapy group (hereafter called the Group) was established as a good enough space with the following aims:

1) To offer a sense of being grounded:

> Development is a challenging process: for a severely traumatised child this development is even more complex (Bettelheim, 1999). 'The child

is therefore dependent on a reliable caregiver or facilitating environment, to help them to organise their experience' (Case, 2008, p. 123). Layado defines this feeling of being grounded as existing when 'adults can create enough of a sense of continuity of emotional containment for the child' (Layado, 2008, p. 156). In this light, art therapy may create a positive impact in the life of the child by providing a secure base (Bowlby, 1988), constructed with coherence and continuity.

2) To heal attachment wounds:

Working towards a renegotiation of attachment was part of the work. The Group itself was thought to represent the attachment figure, providing a secure space and giving a sense of continuity and reliability.

3) To palliate the effects of abuse and institutionalisation:

To palliate is a word that came from the Latin 'pallium' and it means 'to mitigate, alleviate' (Collins Dictionary, 2006, p. 610). 'We cannot change what has happened to children in the past' (Miller, 2008, p. 63); unfortunately, abuse and neglect happened.

4) To be a facilitating environment:

It was hoped that the expression of traumatic experience in the Group would enable the children to gradually de-traumatise and integrate their experiences, and offer them opportunities to share experiences and feelings (Yalom, 1986). Hopefully they would benefit from 'the opportunity to be part of a group with its own culture, which is dependent on the contribution of all its members, and is an important experience to the emotional growth of children, especially those who have not had good experiences in their family' (Prokofiev, 1998, p. 51).

5) To offer communication through art materials and processes:

With the idea that 'art materials and processes can provide an area of concrete negotiation that fosters the development of internal structures leading to therapeutic growth' (Meyerowitz-Katz, 2003, p. 60), it was hoped that the children could find a vehicle for communication, expression and integration of traumatic experiences and sense of self.

The place of the art therapy group within the institution

The Group and the Home were conceived of as forms of 'transitional space' (Winnicott, 2013), spaces between the biological family and the adoptive family where the institution embodied the paternal figure (an important role as so many of the fathers were absent and/or violent), the group the maternal figure, and the children were waiting. The transitional space of the Group was considered to be a holding and containing environment (Symington and Symington, 1996), capable of creating a bridge of understanding for the child, and also for the adoptive parents, between the past and the future.

The Group took place twice a week over a period of eleven months, meeting after the afternoon nap. This routine facilitated the sense of being grounded, which started by providing consistency in the setting: the same therapist on the same days each week, the same box of materials. I even wore the same gown each time. I also provided every child with a box in which to store the things created during the sessions.

The first stages of the Group

For the first few months, the children's communications were largely preverbal and the Group was characterised by abundant mess and chaos. The children used the materials, space and myself to communicate the discomfort of the messy and painful feelings with which they were surrounded. The first session began with a high level of anxiety. Lucas anxiously explored the materials and the space quickly and almost without looking at the objects, finishing by empting the box and spreading the contents noisily and chaotically all around. He seemed calmer when he finished. Jasmin anxiously poured some paint on a piece of paper and started to make some movements in the paint with her hands. She mixed colours repeatedly, painted her arms and clothes and made some noises by tapping the paper.

Denise and Jussef began by drawing with crayons and pens. Jussef moved around the room, exploring the boundaries of the setting, constantly interfering with the work of the others. He painted on Denise's drawing and Jasmin's painting, finishing by sitting on Jasmin's work. This upset her and led to her having a tantrum.

Carmen remained in the corner of the room, colouring with crayons, testing the boundaries by sticking some stickers to the walls of the room.

The Group displayed disorganised attachment and deep confusion about the place. They were confused about where they ended and other people began and didn't seem 'to know where I am: what is inside of me is me, and what is outside of me is not me' (Winnicott, 2013, p. 169).

At this stage the Group was functioning like an archipelago, with the children interacting like separate islands. It seemed that the group was communicating their shared inner chaos and their lack of connection with others. They included me in the messy and painful feelings which overwhelmed them. The use of art and play materials in the group context enabled the communication of deep levels of distress and trauma; art therapy groups of children are characterised by mess making (Prokofiev, 1998). O'Brien concludes that for severely traumatised children mess and chaos are even more common: 'materials used as bodily substances of dirt, conveying feelings of being messed up inside, or as attempts to find boundaries or distinguish between good and bad feelings' (O'Brien, 2004, pp. 4–5).

My countertransference experience was intense. Jung writes that 'emotions are contagious because they are rooted in the sympathetic nervous system. . . . Any process of an emotional kind immediately arouses a similar process in others.' He goes on to say that it is inevitable that the doctor (therapist) will be affected by the emotions of patients, and that he 'cannot do more than become conscious of the fact that he is affected' (Jung, 1954/1982, para. 18). I felt unable to hold such a mess, but I knew that I had to accept feeling chaotic and remain in a state of not-knowing and not even understanding how best to hold the group.

The children found the endings of the sessions extremely difficult, particularly Lucas and Jasmine. Both had a severe tantrum every time the group had to end; this resulted in them breaking and ripping their artwork created during the sessions. Prokofiev writes that 'the ending of the session is often resisted by the children, who need space to express the feelings of separation, loss and sometimes rejection which are aroused' (Prokofiev, 1998, pp. 55–56). Given the unpredictability of their previous lives they may have feared, at the ending of the group, that they would never have this experience of symbolic plenty ever again.

After three months the sessions gradually became less messy and chaotic. They included more sensory play with different textures, movements and noises, and seemed enjoyable rather than painful. The children also seemed to be more open to receiving my reflections. When I intervened, commenting that 'It seems that the group really needs to use the red paint today' the group stopped for a brief second, looked at me and then continued with their task. They were understanding, absorbing and digesting my words, a reflection of the way in which I was trying to do the same with their communications.

Over time, the regularity of the sessions and clarity of the frame meant that the children began to experience a sense of continuity that they could rely on, developing a sense of 'going-on-being' (Winnicott, 1963); and this led to the changes in their play and receptiveness to my comments.

Lucas and Jasmin began to cry at the end of the sessions. The traumatic quality of the endings had dissipated; replaced with grief at the loss of something good. Gradually the children were learning to trust that what was offered was reliable, so that they were sad when it ended but did not desperately fear that it would never happen again.

A co-created group mural

The table was consistently covered with a big piece of paper during every session, and the group had not paid attention to it for weeks until, led by Jasmin, they suddenly used it to paint a mural (Plate 12) and (Figure 9.1).

The children collaborated together, using few words to interact, enjoying sounds, movement and textures. On this occasion I was a witness. They didn't need my help to organise the space and play; my role was to reflect the meaning and provide containment. The group's joint use of the paper and the table symbolised a change in the group process. They worked together, painting and exploring the paper's space individually but also in the presence of each other. Franklin writes, 'some mural artists practice a similar attunement on the collective level by creating

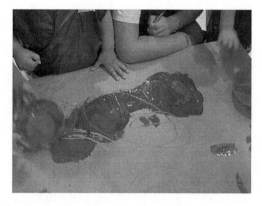

FIGURE 9.1 Co-created mural.

a cultural portrait that successfully locates and renders the emotional centre of the community' (Franklin, 2010, p. 162). They were recognising the boundaries of the space and the other: identifying the group as a symbolic family and as a place where there was 'emotional food'. It seemed that the group was providing a counter to the 'emotional starvation' (Fraiberg et al., 1975, p. 388) in these children linked to the anxiety around food exhibited in the early sessions. My countertransference changed; I felt less overwhelmed and found it easier to contain them.

The middle stage of the group

In the next couple of months there was a lot of change. Jasmin started school and became articulate in both Spanish and Catalan, and her voice in the Group became stronger. Carmen and Denise also started school. These events were significant because in engaging with the outside world the children became curious about their situation and used the Group to ask questions like 'What is this place?' and 'Who is a mommy?' This reflects their use of the space and the room as a place to construct their identity and to think.

There was a change during the sixth month of the group, as the following vignette illustrates.

Lucas was the first to arrive and he looked for the box of materials. He was fascinated with a little toy bicycle that became very important and in the following sessions kept it next to him. He drew with crayons and markers but once in a while stopped to check if the bicycle was still next to him and grabbed it to make the wheels spin. Carmen, Jasmin and Denise engaged in painting with brushes and sponges. They were very amused by the different sounds, textures and mixing of colours. Jussef worked with Play-Doh; he was busy making a path with little pieces that made me think of 'Hansel and Gretel' (Grimm and Grimm, 2008). The little crumbs in his narrative seemed to reflect his sense of loss, recalling that for him being alone was intolerable. There is no worse fantasy for the child than that of being abandoned (Bettelheim,

1999). Stern (2011) states that even the briefest absence of the mother is experienced as swimming in the ocean, where the space becomes bigger and bigger.

At the end of the session, Denise stopped painting and became very interested in organising the different materials inside her box. The interaction had helped her process something, so that she was able to organise the materials as a symbolic form of organising herself. In this session she started to articulate little words which were difficult to understand because she was speaking in secret, but in the next sessions this improved. She started to have conversations with the dolls provided in the Group, describing her day and singing lullabies. This led to her speaking with her peers and then the adults in the Home, including myself.

The changes within the Group were reflected in the children's daily life: behavioural issues became less dramatic, tantrums were less common, sleeping difficulties gradually improved and they ate more. It seems that the assimilating and digesting occurring in the Group processes and the art materials were a representation of getting symbolic food, and the result was the children were accepting and processing real food.

Like Lucas with the bicycle, they began to attach to objects – recognising a piece of clothing or agreeing to sleep with a particular object and carrying a specific toy all the time. The transitional space of the Home and Group was enabling them to develop their own transitional capacities and objects, and with that a renegotiation of their attachment disorders.

The fort

In the seventh month of treatment, the children started to play together during the session. Denise suggested the idea of building a fort. This was spontaneous but the group followed her, as she was the voice at this moment. The children took turns to be the voice of the group in different ways at different times. They built the fort using the boxes of materials and some paper sheets. They co-operated and followed Denise's instructions. Lucas represented the anxious part of the group, as he insisted on getting in the fort before it was finished. On this occasion they asked for my help to organise the fort and make sure that the parts they couldn't reach were in place, inviting me to get in when it was finished.

The dynamic consisted of staying in all together (including myself) for a while. Being inside was funny – everybody laughed, but we were also silent for a time; Jasmin made the sign for silence, as if we were keeping a secret or were in hiding.

This metaphor suggested a defensive state. At this moment information was circulating about adoptions and, although the professionals involved were cautious, inside institutions the information is not completely private. On one hand, the defensive states were composed of resistance and denial, being in hiding and building a space that nobody could penetrate, but they also revealed a feeling of being threatened. The fort was also a symbol of the Home and the Group.

The children subsequently spent time during each session building a 'fort'. The construction of the fort was not always the same; the Group explored the different materials and ways that a fort may be built. For example they often used fabric to cover the boxes, put pieces of cardboard on their heads, hid under the table and blocked the 'entrance to the fort' with the boxes of materials.

They included me in this game, wanting me to be inside the fort with them. However, because of the nature of the materials they used to construct it, sometimes I couldn't get inside or join them when they were hiding under the table, I didn't fit. This made me think about my role inside of the Group. It was evident that I was the different one, but also part of it. The fact that I did not always fit tells us that I wasn't part of the reality of living inside of the Home, but I was present. On the other hand it is also a recognition that I and others are not adopted. By playing with the concept of inside and outside, the children were taking in 'mother' and all she represents in terms of Bion's containment (Symington and Symington, 1996), and having a mother nearby as an attachment figure (Bowlby, 1988).

On a couple of occasions Lucas became violent and tore the fort apart. This upset the rest of the Group; they verbally expressed anger and Jussef cried. As a result they wanted to exclude Lucas from their play. I mediated the situation, validating their feelings and providing an act of reparation, saying, 'I see that what Lucas did is making you feel upset. He didn't know it was going to upset you. I am going to help Lucas to build the fort again and then we can all play together.'

This was a way for Lucas to enact part of his experience and his own material and he was also representing something for the group, to do with intergenerational trauma: 'if the primary carer is unable to control feelings of extreme anger, and expresses their violence through acts of abuse on the child, then these children may well go on to enact similar acts of violence' (Boronska, 2000, p. 2).

Adoption process: the impact of the outside world on the Group

During the eighth month legal decisions started to come from court, and with that came the challenge of preparing the Group for ending. Those decisions didn't come at the same time. The order for leaving the Home was: first Jasmin would be placed with an adoptive family, then Carmen was going to return to her family, Jussef was going to live with his extended family, and finally Denise and Lucas were going to be placed in adoptive families.

The staff team gave a lot of thought as to how to handle the information in an appropriate way in order to avoid making the children feel confused. It was decided to create a 'story tale' with pictures and images of each child in the Home, and to include pictures of the adoptive family. As the Group had been instrumental in supporting their emotional and psychological development, it was agreed that we would start this preparation within the Group. Since Jasmine would be the first to leave, her process would model for the rest of the children what would happen. The session that day started with Jasmine's news; we all gathered to look at the pictures and listen to what she was telling us about her adoption. She expressed excitement and visible anxiety. I put special emphasis on not calling the adoptive parents Mum and Dad. It is vital to do this to help the child to differentiate between the former parents and to allow the child to accept the adoptive parents in his or her own time (Amorós, 2008).

The rest of the Group was present, except for Carmen, who refused to listen and was withdrawn from the group dynamic, doing some drawing. She represented the part of the Group who was not ready and needed more time to digest the news. The children were using the materials with visible confusion and anxiety. More mess was present, and the ending of the session was particularly difficult for everybody as they pretended they were not listening to my instructions and refused to tidy up.

The ending

As the children started to leave the Home, those who remained expressed more confusion and feelings of anger and sadness. Ripping objects and mess making were more present again, indicating understandable regression in the face of separation.

I made sure that everyone took their box of images created in the Group as part of their transition. Lucas and Denise were the last ones to leave, and they had to wait for a couple of months to be matched with their adoptive families. Inside the Group Lucas was really violent and destructive with the material, ripping things and expressing his anger. Then Denise, who was feeling abandoned waiting for her adoptive family, symbolically adopted Lucas. She took care of him and helped him with his daily tasks, like eating and dressing, like a real mother does. This dynamic of members taking on roles as a way of managing their feelings is also a response to the reality of being in a state of having to wait, and also a way to fight against the feeling of abandonment.

Lucas was the last one to leave. He was a bit more verbal and he enjoyed playing with different textures or imitating the sounds of animals and other things. Very often he evoked his former peers, saying their names and pointing to something that reminded him of them. The elaboration of the loss for Lucas was a long process, as he was the first to arrive and the last one to leave. My role consisted of giving him support and reflecting his different emotional states.

Conclusion

After having experienced some form of abuse or deprivation, the children in the Home experienced the trauma of separation from their parents and disintegration of their worlds. This, combined with being institutionalised and awaiting adoption in a very early moment in development, caused attachment disorders and somatisation. The art therapy environment provided them with opportunities for a more favourable outcome.

The art therapy group represented a transitional space between family of origin, the institution and the adoptive family. It became a symbolic family, a secure base that was reliable, and provided holding and containment where the children could build trust. The creation of a symbolic family allowed a sense of togetherness and renegotiation of disrupted attachments, especially when the parent-child relationships were so conflicted.

The opportunity to be part of an art therapy group with its own ethos and the sense of having a symbolic family allowed the children to take turns to be the voice, enacting internal family models and exploring differences and similarities. Working together as a group the children were able to each enrich their own sense of belonging, sense of self, identity and trust in the other.

Within the Group the different stages that characterised the therapeutic process were quite remarkable. The materials and processes acted as a vehicle of communication, negotiation and understanding of different states and experiences. The beginning was characterised by mess, chaos and painful feelings. The use of the therapist as a receiver of the traumatic experience acted as a first moment of holding and understanding. The use of the space and materials allowed for thinking and questioning about the inside and outside world, and with that a fuller identity and sense of self started to develop.

Gradually the Group moved to a stage where changes were evident in the children's daily lives as behavioural and somatisation issues faded. The Group supported their changing needs and development and also facilitated the acceptance of the adoption process. The ending was defined by a strong sense of the cyclic nature of the therapeutic process and attachment behaviours. The return to understandably regressive and aggressive behavioural states was a way to cope in the face of saying goodbye to their peers, the Home and staff. The adoptive families subsequently reported that the boxes and files with the artwork were helping the children by evoking memories and building up a self-narrative.

In art therapy, the context shapes how we work. Providing a specific answer in terms of models of intervention helped these traumatised children to palliate the effects of their experience, in order to give them the possibility of embracing a positive future.

Acknowledgements

I would like to thank my colleagues Olga López, Thijs de Moor and Sarah Wiltshire for their immense help during the preparation of this chapter.

I also want to express my gratitude to Dean Reddick and Julia Meyerowitz-Katz, for their kind invitation to participate in this journey together.

References

Ainsworth, M. (1978) *Patterns of attachment: A psychological study of the strange situation*. Hillside, NJ: Erlbaum.

Amorós, C. (2008) 'Del abandono a la adopción: Un proceso dinámico de diálogo con el desamparo', *Intercanvis*, 21, pp. 7–12 [Online]. Available at: http://intercanvis.es/articulos/13/art_n13_01R.html (Accessed: 01 April 2015).

Bettelheim, B. (1999) *Psicoanálisis de los cuentos de hadas*. Barcelona: Paidós.

Boronska, T. (2000) 'Art therapy with two sibling groups using an attachment framework'. *Inscape*, 5 (1), pp. 2–10.

Bowlby, J. (1976) *La separación afectiva*. Buenos Aires: Paidós.

Bowlby, J. (1988) *A secure base: Clinical applications of attachment theory*. London: Routledge.

Case, C. (2008) 'The mermaid: Moving towards reality after trauma'. In Hindle, D. and Shulman, G. (eds.) *The emotional experience of adoption*. London: Routledge, pp. 121–135.

Collins Dictionary (2006) *Concise dictionary and treasures*. Glasgow: HarperCollins.

Comín, M. (2012) 'El vinculo de apego y sus conecuencias para el psiquismo humano,' *Intercanvis*, 29, pp. 7–17 [Online]. Available at: http://intercanvis.es/articulos/29/art_n029_01R.html (Accessed: 01 April 2015).

Dio Bleichmar, E. (2005) *Manual de psicoterapia de la relacion padres e hijos*. Barcelona: Paidós.

Edwards, J. (2008) 'On being dropped and picked up: The plight of some late-adopted children'. In Hindle, D. and Shulman, G. (eds.) *The emotional experience of adoption*. London: Routledge, pp. 136–147.

Fraiberg, S., Adelson, E. and Shapiro, V. (1975) 'Ghosts in the nursery: A psychoanalytic approach to the problems of impaired infant-mother relationships'. *Journal of the American Academy of Child & Adolescent Psychiatry*, 14 (3), pp. 387–421.

Franklin, M. (2010) 'Affect regulation, mirror neurons and the third hand: Formulating mindful empathic art interventions'. *Journal of the American Art therapy Association*, 27 (4), pp. 160–167.

Freud, S. (1948) 'Más allá del principio del placer'. In Freud, S. (ed.) *Obras completas de Freud*, 1, Madrid: Biblioteca Nueva Madrid, pp. 1089–1117.

Gerhardt, S. (2004) *Why love matters: How affection shapes a baby's brain*. London: Routledge.

Grimm, J. and Grimm, W. (2008) *Hansel and Gretel*. London: Floris Books.

Hass-Cohen, N. (2006) 'Art therapy and clinical neuroscience in action'. *GAINS Community Newsletter*, Spring, pp. 10–12.

Hindle, D. and Schulman, G. (2008) *The emotional experience of adoption*. London: Routledge.

Jung, C.G. (1954/1982) *The collected works*. Vol. 16. *The practice of psychotherapy*. Second edition. Bollingen Series 20. Princeton: Princeton University Press.

Layado, M. (2008) 'Playing out, not acting out: The development of the capacity to play in the therapy of children who are "in transition" from fostering to adoption', in Hindle, D. and Shulman, G. (eds.) *The emotional experience of adoption*. London: Routledge, pp. 155–167.

Meyerowitz-Katz, J. (2003) 'Art materials and processes – A place of meeting: Art psychotherapy with a four-year-old boy'. *Inscape: The Journal of the British Association of Art Therapists*, 8 (2), pp. 60–69.

Miller, L. (2008) 'Understanding an adopted child: A child psychotherapist's perspective'. In Hindle, D. and Shulman, G. (eds.) *The emotional experience of adoption*. London: Routledge, pp. 57–69.

O'Brien, F. (2004) 'The making of mess in art therapy'. *Inscape*, 9 (1), pp. 2–13.

Papadopoulos, R. (2007) 'Refugees, trauma and adversity activated development'. *European Journal of Psychotherapy and Counselling*, 9 (3), pp. 301–312 [Online]. Available at: http://repository.tavistockandportman.ac.uk/159/1/Papadopoulos_-_Refugess.pdf (Accessed: 01 April 2015).

Prokofiev, F. (1998) 'Adapting the art therapy group for children', in Skaife, S. and Huet, V. (eds.) *Art psychotherapy groups: Between pictures and words*. London: Routledge, pp. 44–68.

Robertson, J. and Robertson, J. (1989) *Separation and the very young*. London: Free Association Books.

Shore, A. (2014) 'Art therapy, attachment and the divided brain'. *Journal of the American Art Therapy Association*, 31 (2), pp. 91–94.

Sor, D. (1988) *Cambio catastrofico: Psicoanálisis del darse cuenta*. Buenos Aires: Kargienman.

Spitz, R. (1999) *El primer año de vida del niño*. Madrid: Fondo de Cultura Económica de España.

Stern, D. (1999) *El nacimiento de una madre*. Barcelona: Paidós.

Stern, D. (2011) *El diario de un bebé*. Madrid: Paidós.

Symington, J. and Symington, N. (1996) *The clinical thinking of Wilfred Bion*. London: Routledge.

Vives, A. (2008) 'Identidad y exhilio', *Intercanvis*, 20 [Online]. Available at: http://intercanvis.es/articulos/20/art_n020_04R.html (Accessed: 01 April 2015).

Wassel, S. (2008) 'Why is early development important?' in Hindle, D. and Shulman, G. (eds.) *The emotional experience of adoption*. London: Routledge, pp. 42–56.

Winnicott, D. (1963) *Maturational process and the facilitating environment* [Online]. Available at: www.abebe.org.br (Accessed: 10 July 2015).

Winnicott, D. (2013) *Realidad y juego*. Barcelona: Gedisa.

Yalom, I. (1986) *Teoría y práctica de la psicoterapia de grupo*. Mexico City: Fondo de Cultura Económica.

10

MAKING WAVES

An art therapist's retrospective review of countertransference images and case material that took place in a preschool setting

Julie Green

Setting the scene

In the spring of 2002 I undertook my first student placement as part of my training to become an art therapist. My placement was situated in a preschool in a Sydney suburb with a large proportion of low-income families and with a mix of people from different ethnicities and cultural backgrounds, including recent immigrants from Russia and parts of Asia. The preschool was a not-for-profit, community-based service and was open to the public for attendance by children aged two to five. The preschool's philosophy aimed to provide high-quality early childhood services and offered children with additional needs inclusion into the service. The children at the preschool were identified as coming from high-risk backgrounds. Many of the children experienced emotional deprivation and incidents of physical abuse and neglect. Perry and Szalavitz (2008) speak of the trauma that is associated with high-risk populations as having lasting impact and state that even minor stresses in infancy can have considerable impact on development.

In order to improve the 'holding environment' (Miller et al., 2002, p. 8) and provide the children with a secure base (Bowlby, 1978), the preschool adapted the Circle of Security programme (Marvin et al., 2002). Staff were encouraged to reflect on the inner worlds of the children, to develop their awareness of what might be happening within their relationships with the children and to think about how the children experienced separation. Ainsworth (1967), cited in Karen (1998, p. 136), states,

> Again and again she observed that once they were able to crawl the children would make small excursions away from their mothers, always maintaining consciousness of her whereabouts and returning to her periodically, either physically or with a smile. Using the phrase that would become the

cornerstone of attachment thinking, she wrote, 'The mother seems to provide a secure base from which these excursions can be made without anxiety.'

I was present at the art therapy table for a period of eleven weeks. After the first six
weeks (during which I attended once per week) there was a three-week break, and
then the position was resumed for five weeks before the placement ended. In the
final three weeks I attended twice a week at a parent's request; they were anxious
about my impending departure. I had formed a therapeutic alliance and relationship
with their daughter, Kate, at the art therapy table.

The art therapy table and the open outside setting

The art therapy table was situated in a playground. It was set up with paint, crayons,
colour pencils and collage material. There were six seats at the table and a rack for
drying paintings next to it. There was also a set of swings, an open cubby house,
a sandpit, storage shed and an area for playing with blocks and toys. These areas,
including the art therapy table, functioned as secure base zones and formed the
circle of security (Marvin et al., 2002). Each base had a member of staff present,
providing an attachment figure at a particular activity zone. The staff, including
myself, were encouraged to observe the children as they navigated the circle and
moved from base to base. We were to welcome the children as they approached and
help them to begin to understand their feelings. It was emphasised that we should
stay at our bases as much as possible and in doing so we were creating a predictable
environment for the children.

Berman (2011) oversaw the practice of community art counsellors in the open
setting of a refugee camp. She speaks of the amount of effort required for counsellors to stay in touch with the value of their work and its containing function
in the face of feelings of uselessness and helplessness. Conversely, Reddick (1999,
p. 20) outlines the importance of a separate space for art therapy in a children's
day-care centre and states, 'as Greenwood and Layton (1987) have pointed out
the physical separateness of an art therapy space can resonate with a psychological
separateness.' Reddick explains that the distinctness of different rooms for different
activities in the preschool can be useful for the children who are still developing an
understanding of 'the boundaries between self and other' (Reddick, 1999, p. 20).
The separate room can also be useful for the art therapist in establishing his or her
frame without the distractions or intrusions that might occur when there is no
physical boundary.

Although a discrete separate space for art therapy was absent in the preschool in
which I was placed, the distinct zones supported the possibility that relationships
might form between an adult caregiver and a child within the context of a 'secure
base'.

As Kate's and my relationship developed at the table I was aware that we were
able to establish a connected rapport despite the hectic activity around us. Through

my focus and our shared concentration the awareness of peripheral noise and activity receded. I think of this as an intimate and discrete bubble-like shelter at the art table in which the therapeutic work could happen.

In the playground the bubble-like shelter at the table could be ruptured by another child approaching the table, upsetting the established equilibrium. In this way the table was somewhat like an open group in a structured, open, outside setting. Deco, speaking of the role of the art therapist in the open studio group, speaks of the hard task of 'respect for the idiosyncratic unfolding of the creative in each particular individual . . . held alongside an awareness of the group-as-a-whole' (Deco, 1998, p. 105). At times there was a jostling of children at the table and Kate would push for my sole attention. It was possible that within the relationship between us there was a desire for an exclusive relationship that held the focus of a pre-Oedipal (Laplanche and Pontalis, 1988) mother-baby state.

Harmony and discord: the nature of primitive anxieties

> When I was young enough to still spend a long time buttoning my shoes in the morning, I'd listen toward the hall: Daddy upstairs was shaving in the bathroom and Mother downstairs was frying the bacon. They would begin whistling back and forth to each other up and down the stairwell. My father would whistle his phrase, my mother would try to whistle, then hum hers back. It was their duet. I drew my buttonhook in and out and listened to it.
>
> (Welty, 1995, p. 1)

The foregoing quote is a beautiful description of a young child's awareness of the harmony and interrelatedness of her parent's musical dialogue. Thinking about the dialogue psychodynamically, it could be said that there was a harmonic resonance across a space between a loving couple and their child, within the safety of their home. The resonance was supporting the child to find her way through the difficult task of shoe lacing within the rhythm and music of her parents' connection. This resonance is akin to McNeilly's (2006) concept of resonance in groups that operates on an unconscious level. In the preschool playground there was a resonance that was being shared. Continuing the musical analogy – it held a more discordant interrelational sound, one that is filled with anxiety and fear, something unhoused and much more offbeat and clanging. This discordance is what I heard, felt and worked within at the placement.

A description of the cacophonous mix: my remembering

Feeling overstimulated on an audio level. Sitting at the low children's table. Discomfort, anxiety and concentration. Cascading sounds of screaming children as they tear past my table, running on their way to another destination. Behind them the sounds of children running, children sitting and crying, children laughing and playing. Quieter children self-absorbed in water play in the sandpit. Teachers calling loudly. Visually moving my gaze forwards and backwards between the children in the playground and the piece of paper in front of me that I am painting, drawing and sticking things down on to.

Here I have described my experience of the occasionally overwhelming nature of the movements and sounds in the playground. Amongst the intensity of feeling in the playground I could discern moments where primitive anxieties broke through the children's play. Baradon et al. (2005) informs us that in the event of parenting that is not good enough the infant is exposed to states of overwhelming helplessness. Drawing on the legacy of psychoanalytic thinkers she goes on to say that 'These states have been described as experiences of "falling forever", "unthinkable anxiety" and annihilation anxiety' (Bion, 1962, Winnicott, 1962 in Baradon et al., 2005, p. 8). These uncontained primitive anxieties (Case, 2005) could be felt in the preschool playground.

When introducing the practice of infant observation Rustin describes the students' exposure to the kinds of intense feelings just outlined as 'an emotional force field' in which it is difficult to hold one's balance (Rustin, 2002, p. 8). Rustin states that the observer's own infantile self will be painfully stimulated by the experience of observing the vulnerability of the infant, and by observing the mother-baby couple. The challenge at the preschool was to find my balance amidst the felt discordance and to provide a secure base at the art therapy table for the children.

Remembering: a retrospective view

The following reflections are framed by my rereading of a case study written during my student placement in the preschool. The case material has been changed in such a way as to protect client confidentiality. My memories from that time are suffused with a surprising aliveness, especially in regards to the chaotic and fraught atmosphere of the open setting. Perhaps this aliveness persists because throughout life primitive experience remains with us and aspects of these feelings may emerge if the environment provides the resonant triggers (Waddell, 2009).

My retrospective view has facilitated a new understanding of the artworks, the clients' artworks and my own countertransference drawings and paintings. When reflecting on the retrospective review of client work Schaverien states, 'we can return to an atmosphere which was current and pictured months, even years ago' (Schaverien, 1999, p. 77). Prokofiev (2013), when reviewing work done with a child by hanging all the work chronologically in exhibition style, found that certain facts were immediately made clear and that a narrative revealed itself. Prokofiev also found that the fragments became part of a whole and that she could pick up embodied feeling that could have been previously overlooked. Many of my own countertransference drawings were literally made up of a mass of fragments, and as the work occurred within a three-month period it was curious to see how consistent the fragmented nature of the images remained. In retrospect I think the chaotically fragmented pictures were an attempt to contain and process the primitive emotional and psychological material I was sitting with in the playground environment with the toddlers.

The retrospective review process has provided new insights into the case material, including a greater awareness of the significance and facilitating nature of my maternal mirroring (Wright, 2009) function at the art table. Through the review I have come to understand the images I made at the table as countertransference images (Samuels, cited in Schaverien, 1999), which contain visceral residues of my countertransference experience. This means that I think of them as images that depict and therefore make the unconscious relationship between myself and my patient visible and available for thought (Brown, Meyerowitz–Katz and Ryde, 2003, Meyerowitz–Katz, 2013).

Countertransference drawings and primitive states of mind

The drawings and paintings that I made at the art therapy table were primarily created to attract children to my station. I wanted to demonstrate what could be done at the table and my activities were an invitation to participate at the art therapy zone. My hope was that I was offering a quiet, non–intrusive, relational space for art making, exploration and discovery within the raucous environment of the playground. Marshall–Tierney speaks about how art making alongside clients provides a maternal function (Marshall–Tierney, 2014, p. 99). He also talks about the self-consciousness that might be engendered when the therapist finds herself sitting alone, apparently doing nothing in the work context. My sense of being a beginner and doing nothing may have paralleled the preschool children's experience as they found their way within the playground and I found my way as an art therapist. When children did participate at the art table they would initially be curious as to what I was making. I would encourage them to take their own piece of paper and move my focus away from what I was making towards their exploration with the materials.

As a person who found essential fulfilment in painting and drawing I also felt compelled to make pictures at the table. This resonated with Gilroy's description of her sense of '*profound* connection' to her 'primary discipline' of making art (Gilroy, 2014, pp. 9–10). Perhaps I was preserving and protecting my artist identity whilst learning to be an art therapist and was not yet aware of the complexity that comes with the advent of making art with clients. One aspect of this complexity that continues to resonate with me is the implications of sharing unconscious aspects of the self whilst making art with a client (Marshall–Tierney, 2014). Retrospectively, my desire is to find a link between 'unconscious primitive states of mind being uncontained' (Case, 2005, p. 9) and the many fragmented, scribbly, patchy artworks that I made on paper.

When trying to think about what was happening I wonder how deeply I was affected by Kate's anxiety and how it may have touched a chord with regards to my own early childhood stresses around having a baby sibling with a severe hearing

loss. Although these early memories were not conscious at the time of the placement I am sure they impacted on the relationship that developed between Kate
and myself. I wonder if we shared a form of 'implicit relational knowing' that Stern
et al. define as 'operating outside both focal attention and conscious verbal experience' (Stern et al., 1998, p. 3). It may have been my 'past unconscious' (Sandler and
Fonagy, cited in Stern et al., 1998, p. 3) and Kate's current anxious state that were
meeting within the relationship that formed. It was the finding of a representational
form, both drawn, spoken and felt, that facilitated Kate to begin to find a self shape
for her pervasive anxiety.

A retrospective description of my art making

*Busy hands. Fingers covered in glue gunk. Paste, paint and bits of paper. Stillness of the body
and the busy work of the arms, hands and fingers. Seated at the table in the thick, soupy
atmosphere that was humid with the dampness of the sandpit, the hose, the dribble, urine and
sweat from the bodies of the teaming mass of children. At one time an adult whose station
was near the windows of a classroom made a large bucket of corn flour paste and allowed the
children to throw handfuls of the paste onto the large windows, creating a spattering of vomit-
like white, blobby, thick fluid.*

In this visceral description I have tried to capture the intensity of the sensory
experience of being at the art table in the playground. By using the glue, collage
material, paint and pencils I was using my hands and body to help me process the
amount of primal sensory material I was taking in. Tustin argues that infant experience is predominantly sensory and there is no distinguishing between what is inside
and what is outside the body (Tustin, 1980). At times the sensory experience in
the playground was overwhelming. When making the pictures I was able to focus
on the small area of the paper, thus helping to regulate my own anxiety. It was as
if I was taking the felt experience of the larger environment and putting it on the
page. Perhaps by collaging and sticking things down I was trying to fix indigestible
fragments onto a stable surface.

Developmental considerations

It is the thinking of Fonagy and Greenspan that has helped to shape my retrospective understanding of what was occurring at the art therapy table in the preschool playground within the developing relationship between Kate and myself.
Greenspan speaks of 'feedback loops that can be thought of as opening and closing
circles of communication' (Greenspan, 1999, p. 162). These occur within the matrix
of 'boundary defining gestures, behaviours, and affects' (Greenspan, 1999, p. 161).
Fonagy et al. (2004) describe the four- to five-year-old as beginning to have a self
story or autobiographical self. The 'autobiographical self' and the emergence of a
representational capacity allow for a sense of before and after and the development
of an internal narrative and historic memory.

Stern's micro mapping of present moments has encouraged me to regard the smallest and most subtle of communications as having significant gravity and meaning (Stern, 2004).

Kate's first visit to the art therapy table

The first painting I made at the table was in response to four-year-old Kate's request for water to feed some thirsty toy elephants she was playing with. I painted some waves using thick blue paint on paper and gave it to Kate, who took it to the toy area and then returned and asked for more water. I painted two more pictures of some blue waves. My painted response was useful in that it showed her that a representation of something could be made with art materials. In this case the 'something' was water; it was a representation and a symbol of a needed substance. It was both literal and metaphoric. Kate's need had been expressed with intense urgency; the elephants were dying and they needed water urgently. The message was for me to be quick. The essence of the communication was that something was dying and it needed to be hydrated. I was to find out weeks later that this Kate had a baby sibling who was chronically unwell. The hugeness (elephant-like size) of this baby's needs in the family was something I was subsequently able to see as contributing to Kate's pervasive anxiety. The waves I painted became bigger and more hectic as the request for more water kept coming (Figure 10.1).

In retrospect Kate's communication seems to embody the raw and primitive nature of many of the children's experience. The urgent request for water for the very survival of the elephants in the play resonates with primitive urges and cries for survival in the infant with all its related terror and turbulence (Baradon et al., 2005).

I made Plate 13 later on the same day as the water and elephant play.

Were my paintings a response to the setting and its inhabitants rather than inter-relational moments? Where they a response to the chaotic group dynamic in the

FIGURE 10.1 Water for the thirsty elephants, becoming more hectic on the right.

playground? Or were they a subjective response to the total environment? In retro-spect I think that they were all these things. The painting/collages are both tended to and tatty, so they are both cared for and ragged. I wonder how much I was filling up with primitive anxieties and reconnecting to my preschool self. By continuously making the painting/collages I was trying to find ways to contain and digest these difficult non-verbal states and to manage my own anxiety.

Case material: representation and separation

My aim here is to capture aspects of Kate's development and her emergent abil-ity to share her inner world through her drawing and painting. After the initial interaction between Kate and myself a relationship developed between us. Kate was new to the preschool. Her family (parents and two younger siblings) had recently emigrated from Southeast Asia. Her father was finding it difficult to gain employment and this was causing him considerable stress. Kate's baby sibling was chronically unwell, a further cause of anxiety within the family. Kate spoke English with an Asian accent and at times would tell me words in the language of her country of origin. Sometimes it was difficult to understand what she was say-ing. She presented as a delicate four-year-old with lots of energy and she looked pale and strained. Over the eleven weeks of the placement, as winter turned to spring, I became aware of Kate's eczema on her arms. The eczema appeared to be a somatic symptom of her anxiety. There was a tension for Kate between her intense neediness and her desire to appear independent and wholly capable. Phillips writes of eczema's paradoxically private nature as 'a part of the self that defies intrusion while keeping you in contact with the people you need' (Phil-lips, 1995, p. 44).

A session at the table

Kate's parents had spoken to the preschool staff about their anxiety about Kate's mess making at the table and sandpit. Retrospectively I wonder how uncon-tained Kate's parents might have felt with the messiness of their immigration, the demands of their young family and the stress and worry about their chronically unwell baby. Mess can be a communication of uncontained or traumatic experi-ences (O'Brien, 2004, Reddick, 1999). Further to this there is a degree of anxiety that can collapse the capacity for play (Winnicott, 1999). The parents' difficulty in understanding the mess may also have been an indication of their level of stress and anxiety. There was a sense that the family needed containment. The preschool did provide some occasional parent consultations. This was helpful for this family and it encouraged Kate's parents to come and see her and other children playing at the preschool.

At the art table Kate struggled with messy hands and made multiple trips to the bathroom to wash them. Three weeks into the placement I made some textured paint with sand mixed into it. Kate found the sandy liquid mix confronting and

I gently coaxed her into exploring what it did on the paper using a brush. She painted a large mass on a piece of paper (Figure 10.2). The undifferentiated gritty blob was an adventurous exploration which happened in relationship with myself at the table. In showing Kate that the gritty mass of paint was safe to use and explore I was showing her that she could make a mess within our 'being together' and that we could survive it. It is helpful to think of the mess as something that embodied Kate's fears in direct relation to her parents' concerns about the sandpit play. The fact that the result was held on the page on the table within the growing relationship was of tremendous help to her. She began to seek the relationship with me and the art table during my weekly visits.

At the art table Kate pushed in to me as if she wanted a cuddle. She seemed to be pushing in because she wanted to join up with me and she may have been seeking an earlier, more infant-like nuzzling-in for comfort and safety. I was aware that Kate wanted me to do things for her and that the pushing in was part of that too. For example she would say 'you draw all the planets' and in this case 'you draw the dog.' I resisted these commands, although they were strongly expressed. I think I instinctively knew that it would not help if I made pictures for Kate. Instead I wanted to allow for therapeutic interactions that would facilitate Kate drawing for herself inside the conversation that was developing within our relationship. My sense was that Kate wanted to see what I would do and then try to copy me so that she could protect against exposing her vulnerability. Perhaps she wished to merge

FIGURE 10.2 The undifferentiated gritty blob.

with me at that moment too. Matthews opposes copying as a way for children to learn to draw (Matthews, 2003, p. 157). He believes it is counterproductive to a child's development in the deepest sense and that it inhibits the expressive use of the body whilst making marks.

There were echoes of early and continued maternal mirroring (Wright, 2009) in the interactions that followed. Whilst pressing in to me Kate asked me to draw a dog for her. I asked what she thought of when she thought of a dog, I waited and 'hmmmnned', and we wondered together. Then Kate replied, 'the ears'. I took my hands above my head and positioned and shaped them as if they were the ears of a dog. Kate looked at me, then took a pink pencil to paper and drew two very small arcs next to each other, open side down. The next item that was drawn was the nose, also drawn in pink. We then moved through the parts of the body that Kate spoke out loud when I wondered with her what else the body of the dog might have. Slowly a rudimentary dog took shape in a brown pencil line drawing as all the dog parts were linked up with the big rectangular shape of the body. This was a very exciting and liberating moment for Kate. It was as if in my miming of the dog body parts I was saying through my actions, 'I know something about "dog" and I hold in my mind that you might know (something about) "dog" and I am inviting you to find in your bodymind (Meyerowitz-Katz, 2013) your dog representation.' Here representation is the end part of an inner gathering up of sensory memory, including 'visual, auditory, tactile, olfactory, vestibular and proprioceptive' (Greenspan and Wieder, 2006, p. 31) memories that bear a latent bodily expressive gesture that is then born/drawn or expressed in the image. In retrospect I regard the drawing of the dog (Figure 10.3) as a culminative developmental moment when symbolic thought and the ability to articulate (draw) what one carries inside began to emerge and emerge as safely separate to the other. It was as if Kate had been at the cliff edge of developmental growth and made a leap to representational drawing.

Kate frequently checked in with my face and gaze as she drew and I nodded reassuringly at those moments. We alternated brief moments of being separate with brief moments of being together. Greenspan (1999, p. 164) says, 'the glances exchanged between two people are an acknowledgement of their mutual existence.' I would add to the sense of acknowledgement that I had faith in Kate's developmental abilities and that she could make something from a state that might have felt like messy non-sense. This checking in with gentle certainty may have helped her regulate her affective state (Stern et al., 1998), most likely an inner sense of unease, whilst mastering this new ability, and may also have helped her out of a regressed pre-symbolic state.

I am also intrigued by how Kate drew the ears and nose with the pink pencil and the rest of the body with the brown pencil. The sensory parts have been articulated as different to the outline or skin/fur of the dog. Smell and sound may have carried particular meaning and sensitivity for Kate. Further images were drawn on the page, another dog appeared, the yellow sun was drawn and then a person and

FIGURE 10.3 The drawing of the dog (redrawn by author).

a tree, all with this *brand new* ability to articulate in drawn pictures what was being thought and talked about within the therapeutic relationship. The picture of a person has a pram-like shape inside its body. Kate has drawn a person carrying a baby around with them and inside them. This could be Kate carrying a baby around, her own baby self and her anxiety about her baby sibling. It could also be Kate representing her mother's preoccupation with the unwell baby. The image is also a transference image of Kate and myself, the pram shape representing baby Kate and the larger figure being myself as safe container for Kate's baby self. For Kate, I was both a real person and in the transference an imagined one (Schaverien, 2005) that carried aspects of other attachment figures. Here I am thinking of transference as 'The repetition in the present of significant aspects of a person's relationships with earlier attachment figures, usually but not exclusively, parental figures' (Baradon et al., 2005, p. xxii).

Our transference relationship

The nature of the transference relationship emerged in a session prior to my scheduled break from the preschool. It was one of being like a loved aunt who was present and available. Kate told me that she wanted to write a letter to her aunty. She took a small, square piece of paper and asked me to write for her. I told her I would help her write the note – that we would do it together. Kate struggled with her words and appeared fraught. Witnessing her struggle I felt pain and sadness. Letter by letter we worked our way through her communication. Much of the letter formation was done while I very slowly, phonetically and repeatedly sounded out each word that she spoke, with little breaks between the letters and then the whole word sound. Kate wrote in capital letters:

DEAR
JANET
I LOVE
YOUIWANT

And the reverse side said,

YOU IWANT
I YOU
SO TO WITH
ME COME
MUCH

On the reverse side the words were quite higgledy-piggledy on the page and there was an interesting shape between the words YOU and IWANT. It looked like Figure 10.4.

Kate was struggling with the prospect of us separating for the break as well as her and I being separate in the present moment of the writing of the note. In her effort to communicate how hard it was she drew a '2' and an 'I' joined up.

Kate was communicating her sadness and anxiety to me about my impending departure for the break (Edwards, 2007), and it emerged in the transference. Further to this there was an amalgam of '2' and 'to' as Kate wrestled with numbers and letters.

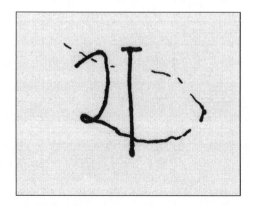

FIGURE 10.4   The shape between the words YOU and IWANT (redrawn by author).

Concluding thoughts

The making of the countertransference images at the time of the student placement helped me work with the children by providing a containing space (the art materials) for my anxiety. As a consequence I was able to be present as a maternal attachment figure for Kate and to provide a mirroring presence for her that enabled a leap in her development. The arrival of symbols for Kate facilitated communication between us that held imaginative interpretations and associations and meaningful exchange.

The retrospective view has allowed me to have further insight into the complexity of Kate's and my relationship. Weiner's 'contemporary Jungian metaphor' of the 'transference matrix' (Weiner, 2009, p. 96) can be applied to the dynamics of our together-ness. Weiner defines the transference matrix as 'a co constructed place with structure, form and energy'. She says that it 'is a structure that contains the psyche's capacity for both relating and creating' (Weiner, 2009, p. 96).

Within the transference matrix elaborate interactions of transference and countertransference can occur. I wonder if the moment of making the blue waves for Kate and myself was a first, singular, condensed transference matrix moment in which transference (Kate's) and countertransference (mine) happened in a brief exchange made manifest by the painting of the blue waves and the giving of them to Kate. The transference matrix was activated and constellated in Kate's first approach, and it was enabled and contained by the presence and use of the art materials.

References

Baradon, T., Broughton, C., Gibbs, I., James, J., Joyce, A. and Woodhead, J. of the Parent Infant Project at The Anna Freud Centre (2005) *The practice of psychoanalytic parent-infant psychotherapy: Claiming the baby.* London: Routledge.

Berman, H. (2011) Quoted from 'Safe spaces – Witness to violence' video written and directed by Graham Young, produced by art therapist Michelle Altlas and Graham Young. *ATOL. Art Therapy OnLine,* 2 (2). Available at: http://journals.gold.ac.uk/atol/backissues.html Accessed 1.12.15.

Bion, W.R. (1962) *Learning from experience.* London: Heinemann.

Bowlby, J. (1978) *Attachment and loss, volume 2: Separation: Anxiety and anger.* Middlesex: Penguin Books (Penguin Education).

Brown, C., Meyerowitz-Katz, J. and Ryde, J. (2003) 'Thinking with image making in supervision.' *Inscape,* 8 (2), pp. 71–78.

Case, C. (2005) *Imagining animals: Art, psychotherapy and primitive states of mind.* New York: Routledge.

Deco, S. (1998) 'Return to the Open Studio Group: Art therapy groups in acute psychiatry', in Skaife, S. and Huet, V. (eds.) *Art psychotherapy groups: Between pictures and words.* London: Routledge, pp. 88–108.

Edwards, D. (2007) *Art therapy* (2nd edition). London: SAGE.

Fonagy, P., Gergely, G., Jurist, E. and Target, M. (2004) *Affect regulation, mentalization and the development of the self.* New York: Other Press.

Gilroy, A. (2014) 'Taking a long look at art: Reflections on the context of production and consumption of art therapy.' *ATOL. Art Therapy OnLine*, 5 (2), pp. 1–36. Available at: http://journals.gold.ac.uk/atol/backissues.html Accessed 1.12.15.

Greenspan, S.I. (1999) *Developmentally based psychotherapy* (2nd edition). Madison, CT: International University Press.

Greenspan, S.I. and Wieder, S. (2006) *Infant and early childhood mental health: A comprehensive developmental approach*. Arlington: American Psychiatric.

Greenwood, H. and Layton, G. (1987) 'An out-patient art therapy group.' *Inscape*, Summer, pp. 12–19.

Karen, R. (1998) *Becoming attached: First relationships and how they shape our capacity to love*. Oxford: Oxford University Press.

Laplanche, J. and Pontalis, J.B. (1988) *The language of psychoanalysis*. London: Karnac Books.

Marshall-Tierney, M. (2014) 'Making art with and without patients in acute settings.' *International Journal of Art Therapy: Formerly Inscape*, 19 (3), pp. 96–106.

Marvin, R. Cooper, G., Hoffman, K. and Powell, B. (2002) 'The Circle of Security project: Attachment-based intervention with care-giver-pre-school child dyads.' *Attachment & Human Development*, 4 (1), pp. 107–124.

Matthews, J. (2003) *The art of childhood and adolescence: The construction of meaning* (Transferred to digital printing 2003). London: Routledge Falmer.

McNeilly, G. (2006) *Group analytic art therapy*. London: Jessica Kingsley.

Meyerowitz-Katz, J. (2013) 'Consciously forgotten, unconsciously remembered relationships made visible: The therapist's use of art making to understand the embodied transference-countertransference relationship.' ANZATA Conference, Sydney, October. Unpublished paper.

Miller, L., Rustin, M., Rustin, M., and Shuttleworth, J. (2002) *Closely observed infants*. London: Gerald Duckworth.

O'Brien, F. (2004) 'The making of mess in art therapy. Attachment, trauma and the brain.' *Inscape*, 9 (1), pp. 2–13.

Perry, B.D. and Szalavitz, M. (2008) *The boy who was raised as a dog: And other stories from a child psychiatrist's notebook: What traumatized children can teach us about loss, love, and healing*. New York: Basic Books.

Phillips, A. (1995) *Terrors and experts*. London: Faber and Faber.

Prokofiev, F. (2013) 'Allowing the artwork to speak: The use of visual display as a research method in a retrospective study of four years' artwork in art therapy with a four-year old boy.' *ATOL: Art Therapy OnLine*, 4 (1), video portion of paper.

Reddick, D. (1999) 'Baby-bear monster.' *Inscape*, 4 (1), pp. 20–28.

Rustin, M. (2002) 'Encountering primitive anxieties', in: Miller, R., Rustin M., Rustin, M. and Shuttleworth, J. (eds.) *Closely observed infants*. London: Duckworth, pp. 7–21.

Schaverien, J. (1999) *The revealing image: Analytical art psychotherapy in theory and practice*. London. Jessica Kingsley.

Schaverien, J. (2005) 'Art and active imagination: Reflections on transference and the image.' *International Journal of Art Therapy: Formerly Inscape*, 10 (2), pp. 39–52.

Stern, D.N. (2004) *The present moment in psychotherapy and everyday life*. London: W.W. Norton.

Stern, D.N., Sander, L.W., Nahum, J.P., Harrison, A.M., Lyons-Ruth, K., Morgan, A.C., Bruschweilerstarn, N. and Tronick, E.Z. (1998) 'Non-interpretive mechanisms in psychoanalytic therapy: The "something more" than interpretation.' *International Journal of Psycho-Analysis*, 79, pp. 903–921.

Tustin, F. (1980) 'Autistic objects.' *International Review of Psycho-Analysis*, 7, pp. 27–39.

Waddell, M. (2009) *Infancy*. Available at: http://backdoorbroadcasting.net/2009/03/states-of-mind-development-and-the-life-cycle/ Accessed 28.11.2015.

Weiner, J. (2009) *The therapeutic relationship: Transference, countertransference, and the making of meaning*. College Station: Texas University Press.

Welty, E. (1995) *One writer's beginnings*. Cambridge, MA: Harvard University Press.

Winnicott, D.W. (1999) *Playing and reality*. London: Routledge.

Wright, K. (2009) *Mirroring and attunement: Self-realization in psychoanalysis and art*. Hove: Routledge.

11

SIDE BY SIDE

An early years' art therapy group with a parallel therapeutic parent support group

Alice Rayment

Introduction

In this chapter I explore a side-by-side model in which an art therapy group for two- to three-year-olds ran in parallel with a therapeutic parent support group. I describe the setting, a family centre within a Jewish charity. The therapy is contextualised in a discussion of relevant literature addressing art therapy groups with children and art therapy in the early years, as well as children and parent groups and simultaneous toddler and parent group work.

The clinical material describes the group processes and how both children and parents were supported. I focus on two children and their parents and explore the parallels and interplay between the groups. The measuring of outcomes of this side-by-side model of art therapy intervention is presented. The development of the early years' art therapy group and parallel parents' group has been a joint enterprise involving a meta-family made up of a range of professionals who have co-operated in thinking about the complex material, assessing risk and supporting the families attending the groups.

Setting

This well-established Jewish charity provides a wide range of services, including a number of family centres serving different geographical areas and, consequently, different parts of the community. The charity predominately serves the Jewish community whilst the workforce is made up of Jews and non-Jews. The Anglo-Jewish community is diverse in terms of identification: religious, ethnic and cultural affiliations. The community that makes use of the charity's services includes the religious members of the ultra-orthodox, orthodox, reform and liberal communities. These are further defined through ethnic backgrounds of Ashkenazi (Eastern European) and Sephardi (Spanish and Portuguese). There is also a secular cohort who identify themselves as culturally Jewish but who do not observe religious traditions. The socio-economic divide in the community is equally diverse.

The family centre serves the wider Jewish community, which encompasses religious and secular Jews. The family centre is kosher (following religious dietary laws), which is required in order for the Haredi (ultra-orthodox) community to access the services that are offered. These include a nursery, a family support team, including social workers, and parent and toddler groups. The centre also provides a special education needs service for children. Art therapy has been present within the special educational needs department for over twenty years, providing individual and group work. Reflecting the culture of this charity and its position within the community, funding for this programme has come from within the Jewish community.

Theoretical underpinnings

A number of authors describe various approaches to group art therapy with children (Deco, 1990, Dalley, 1993, Prokofiev, 1998, Boronska, 2000, Reddick, 2008). Prokofiev (1998) suggests that the art therapist should take age and emotional development into account. Baradon et al. (2005) points out that the parent's capacity to tolerate a toddler's emotional life is of central importance to his development. While Reddick (1999) and Meyerowitz-Katz (2003) have described individual art therapy with children under five, O'Brien (2008) describes simultaneous individual work with a carer alongside an older child's art therapy in which containment of the carer impacts on the outcomes of the work. Proulx (2002), Hosea (2006), Hall (2008), Choi and Goo (2012) and Arroyo and Fowler (2013) describe group art therapy with parents and young children making art together.

Schamess (1987), describing how the parent group offers a holding environment within a protective, symbolic family, explores parallel mother and infant groups. Bower (1995) suggests that a separate children's group can provide children who may be aggressive or withdrawn with new experiences of socialisation and play. She describes working with a therapeutic group for depressed mothers and a separate under-fives group for their children in a family centre. Bower provides an account of how the parents' group enables an experience where difficult feelings can be understood and processed rather than punished and judged (Bower, 1995). Musitano and Rosenman (2012) explore a separate mother's group and a group for children from birth to three running next to each other in the same room. This allows the mother and child to be connected whilst also achieving a degree of separation.

The side-by-side art therapy programme

The side-by-side art therapy programme was supported by a meta-family of professionals. Besides the co-workers who facilitated the group sessions, there were also social workers, centre staff and volunteers who worked in the crèche with siblings. At the time of writing we were running the third, year-long, early years' art therapy and parallel parents' groups. I have co-worked the three art therapy groups with a drama therapist for two groups, and with a social worker, who had trained as an art therapist, for the third. A parent worker has facilitated all three parents' groups. The art therapy group co-workers and the parent worker met pre- and post-groups in order to discuss and think about what was happening in the groups, and we were supervised together by an external child psychotherapist/art therapist.

Referrals were predominately made by professionals from the preschool, the family support team within the centre and other early years' settings in the wider community. Children were referred because there were concerns about their emotional well-being. They may have presented as withdrawn, displaying aggressive, chaotic behaviour (biting/hitting), not thriving in a larger group setting, such as in nursery, or having poor or delayed language development or poor or delayed development of social skills. Alongside the child's presentation there were a range of parental issues, such as family breakdown, postnatal depression, mental health issues, illness and/or bereavement in the family.

The art therapy groups comprised five to six boys and girls. As we developed our work, we took on referrals that clustered in age and the cohort usually fell around two and a half to three years old at the point of referral. This was to try to support the function of the group in aiming to address the children's developmental needs, even though, as Mahler (1975) points out, developmental processes are not linear.

Between the ages of two and three, a separation-individuation process occurs in which a child emerges from a fusion with mother and achieves a psychological sense of being separate (Mahler, 1975). At two, toddlers move from parallel play to being more interactive, increasingly seeking out playing with others. By around three they are becoming more sociable. Siblings, peers, toddler groups and nursery settings offer opportunities for developing skills in compromise, negotiation, quarrelling and making up. Mahler (1975) suggests that in the third year gender identity seems to take place.

Assessments

Each referred child and the family were offered an assessment by the group facilitators from both the children's group and the parents' group in order to consider the family's needs. The assessment could include a nursery observation. At this point we thought about how parents/primary carers could make use of the parents' group. Fathers were encouraged to join the parents' group, as a child will be preoccupied with both mother and father in the development of his or her internal world (Trowell, 2002). If it was felt that neither parent could make use of the group process, then the family was referred to alternative services in the centre.

On accepting a place in the art therapy group it was made clear that parents were required to attend the parents' group as well as termly reviews. We explained that there was an additional layer of thinking about the therapy and this was in the form of confidential supervision. Clinical material from both groups was to be shared by the three facilitators, who met before and after the groups to think about and process the material. There was an outside supervisor who met regularly with the group facilitators.

Spaces

The art therapy group met in a small art therapy room usually used for individual work. We found the small size helpful in observing the often fast interactions, and it promoted the children's playing and art making with each other. It was set up with cushions, beanbags and art materials. Over time we learnt to adapt the art materials according to group membership. Whilst working with the qualities of the materials and inevitable mess we maintained the capacity to think and use each other as co-therapists. Each child had a folder in which to keep artwork, and there was a group folder where everything produced together was stored. Playing and art making happened on the floor and the group ran for an hour.

The materials offered included wet and dry sand, a low sink for water play, small figures, dolls, blankets, bottles, a doll's house and construction toys. A soft, football-sized ball was used at the start and end of the session, ritually defining the beginning and the end of each session.

On entering the art therapy room the children were encouraged to sit in a circle on cushions. The ball was rolled between group members. After this children chose their space and materials to play with, sometimes with others or on their own. Towards the end of the group we packed away together and looked at the artwork.

The ball was used to increase cohesiveness in the group. It provided a concrete way of connecting and nurturing a to-and-fro movement between group members. The ball could promote playfulness and humour: it could be rolled and bounced, thrown, sat on, hidden, lost and found. New skills could be discovered, experimented with and marvelled at. Sharing and turn taking could be negotiated. Mahler (1975) noted that ball play lent itself well to both social interaction and feelings and fantasies of parting with and re-finding an object. Equally the ball could evoke rivalry, desires for control, frustration and anger – all useful emotions to be considered in the group. Sometimes the ball rolled away and did not return. This offered opportunities to consider feelings around loss. The ball could be held onto or let go of, and this seemed to link to holding onto and letting go of in terms of bodily function and toilet training.

During the life of the groups most children negotiated toilet training and the art materials could reflect this process. The experience of the materials, water play, paint and glue with their qualities of leaking, oozing and dribbling linked to a sense of being or not being in control.

Attention to the outside spaces and separations

Holding and containment of the group began outside the group spaces. Before the groups started younger siblings were settled in a crèche run by volunteers. In order to facilitate a less public separation of parent and child than would have occurred in the reception area, parents and the child attending the art therapy group were collected from reception by one of the facilitators. The children continued down the corridor for a short distance to the art therapy room.

In the first weeks of the groups, parents might come down to the art therapy room where the separation happened as the group started. Although we held a boundary at the threshold of the room (i.e. no parents came into the room) the door could be open whilst the child said goodbye to the parent as the group started. On occasions the ball could be used to roll from the group to the child and parent at the door, serving as a transitional object (Winnicott, 1971) as the child moved from the parent into the group.

The group as a whole was encouraged to voice feelings around separation. This would shift; sometimes children would run ahead of parents, bursting into the art therapy room, and at other times, they needed time to separate and settle into the session. Parents were asked to encourage children to go to the toilet before the session. However, there were times early on in the group when children wanted a parent to accompany them to the toilet. Very soon we were called upon to accompany children. During the year of the group, children were striving to manage becoming independent in going to the toilet. A trip to the toilet allowed children to have a facilitator to themselves, and if something was shared with the facilitator on the way to the toilet the child was encouraged to share it with the rest of the group on returning to the group.

When we returned with the children to the parent group, we sometimes found that we fell into the role of nursery staff, drawn into passing on how the group had been for the child. Over time we felt that it was more helpful to allow children to share their experience of the group with their parent.

Therapeutic parent support group

The parents' group became regarded as a therapeutic parent support group. The boundaries of the group – timing, confidentiality and not socialising outside during the life of the group, as well as respecting and awareness of others' feelings – were all discussed and agreed upon at the start of the group.

Depending on the group membership, different themes emerged at different times. These included guilt or anxiety around not being a 'good enough' parent, how parents were themselves parented, parenting together or separately, responding to their child's needs, the feelings evoked when a child was upset crying or angry and the child biting or hitting others. In addition parents discussed their efforts to find time and space to attend to their own or their partner's needs, having older children and managing siblings' feelings. An important theme emerged around losses, their own and their parents'. This included miscarriages and deceased babies. Parents shared experiences of their wider family relationships and support networks in the community. Discussions in the parents' group also included practical advice and sharing of strategies for boundary setting, sleep patterns, toilet training, tantrums, crying, biting and sibling relationships.

The style and ability of the facilitator to nurture and contain projections and anxieties without shaming were fundamental to the outcomes of the work. Clulow (2014) describes a proven dip in couple satisfaction when parenting a child under five. He suggests that supporting parents to deal productively with problems and impasses supports the social and emotional well-being of the child. He stresses the importance of considering the quality of parenting styles rather than purely delivering strategies.

The parent group facilitator extended her approach from a parenting course, such as 'strengthening families' (Steele and Marigna, 2000), to a more psychodynamic approach. The idea of extending her approach evolved through the pre- and post-discussions around the group work and in clinical supervision. The development of the co-working process in and between the groups grew in a similar way.

Developing relationships between group facilitators

Often the communication between the facilitators gave an insight into the child-parent relationship. An example of this was Gabriel, who over two sessions in the art therapy group had periods of lying on his back, kicking against the door, throwing materials around the room and growling. I and my co-worker felt we were struggling to keep him and the other children safe. In supervision we explored feelings of being overwhelmed with the behaviour and frustrated that the other was not helping. We both felt quite abandoned by the other and ineffectual in both managing Gabriel and thinking about the rest of the group.

The parents' group facilitator reminded us that Gabriel was one of five children. We reflected that Gabriel's mum had expressed similar feelings to us; she was cross with Gabriel as he was taking up so much of her time and cross with his dad as she felt alone with managing Gabriel's behaviour. We considered how as co-workers we could become more effective in managing this behaviour. Although his dad was not a member of the parents' group, the parents' group facilitator felt it would be useful to explore with his mum how they could support each other in managing at home. Over the next three sessions our thinking as co-therapists supported the work of the parents' group in helping Gabriel's mum. A month later his dad attended a review with his mum where we drew from this material to support healthier functioning within the family.

It seemed particularly helpful for co-workers to verbalise the group process during the group, reflecting their observations on how individual children might be experiencing the group at a given time. This also helped to promote interactions between the group members, managing boundaries and more challenging behaviour. In a similar way Westman (1996) suggested that co-therapists model parenting, allowing children to hear and experience adults' thinking about options together and jointly deciding on a path of action and following it through.

Discussions between workers within supervision supported the holding of the groups and the group process; this ultimately supported the children. For example in one group a set of parents were taking it in turns to attend separately. This splitting was occurring outside of the group, with Mum contacting one worker and Dad another. We were able to think together about these communications in supervision. This had the effect of supporting both parents to attend together. We decided that if there was to be any communication between sessions by parents this would be done through the parents' group facilitator.

Sara

Sara was referred by the family centre's nursery as they were concerned that she was withdrawn. She engaged in solitary play and there was limited communication between her, her peers and nursery staff. It had been difficult to assess any possibilities of language delay. At the time of referral the family was also supported by a social worker.

During the assessment Sara stayed close to her mum, Orli, and did not explore the space or any of the materials. She was the youngest of four. Orli was an Ortho-dox single parent. Whilst Orli was supportive of Sara joining the group, she felt that she could not attend the parents' group as she had a work commitment at that time.

My co-worker had previously worked with the family and felt strongly that Sara would benefit from the group. We felt that Orli was isolated and that she would benefit from engaging in the group. Yalom (2005) points to evidence that those suffering from stigma or social isolation can gain the greatest benefits from group work. We wondered about this mum's resistance to joining the group. We offered the place to Sara, expressing our hope that Orli would join the parents' group further into the work. At this point we were mostly concerned about how this would impact on the other parents when we had made it clear that offering a place to the child meant a commitment to attending the parent group. We booked a meeting with Orli six weeks into the group to consider her joining the parent group.

Initially Sara came directly from the nursery in the centre to the group. She was quiet and played alone with the doll's house and dolls, moving away from the doll's house if another child joined her, shrinking away to the edge of the group. Sometimes we struggled to remember where she had been or what she had been playing with when we reflected on the session.

Sara spoke with a whisper and we often had to lean towards her to hear. Our concerns around the absence of Sara's mum, Orli, did not appear to impact negatively on the parents' group. However, my co-therapist and I were finding it difficult to work with this absence in the art therapy group. The rest of the group was arriving and separating from their parents at the door. Within the group, children would wonder about what the mummies and daddies might be doing, and the children often imagined them to be together 'eating biscuits'. We might then reflect that perhaps the mummies and daddies were thinking about the children. At the end of our group we took the children into the group room to the parents, where the children rushed in to be greeted and lifted onto laps; often children would tell parents what they had been playing with. One of us took Sara to reception, where Orli met her.

Sara seemed to be on the edge of the group. At the six-week meeting with Orli we were able to reflect on this with her. We shared with her that we felt her joining the parents' group would significantly support our work. Orli expressed several anxieties around this that partly related to her status as a single-parent, Hebrew-speaking, Orthodox Haredi Jew mixing with less religious Jews and a lack of confidence in her spoken English. We felt that Sara's marginalisation in the group echoed Orli's anxiety about her sense of not fully belonging to the community.

The following week Orli arrived with Sara, who bunny-hopped ahead of her down the corridor and, on reaching the group room for the parents, pointed to the room. Orli laughed and asked, 'Is that where I am meant to go?'

In our post-group meetings we thought about supporting Orli's integration into an already established group. As Orli gained a sense of belonging in the parents' group Sara became more engaged in the children's group; she became more experimental with art materials, in particular with her use of paints. She joined others in play and she also initiated play, thus building her resilience and confidence with her peers and supporting her verbal interactions with them. Her language developed noticeably. There was a parallel process that benefitted Sara at home and at school: Orli reported that this shift had also happened in the home and school setting.

In the third term of our groups Sara moved to a new nursery in a school setting. The work of the groups supported this transition. In the final review the social worker reported that the new nursery currently had no concerns around Sara's social and developmental progress.

Meir

At the time of referral Meir was aged three. A social worker from the family support team made the referral specifically around concerns that Meir did not respond to invitations to play. There were questions around language delay and a referral had been made for speech and language therapy. The social worker had observed Meir screaming when he seemed frustrated and felt the family could benefit from the groups. The social worker also expressed his concern about whether the family would engage with the service.

Mum, Dad, Meir and his brother, Saul, aged ten months, arrived late for the assessment. During the assessment Meir kept his coat and rucksack on and Mum reported that he would often remain wearing these in new situations. He did not engage with any of the play nor art materials available and remained non-verbal throughout the assessment. Mum expressed feelings of not understanding Meir and described 'big tantrums' where he 'screeched'. She described having to put him alone in his room as she was unable to understand what he wanted. She expressed her wish to be able to further understand him and also expressed her concerns that perhaps there was something 'organically' wrong with him and there could be no change. Dad held a different view that this was a 'phase' that they needed support to help Meir through. Both parents expressed concerns around his limited speech and that he was hitting Saul. Both Mum and Dad agreed to join the parents' group. We were also able to offer a place for Saul in a crèche run by volunteers in the centre.

In the first session Meir sat quietly on the edge of the group, remaining in his coat and rucksack. He watched other group members at play; at one point the ball was rolled towards him and rested by his feet. Another child rushed over and scooped it up and Meir remained watching the spot where the ball had been. I sat close to Meir and described my observations of what was happening within the group. In the second session he wriggled his feet when the ball rested by him. Over the next two sessions Meir responded to the invitation from the facilitators of join-ing the group in the ball game. Meir appeared to enjoy rolling the ball to and from the facilitators and to the children, and this became a real way of enabling him to begin to connect to the group members.

The ball helped draw Meir into the group and connect with other group mem-bers. He was delighted and excited that he could roll the ball away and that it would be returned. Linking the ball game to Winnicott's (1971) idea of play, Case (2008) suggests that the ball game in psychotherapy can be used to meet those who are hard to reach halfway: it takes place in the overlap of two areas of playing, that of the patient and that of the therapist.

The family did not attend session five and they arrived late for the sixth session. This appeared particularly disorientating for Meir. He arrived when the group had moved on from the ball game and the children were moving freely around the room, making use of the art and play materials.

In supervision we considered our concerns around Meir's family's absence and late attendance alongside another family who had attended ten minutes late for a number of sessions. The parent worker felt that both families were vulnerable to feeling shamed and rejected. We felt that perhaps if the parent worker shared more about the process of the art therapy group and the children's experience it might open up some thinking about the impact of inconsistent attendance and arriv-ing late. The parent worker took this to the parents' group, and in the post-group meeting she felt it had opened up an area for all parents to consider the impact of lateness and inconsistency on the child's experience. Helpfully a parent drew from her experience as a child in always feeling as if she was missing out due to parental lateness.

In his ninth session, Meir began to tentatively make marks. To begin with he often chose to use the paints next to a girl who was very able with selecting, squeezing and mixing her paints so that he could use them. However, as time went on he became more confident in his use of the play and art materials, enjoying in particular the sand, water play and the paints. Through the ball games, art and play materials he started to interact non-verbally with others in the group. These interactions were observed and often shared with the group as the co-worker and I spoke to each other about what we noticed; in this way we actively supported his emerging capacity to interact non-verbally with the other children and to play.

In the post-group debriefs we described Meir's emerging capacity to play to the parent worker. The parent worker wondered how to support Mum and Dad to enable and nurture this emerging play at home. We felt that there was some urgency in bringing them alongside and experiencing these changes. We felt in this case it might be helpful to be more directive in the next parent group session regarding the value and benefits of play. The parents' group took up the themes of play, being available and child-led play.

After a period of time Meir became more playful and started to 'babble'. This developed into him experimenting with humming, giggling and singing, often mirroring others in the group. Significantly, he began to make demands of the group – for example holding his arms out wide for the ball, calling out, 'Me . . . me, me'.

We shared these new demands, which we viewed as particularly positive, with the parent worker in the post-group debrief. She said the demands had begun to be felt at home but had been viewed in a different light by Mum. At this point the parents' group played a crucial role. Mum and Dad's experience resonated with a number of parents in how to respond to the changing demands and needs of their toddlers. Positive shifts made by Meir were experienced by Mum as being more challenging. She requested particular support in how to respond to these new demands. The members of the parents' group considered these 'new' demands and discussed ways of meeting them.

In our first end-of-term review Mum and Dad reported that the 'tantrums' and hitting of his sibling had greatly reduced and Meir appeared to get less frustrated. Meir and his brother played together, and Meir was responding to his brother's invitations to play. In the second and third term Meir became an integral member of the group. He began to extend his use of language, mirroring others. He became more resilient and robust in his interactions, he joined in play and he also initiated play with others.

After session twenty, prior to a two-week break, the parents' group worker came into the art therapy room for our end-of-group meeting. The room looked chaotic and I and the co-worker were struggling to clear away. The parent worker jokingly said that 'You two look like how the parents in my group feel.'

In the parents' group, Meir's parents had described him testing boundaries at home; they had differing views on how to manage this, creating tensions between them. Our group had parallel material. Meir and two other children had been tipping out materials and swinging on the group door. In supervision we discussed how boundary testing was a theme occurring simultaneously in both groups. Children's testing of boundaries was putting both parental relationships and relationships between workers under pressure. This was a parallel process that needed to be thought about.

In the final review of our work it was observed that Meir and his sibling played together; Meir was a happier child. Mum and Dad felt more equipped to respond to his needs. The group had also supported Meir's transition into nursery, which he had been attending for the last term of the group. It was reported that he had settled well into this new setting.

Measuring outcomes

Assessment of outcomes was multilayered. These included termly reviews with families and post-group discussion between facilitators and the supervisor. At the start and end of the groups we used the Strength and Difficulties Questionnaires aged 2–4 years (Goodman, 2005) and a parental feedback form was completed.

According to the evaluation and feedback, the parallel toddler art therapy and parents' groups supported two- to three-year-old development and emotional well-being. We observed within the art therapy groups how the group process enabled toddlers to extend their social, emotional and verbal skills. The group work supported nursery placements and transitions into nursery and school settings. The groups helped children and parents to strengthen communication in their families and in the wider community.

Through evaluation it became increasingly clear that the role of a parallel parents' group creates a space that strengthens the bond between parents and child. A parent group evaluation response was 'I am able to understand and connect more to my child. My child is able to communicate better and connect with his sibling and others better.' There is a positive impact on the wider relationships of the couple and other siblings that demonstrates the benefits of this practice to effect change and healthier functioning within families.

The value of a side-by-side model of an early years' intervention

The development of our psychodynamic side-by-side model that depends on a meta-family of a range of professionals was made possible because of the respect for and understanding afforded to art therapy and psychodynamic thinking and practice within the charity and children's centre. Art therapy and psychodynamic work with children and families had a presence within the family centre for over twenty years. Consequently, we, as a staff team, were trusted and therefore enabled to develop our model over a period of four years, as a response to the needs of the families and children. Our side-by-side model had its origins in a 'children with low immunity' art therapy group and an informal parents' group. The curative factors in the model were complex and depended on a joint enterprise of multilayered, careful thinking by the meta-family, who were supported in the family centre by the wider Jewish charity. The charity in turn was supported by the Jewish community. The meta-family co-operated in thinking about the complex material, assessing risk and supporting the families attending the groups.

Differences in faith, class, economic status, gender and ethnicity were present in the groups, and the group workers came from different trainings and disciplines. Working with difference is a dynamic aspect of group work. The pre- and post-group meetings and supervision were essential in addressing splitting that occurred in the parallel processes. Understanding splitting as parallel process was a core component of our therapeutic approach. Echoing this, there were differences within the parents' group, and the religious and secular Jewish members found that a closed group offered a safe place to think about issues like loss, mental health and divorce. Confidentiality and safety in this group were vital because of stigma surrounding these issues.

Over time, we found that a potential space (Winnicott, 1971) developed between the groups through the process of the co-workers playing with ideas, issues and difficulties that arose inside and in between the groups. We felt that this potential space was an important arena in which to manage conflict and difference. We also came to realise that we were role modelling something important for the families: it is often the lack of potential space, which functions as a joint thinking space, which causes so much trouble in family dynamics. The children's sense of being held was supported with the knowledge that their parents were thinking about them nearby.

Within the meta-family, our psychodynamic approach, with its attention to both conscious and unconscious processes, allowed for a deep understanding of the complexities of parent-child and family relationships. This approach facilitated the emergence of our understanding of the layers of conscious and unconscious parallels and resonance between the children's group, the parents' group, the staff team and the families' home experiences. The co-workers' relationship and countertransference experiences in the art therapy group could reflect the parents' struggles. When shared with the parent group worker these understandings could inform the work in the parent group if we felt they were relevant. Once these layers of parallel processes became conscious and therefore visible, they could be usefully thought about and they then informed our interactions with the children and families. In this way we were able to develop a model that endeavoured to be attuned to the changing needs of the children and families, and by so doing, was successful in facilitating improved relationships and family functioning for the children and families who used the service.

References

Arroyo, C. and Fowler, N. (2013) 'A mother and infant painting group.' *International Journal of Art Therapy: Inscape*, 18 (3), November 2013, pp. 98–112.

Baradon, T., Broughton, C., Gibbs, I., James, J., Joyce, A. and Woodhead, J. (2005) *The practice of psychoanalytic parent-infant psychotherapy*. London: Routledge.

Boronska, T. (2000) 'Art therapy with two sibling groups using attachment frame work.' *Inscape the Journal of the British Association of Art Therapists*, 5 (1), pp. 2–10.

Bower, M. (1995) 'White city toy library: A therapeutic group for mothers and under-fives', in Trowell, J. and Bower, M. (eds.) *The emotional needs of young children and their families*. London: Routledge, pp. 112–124.

Case, C. (2008) 'Playing ball: Oscillations within the potential space', in Case, C. and Dalley, T. (eds.) *Art therapy with children: From infancy to adolescence*. London: Routledge, pp. 103–122.

Choi, S. and Goo, K. (2012) 'Holding environment: The effects of group art therapy on mother–child attachment.' *The Arts in Psychotherapy*, 39, pp. 19–24.

Clulow, C. (October 2014) *Parental conflict and attachment theory*. A seminar with Dr Christopher Clulow, Ambassadors Hotel Bloomsbury, London.

Dalley, T. (1993) 'Art psychotherapy groups', in Dwivedi, K.N. (ed.) *Group work with children and adolescents: A handbook*. London: Jessica Kingsley, pp. 136–158.

Deco, S. (1990) 'A family centre: A structural family therapy approach', in Case, C. and Dalley, T. (eds.) *Working with children in art therapy*. Routledge: London, pp. 115–130.

Goodman, R. (2005) *Strengths and Difficulties Questionnaire*, UK. Available at: http://www.sdqinfo.org/

Hall, P. (2008) 'Painting together: An art therapy approach to mother–infant relationships', in Case, C. and Dalley, T. (eds.) *Art therapy with children*. London: Routledge, pp. 20–35.

Hosea, H. (2006) 'The brushes' foot marks: Parents and infants paint together in a small community art therapy group.' *International Journal of Art Therapy*, 11 (2), pp. 69–78.

Mahler, M. (1975) *The psychological birth of the human infant*. London: Maresfield Library.

Meyerowitz-Katz, J. (2003) 'Art materials and processes: A place of meeting.' *Inscape: The Journal of the British Association of Art Therapists*, 8 (2), pp. 60–69.

Musitano, J. and Rosenman, A. (2012) 'Separate and connected: A side-by-side model for intervening with mother-child dyads in small groups.' *Journal of Infant, Child and Adolescent Psychotherapy*, 11 (2), pp. 96–112.

O'Brien, F. (2008) 'Attachment patterns through the generations: Internal and external homes', in Case, C. and Dalley, T. (eds.) *Art therapy with children from infancy to adolescence*. London: Routledge, pp. 36–53.

Prokofiev, F. (1998) 'Adapting the art therapy group for children', in Skaife, S. and Huet, V. (eds.) *Art psychotherapy groups*. London: Routledge, pp. 44–68.

Proulx, L. (2002) 'Strengthening ties, parent-child-dyad: Group art therapy with toddlers and their parents.' *American Journal of Art Therapy*, 40, pp. 238–258.

Reddick, D. (1999) 'Baby-bear monster.' *Inscape: The Journal of the British Association of Art Therapists*, 4 (1), pp. 2–28.

Reddick, D. (2008) 'Working with the whole class in primary schools', in Case, C. and Dalley, T. (eds.) *Art therapy with children*. Routledge, London, pp. 86–102.

Schamess, G. (1987) 'Parallel mother/infant/toddler groups.' *Journal of Social Work Practice*, 2 (4), pp. 29–48.

Steele, M. and Marigna, M. in collaboration with Tello, J. and Johnson, R. (2000) *Strengthening families, strengthening communities: An inclusive parent programme facilitator manual*. REU.

Strengthening Families Programme (SFP 10–14) Parenting programme evaluation, research report DFE-RR121. (2010) Available at: www.gov.uk/governments/uploads/system/uploads/attachment_data/file/182715/DFE-RR121A.pdf

Trowell, J. (2002) 'Setting the scene', in Trowell, J. and Etchegoyen, A. (eds.) *The importance of fathers*. London: Routledge, pp. 3–17.

Westman, A. (1996) 'Co-therapy and re-parenting in a group for disturbed children.' *Group Analysis*, 29 (1), pp. 55–68.

Winnicott, D.W. (1971) *Playing and reality*. London: Routledge.

Yalom, I.D. (2005) *The theory and practice of group psychotherapy*. New York: Basic Books, 5th Ed.

CONCLUSION

Art therapy: A transformational object

Julia Meyerowitz-Katz and Dean Reddick

> *The effect in sickness of beautiful objects, of variety of objects, and especially of brilliance of colours is hardly at all appreciated . . . People say the effect is only on the mind. It is no such thing. The effect is on the body too. Little as we know about the way in which we are affected by form, by colour and light, we do know this, that they have an actual physical effect.*
>
> (Florence Nightingale, c. 1860, cited in Hill, 1945, p. vii)

We view this conclusion as an opportunity to draw together particular threads emerging from the case studies in the book and which focus particularly on that which is unique to art therapy: the role of the art materials, the artworks, and the nature of the interactions and processes around them. We begin by discussing the contexts of the art therapy that is represented in the book before going on to elucidate the nuanced relationship between art making, play and symbolic development. We suggest that art making in art therapy is essentially a psychosomatic activity that links the bodies, minds and brains of the participants within the context of a therapeutic relationship. We consider the nature of the art and play materials offered. As mess in art therapy with young children is ordinary and because it also signals distress, we explore the complexity of mess. This includes the impact that the toddler's or infant's mess has on parents and therapists. We explore an aspect of the work that is raised by all the contributors: the nature of the thinking and digesting that occur outside art therapy sessions.

The chapters in this book contain careful observations of the interactions around, and engagement in, art making. Reflections on these have led us to propose that there is a fourth element to add to the traditional triangle of art therapist–client–art object. When taking all these different elements into account, it seems to us that art therapy represents a form of layered, embodied thinking which is inherently transformational and which provides the experience of a living, transformational psychosomatic object which can be internalised.

All references to the contributors are taken from this book.

Context

Art therapy, like ordinary life, always takes place in a context and context is an important theme in the chapters throughout the book. The art therapy presented takes place in a variety of settings. The nature of the institution, the history of art therapy within it and the nature of the support that the art therapy receives from the institution have a profound impact on the clinical work that is carried out. Context encompasses the interpersonal, cultural, economic and political situation within which the adult–infant/toddler dyad and the family exist. Stresses and influences on the adult from the external environment and the adults' own internal environment impact on the adult–infant/toddler dyad. Dynamics within the adult–infant/toddler dyad include the transmission of intergenerational trauma and the transmission of ideology upon which culture depends. All of these contextual layers can impact on the dynamics and content of art therapy.

Much of the art therapy depicted in this book reflects practice which has emerged in settings where it has been well supported over time. Hosea points out that groups that run continuously in communities over years develop their own culture and status and become reliable objects for the wider community. Hosea describes 'circles of containment' of professionals working to support families. Within this, the art therapist embodies a 'grandmotherly' role, functioning as a containing elder for mothers, fathers and babies and for Sure Start workers, who themselves form a community, containing and supporting each other as well as their clients. Rayment portrays working in an institution with a long history of supporting art therapy. Over time, and with the support of the institution, a 'meta-family' of professionals, supporting a 'side-by-side' model of art therapy groups for the children and therapeutic groups for the parents, evolved. Similarly, Hendry writes about the development, through research by a multidisciplinary team, of a 'package of support' that is offered to adoptive families.

Referring to art therapy within a family centre that was part of a Sure Start programme, and which was an adaptation of the Parent-Infant Project (Baradon et al 2005), Dalley and Bromham explain a dual role for the supervisor. The supervisor holds a space which enables clinical thinking while managing the complex relationships between the different professionals involved in the case.

Meyerowitz-Katz describes working intensely with small groups of children and parents as part of a psychodynamically orientated staff team working together to support the children and parents, individually and as mother-infant/toddler dyads. Support from the medical staff, as well as nurturing a relationship with her client's parents, is crucial in supporting the art therapy Rudnik carries out in a hospital setting. As Rowe elaborates, when working in a preschool, thinking and discussion with other members of staff are important in supporting the art therapy. Reddick explores the provision of art therapy for a child transitioning from nursery to primary school, which depends on the support, cooperation and good communication between these state provisions and parents.

Art therapy can become a secure base for children's attachment needs: Andrade del Corro views the art therapy group in relation to the institution as a holding and containing environment that provided a secure base for the children within the institution; and she describes how it mediates between the children's experience and the wider institution. Green describes how art therapy can become a secure base within a busy and chaotic preschool playground.

Art making is essentially a psychosomatic activity that links body, mind and brain

Beginning in utero and then with the physical experience of birth, of being held, with feeding and with looking, infants and toddlers engage with and explore the world sensorially, through their bodies (Piontelli, 1992). As they grow and develop, they interact with the material environment. Their experience of the way in which the material environment, which is infused with the available emotional and psychological responses, responds to them provides or denies opportunities for growth and development, including speech and symbolic play. Engaging with art materials in art therapy is part of this process and can lead to the development of transitional phenomena, which in turn lead to the development of play and symbol formation where that is lacking.

Wright (1998, 2009) equates the artist's medium with Winnicott's (1967, 1971) 'adaptive mother', whose responsiveness to her infant's categorical affects and vitality affects (Stern, 1985, Wright, 1998, 2009) gives the infant a sense of him- or herself. The adaptive mother simultaneously offers her own aesthetic and form as a 'rudimentary mental structure' (Wright, 2009). 'Vitality affects' refer to the infant's background, almost microcosmic feeling states, which are different from their more obvious, major 'categorical affects'; they are 'ongoing shifting psychosomatic states of arousal' (Wright, 2009, p. 6). In order for them to be manageable, meaningful and potentially recalled by an infant, they must first be captured and contained within a maternal 'form' and fed back to the infant.

Within art therapy, the art materials, like the mother, have a life of their own and are not under the omnipotent control of the infant/toddler. The formal qualities intrinsic to art materials function like the infant's experience of the resonant adaptive mother, providing an immediate experience of self-agency and feedback, echoing processes of mirroring and attunement (Stern, 1985, Wright, 2009) which are not mere mimicry. Engaging with the art materials involves bodily engagement with a substance which has some of its own intrinsic qualities; these might be runny paint, hard crayons, wet, sticky, clay or flimsy tissue, and these qualities provide feedback to the infant/toddler, allowing him or her some sense of the materials as 'other'. This is an 'other' which has physical qualities that in their responsiveness offer moment-to-moment resonance with the infant/toddler's shifting states of arousal. In art therapy, the experience of interacting with this 'other' is layered because it is contextualised within the facilitating, psychoidly attuned bodymind of an art therapist who is trying to make sense of her and the infant/toddler's moment-to-moment experience. For instance, Conolly and King describe a three-year-old's fascination with the way in which the paint, glue and water behaved. They refer to her pouring paint so that it overflowed and slurped; mixing it, transforming it and soothing and layering paint and glue in a manner 'which had an almost meditative quality' (Conolly and King, this volume, p. 70), as if she was soothing herself. They refer to the importance of the shared experience, between therapist and child, of their mutual 'fascination' with the paint.

Provision of art materials and toys

Supporting Prokofiev's view that 'different aspects of making art in art therapy can help a child access a range of experiences missed in early life which can support a better sense of self' (Prokofiev, 2011, p. 22), contributors to this book describe a varied range of age-appropriate materials which offer opportunities for tactile, sensory experiences. These are considered to be fundamental elements in enabling therapeutic change.

In addition, carefully chosen play materials are often offered alongside the art materials. The relationship between play with objects, imaginative play and art making in art therapy is complex. Art processes and play processes are similar but there are essential differences. Play at this age tends to be deeply felt and of the moment. Children will repeatedly return to games with their peers, adults and therapist so that narratives exist and can be developed over time. But ordinarily, play with objects rarely leaves a concrete record for further reflection – toys are tidied away at the end of the session – and play with objects does not necessarily mean that the objects and toys themselves are irrevocably changed, although their meaning for the child may change over time.

There is value in offering toys alongside art materials within art therapy. Rayment describes the use of a soft ball to mark the beginning and ending of group sessions and to provide opportunities for interactions that support emotional and psychological experiences and development. Within the art therapy group facilitated by Andrade del Corro, toddlers developed attachments to toys and other objects; this supported their recovery from their attachment disorders. Reddick describes how a toddler's play with dolls' furniture communicates aspects of his client's 'twinning'. As portrayed by Dalley and Bromham, toys can be painted, becoming incorporated into the art making and layered with meaning.

Art materials are adapted to suit the context and the client group, and to address specific developmental needs. Sometimes large sheets of paper are supplied and the art making might take place on the floor. This accommodates the crawling of infants and toddling of toddlers. This means that they can negotiate their physical proximity with their mothers and each other, as well as their engagement with the art materials. This kind of provision offers them opportunities to explore their own sense of agency within a safe environment. Hendry refers to providing art materials to address attachment needs, and Hosea refers to the use of the photo frame to provide sensitive feedback to mothers and their infants; Meyerowitz-Katz describes how a toddler's engagement with clay plays a pivotal role in enabling therapeutic change around his understanding of the relationship between his body and the outside world. Engagement with the art materials provides the child with physical, bodily sensations that are essential components of developing a healthy psychosomatic partnership.

Making art offers infants and toddlers rare opportunities to produce cultural artefacts which can be admired and displayed. This can be an empowering experience that is not present in the same way in the hours of play in which children engage. This provides the child, the therapist and the parent, if present, with opportunities to view and reflect on something that is in the outside world and, therefore, is shared. Similar to play, these opportunities for reflection occur during the making of the art object. Uniquely to art making and different to play reflection can continue after the art work is complete.

Art making can support a mother–infant dyad. Hosea describes how a child's messy hands can be printed on paper to provide a record that both mother and child can enjoy. In Meyerowitz-Katz's account, a portrait made by a mother and her toddler in a therapeutic playgroup, in which it is witnessed and thought about by the staff and the group, is pivotal in facilitating understanding of the unconscious confusion between them, thus enabling change. Hendry writes that a mother and child manipulating play dough, materials with which they both feel safe and enjoy, can help them enjoy each other.

The child's engagement with art materials can be mirrored, amplified and used in order to support communication and the parent–child relationship – for example:

> The infant drumming with her paint brush may not immediately draw a response from her mum, but when the nursery nurse replies with movement, her mum may invent a further expression with her voice, 'dum-de dum', and, sitting opposite, may extend her child's finger-tip printing when she drops the brush and thrusts her hands into the palette.
>
> *(Hosea, this volume, p. 109)*

Making art can foster new capacities for representation and reflection, which develop into symbolic functioning and therefore communication. As Green writes, 'Further images were drawn on the page, another dog appeared, the yellow sun was drawn and then a person and a tree, all with this *brand new* ability to articulate in drawn pictures what was being thought and talked about within the therapeutic relationship' (Green, this volume, p. 160). But equally, as Dalley and Bromham elucidate, the development of play and visual symbolisation can occur in parallel: They suggest that there is a relationship between Oliver's joined-up scribbles and his growing capacity to make links between thoughts, ideas and feelings.

Provision of art materials and interactions around them have to do with holding and containment

Rudnik refers to the significance of the child's art therapy folder, the box of materials, the trolley and the clock that she uses, as well as the art materials themselves in a hospital setting. These are concrete things that stay the same, offer continuity and allow the child to develop a sense of trust and containment even in the briefest of therapeutic encounters. Similarly, Rowe writes that 'Because the art materials and toys were stored safely for her in between sessions, and available in each session, Lara was able to make use of them to develop linking capacities and build connections between her internal and external experience' (Rowe, this volume, p. 37). In addition, within an unpredictable setting like a hospital ward, the reliability of the art materials represents a form of containment for the therapist's anxiety (Rudnik).

This use of materials links to ideas represented in the literature that refer to work with adults where the concrete nature of materials and the setting provide containers for primitive, pre-symbolic experience (Killick, 1993, 1997, 2000, Wright, 2009). Robbins (1987) views art materials as an extension of the holding environment that links clients to the 'primary creativity' that Winnicott (1971) delineates.

Within individual art therapy, interactions around art processes between the child and therapist can provide psychosomatic containment for young children (Meyerowitz-Katz, Reddick, Rowe, this volume). This is particularly the case with experiences that are unrepresented in the child's mind because they have not been adequately thought about and transformed in the parent-child dyad. They are experienced and expressed as primitive, bodily, sensory experiences that are stuck psychosomatically at an autistic contiguous level.

Interactions around art processes between parent and child in the presence of a therapist within a group provide containment which supports the relationship between parent and child. For example, Hosea describes the therapist pointing out 'moments of meeting' between mother and child in the photos and says that 'Art materials seem ideal for expanding mother-infant reciprocity' (Hosea, this volume, p. 109). Hendry gives an account of the sense of connection that child and mother experience when using art materials in the presence of the art therapist.

Because of the age and development of the children, engaging with art materials is often linked to or resonant with being cared for. This represents a non-verbal therapeutic intervention, indicative of the holding, containing, mirroring, attuned and reciprocal care which leads to the development of the self as an interpreting subject with the capacity for symbolic functioning and play. Simple tasks, such as opening a bottle of paint or lifting a bag of clay, or washing their hands, actions that older children can manage, can be beyond the toddler's capabilities. A child may therefore need a therapist to intervene in a physical way; Hosea refers to washing the children in the warm soapy bubbles at the end of the group. Intervening physically during play or art making might also be important, such as Reddick's description of playing at 'pulling' the child out of the mud or Rudnik's modelling of a clay family for a child who needed her therapist to literally manage her struggle by manipulating the clay for her.

Making art depends on an interaction between the maker and some 'stuff' in the real world; 'the intrinsic values of primary matter' (Smithson, 1965, in Meyer, 2000, p. 210). Art materials offer the maker opportunities to relate to something real, like a body, with mass, texture, density, colour and shape. An infant's or toddler's engagement with art materials in art therapy can be varied – for instance wielding a paintbrush loaded with paint, pouring paint or water, manipulating clay or play dough or smearing paint onto a surface with their hands. Their engagement with the art materials is primarily one in which they engage bodily with the form of the materials and the form then exists as the content. This engagement can be accompanied by sounds that may or may not be linked to words that have a shared symbolic meaning.

The idea that art making and play support the visual and verbal developmental achievements of the capacity to symbolise recurs through the book. Historical and contemporary notions of symbols and symbolic processes are complex and complicated, and there isn't space to comprehensively review them all here. However, a working understanding of symbolic communication as it is represented in this book is that symbols function in an area of meaning that is shared between infant/toddler and his or her parents and/or therapists, and symbols have to do with representing something else, so that a word can represent a feeling, and a colour or a collection of lines on a page can represent a person, an internal dynamic and/or a relational dynamic. In this way, symbols occupy a third position which isn't only one or the other but a combination of the two, which is something new.

This is represented by Conolly and King when they describe Kara's mixing of red and white paint: colour plus the idea of a process. In this case, mixing two colours equals a representation of Kara and her therapist 'mixing' together in a relationship (Plate 6). It seems that in this process, which eloquently represents art making as a form of thinking, Kara is symbolically exploring an idea which has to do with not relying only on herself (red) because she has the relationship (pink) with her therapist (white); her engagement with the paints conveys her understanding of the dynamics and value of relationship with another person, as well as her capacity to symbolise.

This is different from concrete communications where art materials are used in a pre-symbolic way. Echoing Matthews (1986, 1989, 1990, 1994) and Rubin (1984) and in contrast to theories that refer to the development of children's art making beginning in infancy, and which focus on graphic development from scribbles to symbolic representations of the world (Eng, 1931, Lowenfeld, 1957, Harris, 1963, Koppitz, 1968, Kellog, 1970, Goodnow, 1977, B. Edwards, 1979, Cox, 1997, Burkitt et al., 2009), almost all the contributors in this book describe infants and toddlers engaging with the sensory, pre-symbolic qualities of the materials for their own sake and not necessarily in order to reconstruct or replicate what they see or even what they 'know' of the external world, nor to externalise a mental image. This is evident in Andrade del Corro's representation of a three-year-old girl anxiously pouring paint onto a piece of paper and then moving her hands through the paint, mixing the colours before covering her arms and clothes with paint and noisily tapping the paper. This can be understood as an example of Segal's (1950, 1957, 1978) symbolic equation, where the use of the paint is a concrete representation of her experience of herself.

Paint can be used to explore the skin: a primary sensory organ. Hosea discusses the skin offering the child primitive experiences of being a boundaried self (Figure 7.1). Sometimes, as Meyerowitz-Katz describes, the lack of a sense of a boundaried skin causes the experience of a material such as wet, mucky clay to be experienced as a terrifying intrusion. Reddick proposes that a child's use of water can include the self-soothing behaviours characteristic of the closed and auto-sensory world of autism in a desperate attempt to create sensation at the skin boundary as a way of providing a basic experience of being a boundaried self.

Dalley and Bromham describe how the development of representation through painting plays a vital role in negotiating Oedipal problems and helping the toddler untangle from his relationship with his mother and develop language. In Figure 5.1 the series of black marks suggests some sort of movement across a surface. In the context of the interpersonal dynamics in the session they were understood to represent the child's steps towards becoming a more separate, independent person – a movement away from his over-close relationship with his mother, which was inhibiting his individuation and development.

FIGURE 7.1   A young child focuses on his experience of paint.

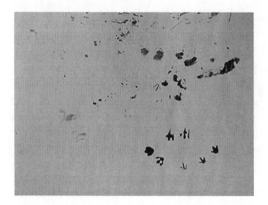

FIGURE 5.1   Dipping! Blue!

Andrade del Corro delineates how changes in the way the art materials are used reflect changes in the internal organisation of individual members in the group, changes in the relationships between members of the group and a corresponding change in the group culture. These changes are developmental, occur within a transitional space and foster the development of transitional objects, verbal communication and symbolisation. She noticed that over time, the group dynamic changed from being a collection of disparate individuals, an 'archipelago', to a unified group, symbolised by their collective efforts in creating and recreating a 'fort'.

The complexity of mess

Mess is ordinary

Mess making is frequently referred to in this book (Reddick, Rowe, Rudnik, Conolly and King, Hosea, Andrade, Green, Rayment). Mess is ordinary when young children are offered art materials, and as Hosea writes, in this context, it is inevitable. The tactile nature of mess evokes basic somatic experiences and needs. Mess speaks to the lack of control and mastery which infants and young children normally experience, nappies full of urine and faeces, runny noses, dribble, vomit, tears, burps, hiccups and flatulence, all emerging from the body. All of these are initially beyond the infant's control and understanding. Mess making gives the very young child opportunities to experiment with mastery, of the feelings of spilling and overflowing and of the stuff of the body and perhaps the body itself needing containment, and as such offers opportunities for development.

This means that engagement with the inherent messiness of art materials by the young child offers an opportunity to communicate experience that is unformulated. Mess frequently has no content and very little form and, as such, is a very effective way of communicating unformulated experience. When mess emerges in art therapy, and when it is received as a communication, understood and thought about, rather than being managed, mess represents a potential for something new to emerge; it offers opportunities for transformation and the development of symbolisation. The mess is akin to a formless ooze out of which new forms will emerge.

Mess signals trauma

However, mess is complex. It is ordinary and inevitable and is a starting point for elaborating form and meaning. It can also signal that matters are not well and can be part of regressed experience. In existing art therapy literature there is a strong link between mess and trauma (Russell, 2011), including relational trauma (Reddick, 1999, O'Brien, 2004), domestic violence (Malchiodi, 1990, Case, 2003), sexual abuse (Sagar, 1990, Murphy, 1998, Gillespie, 2001) and hospitalisation (Lillitos,1990) and can represent a way of denying separateness and difference (Lillitos, 1990, Sagar, 1990, Aldridge, 1998, Murphy, 1998, Reddick, 1999, Case, 2003, Drucker, 2001, Gillespie, 2001, O'Brien, 2004). Art materials and art processes are vehicles that embody relational experiences and traumas and offer opportunities for repair because of the potential for the reconnection of neural pathways (O'Brien, 2004). Rowe refers to O'Brien's concept that mess is a form of dissociation and a means of retreat from being with an 'other'.

Mess making can be a desperate communication of distress along the lines of 'no one has helped me figure out and name what all my experiences mean and so I don't know what to do with them.' It can leave the therapist feeling as helpless as the child. Mess can feel like an attack on the bodymind of the therapist, where it communicates that there has been a failure of containment. In these cases mess is used to attack linking or prevent thinking and is accompanied by projective identification as a means of attack rather than as a means of communication. Mess is strongly linked in several chapters with strong countertransference experiences. Green and Rowe both use art making, including aspects of messy art making, as ways to help understand the mess of the young children they work with. It is as though one of the unconscious purposes of making mess is to communicate strong affect to the therapist.

Thinking continues outside the art therapy sessions

Mirroring the need for carers and infants to be supported in order for infants to survive and thrive, art therapists working with this age group within institutions are frequently supported by thinking with other professionals. This means that a lot of thinking happens outside of the art therapy sessions, as well as within them. This can be in the form of consultation with other professionals involved in the case, reviews with parents, peer supervision, individual supervision or group supervision. Supervision is described by Rayment as an additional 'layer of thinking'. Rowe refers to the importance of supervision in holding primitive chaotic material when working in an early years setting.

Countertransference: the therapist's process

Contemporary notions of transference and countertransference are varied, complex and complicated (Wiener, 2009). A useful working definition of countertransference as it is represented in this book is that it is the therapist's responses to alive and vital, non-verbal communications from their client which are contagious and can lead to a shared *participation mystique* (Jung, 1971) with the child where boundaries between them are blurred (Andrade del Corro, Rowe). Countertransference comprises the therapist's unconsciously led emotional, psychological as well as psychosomatic responses to a client that dominates the therapist's felt experience of the therapy, impacts on his or her capacity to think and must be digested and transformed in order to support the thinking on which the client relies. Being receptive to the influence of countertransference means being open to the way in which a client unconsciously lets their therapist know what it feels like to be him or her from the inside. The therapist's task then is to receive and metabolise this responsive experience so that he or she can resume thinking (Brown et al., 2007).

Part of the felt response to these powerful, primitive and unconscious communications is clearly bodily. Rudnik goes running to help process her bodily countertransference, which was causing her to feel sad and paralysed with anxiety. Reddick describes his powerful somatic countertransference of feeling numb, which momentarily stopped him in a session. Unusually, he finds himself crying as he writes his notes. Meyerowitz-Katz carried an embodied countertransference feeling for several years before it was metabolised, when she understood it as a psychoid communication.

Green and Rowe both understand their responsive art making as a bodily process which offers a way to process their countertransference. Rowe's art making after the sessions helped her put language to the primitive experience that her client communicated to her (Figure 2.2). Green (Figure 10.1) found that her images,

FIGURE 2.2 Art response to ninth session with Lara.

FIGURE 10.1 Water for the thirsty elephants, becoming more hectic on the right.

made during the session while the children were present and, subsequently, after sessions, contained the transference matrix within which elaborate interactions of transference and countertransference occurred (Figure 10.1, Figure 2.2).

Dalley and Bromham give an account of the usefulness of parallel process occurring in supervision where the child's difficulties in expressing himself were brought into the supervision by the therapist, who found herself unable to give voice to her experience. Through projective processes the child had given her a very good experience of what it was like to be him from the inside – wordless and voiceless – and this experience emerged in supervision, where, through shared thought and discussion, it could be made conscious and understood and so be effectively taken back into the therapy. In addition, the experience of supervision meant that the therapist and supervisor shared the vagaries of the emotional experience of the therapy.

There are strong emotional responses to the process of engagement with materials

A theme that has emerged in the book is that the relationship of the therapist(s), parents and children with the process of making art, as well as to the art work, adds layers of complexity to art therapy. There is a tension here between two threads; one has to do with the communicative nature of the artwork as an object in the outside world – its content and symbolic meaning when viewed. The other points to the sensory nature of art making – the process of making art and the way in which an artwork, by virtue of the traces left on it by its maker, can be a record of how it was made. Stern suggests that works of art can provide vitality effects for the viewer to relate to based on the formal, stylist qualities of the artwork, as opposed to the narrative content of the work (Stern, 1985).

The emphasis on the process of engagement with materials is related to the complexity of the relational and aesthetic dynamics in art therapy and is a fourth dimension to add to the traditional three-way triangle.

Art therapy: a transformational object

In her seminal work, Schaverien (1992, 1995, 2000, 2015) draws attention to something that is unique to art therapy: the complexity of the relational and aesthetic experiences within the three-way, 'triangular relationship' between therapist, client and artwork. Schaverien (1992, 1995, 2000, 2015) describes this triangular relationship taking different forms in different settings. It is an alive and vital third element that is not present in the 'mind to mind' (Baradon et al., 2005) transference matrix in child psychotherapy. Schaverien suggests that the process of making an artwork in which an internal image is externalised, delineated as the life 'in' the picture, and the meaning associated with the final product, conceptualised as the life 'of' the picture, are complex and merit equal attention (Schaverien, 1992).

The value of approaching art in terms of its symbolic content, which is available for interpretation, is an essential component of art therapy. However, interpretation of art without acknowledging the sensory, concrete and formal qualities of the art materials and art-making process relies on the belief that an artwork is necessarily made up of content which is interpretable.

The close observations of and deep thinking about infants', toddlers' and their parents' engagement with art materials within art therapy as it is presented in this book offer a route to amplifying the meaning inherent in the concrete aspects of art making. This avoids risking taking the 'sensory experience of the work of art for granted', and proceeding from there (Sontag, 1964, pp. 201–202). Sontag and artists such as Donald Judd (Sontag, 1964, Elger, 2000) draw our attention to the value of art as a thing in itself, which is not dependant on what the art says, or how we interpret what we think it says, but our sensorial experience of it. This sensorial experience is a fourth element in the complex relational and aesthetic matrix that comes alive in art therapy and which is a striking element when working with infants and toddlers. Extending Schaverien's ideas in this area, we suggest that this is the '*life in and of the art making*' of the artwork in art therapy.

Bollas' (1979, 1987) postulates the idea of an 'aesthetic moment' – a non-symbolic form of 'experiential knowing' which predates representational knowing and relies on a state of fusion with a transformative object-as-process. 'The mother's idiom of care and the infant's experience of this handling is [sic] one of the first if not the earliest human aesthetic. It is the most profound occasion when the nature of the self is formed and transformed by the environment' (Bollas, 1987, p. 32). Identifying the transformational object as an 'object as process', Bollas describes it as 'the experience of an object that transforms the subject's internal and external world' (Bollas, 1987, p. 28). It is an experience of psychosomatic transformation which is achieved when an infant experiences his or her self being transformed by the mother's caregiving (Bollas, 1979, 1987).

Art making is essentially a process where something is changed; some material in the outside world is forever altered, and in the process of altering it, something in the maker is altered too. This means that art making has change and transformation at its core. Through the maker's and the viewer's unconscious identification and resonance with the transformation of materials and images, art making offers core experiences of transformation of the self. In addition, the resultant artwork holds traces of gesture and vitality and is available to be reflected on in a shared area of experience. Art making offers opportunities for neural integration (O'Brien, 2004). But as we know, 'Neurons do not stop at the border of the skull – they reach into the furthest and deepest parts of the body; neurological integration can then perhaps be considered a psychoid matter' (Meyerowitz-Katz, this volume, p. 129). Art making within a therapeutic relationship becomes part of a shared unconscious psychosomatic potential and process, a form of layered, embodied thinking which is inherently transformational and which provides the experience of a living, transformational psychosomatic object which can be internalised.

Art therapy with this client group is a specialised form of psychotherapy in which there is body-to-body contact with art materials. We began this conclusion with quotes that refer to the importance of vision and apperception, and we would like to end it with a quote which conveys the importance of the embodied experience of making:

> *Thinking is through the hands as well as the head.*
>
> *(De Waal, 2015, p. 220)*

References

Aldridge, F. (1998) 'Chocolate or shit: Aesthetics and cultural poverty in art therapy with children'. *Inscape*, 3 (1), pp. 2–9.

Baradon, T., Broughton, C., Gibbs, I., James, J., Joyce, A. and Woodhead, J. (2005) *The practice of psychoanalytic parent-infant psychotherapy*. London: Routledge Taylor and Francis.

Bollas, C. (1978) 'The aesthetic moment and the search for transformation'. *The Annual of Psychoanalysis*, 6, pp. 385–394.

Bollas, C. (1979) 'The transformational object'. *International Journal of Psycho-Analysis*, 60, pp. 97–107.

Bollas, C. (1987) *The shadow of the object: Psychoanalysis of the unthought known*. London: Free Association Books.

Brown, C., Meyerowitz-Katz, J. and Ryde, J. (2007) 'Thinking with image making: Supervising art therapy students', in Schaverien, J. and Case, C. (eds.) *Supervision of art psychotherapy: A theoretical and practical handbook*. London: Routledge, Taylor and Francis, pp. 167–181.

Burkitt, E., Barrett, M. and Davis, A. (2009) 'Effects of different emotion terms on the size and colour of children's drawings'. *International Journal of Art Therapy, Formerly Inscape*, 4 (2), pp. 74–84.

Case, C. (2003) 'Authenticity and survival: Working with children in chaos'. *Inscape*, 8 (1), pp. 17–27.

Cox, M. (1997) *Drawings of people by the under fives*. London: Falmer Press.

De Waal, E. (2015) *The white road: A pilgrimage of sorts*. London: Chatto and Windus.

Drucker, K.L. (2001) 'Why can't she control herself?' in Murphy, J. (ed.) *Art therapy with young survivors of sexual abuse: Lost for words*. London: Brunner-Routledge, pp. 101–125.

Edwards, B. (1979) *Drawing on the right side of the brain*. Los Angeles: J.P. Tarcher.

Elger, D. (ed) (2000) *Donald Judd Colorist*. New York. Hatje Cantz.

Eng, H. (1931) (reprinted 1999, 2001) *The psychology of children's drawings: From the first stroke to the coloured drawing.* Abingdon: Routledge.

Gillespie, A. (2001) 'Into the body: Sand and water in art therapy with sexually abused children', in Murphy, J. (ed.) *Art therapy with young survivors of sexual abuse: Lost for words.* London: Brunner-Routledge, pp. 86–100.

Goodnow, J.J. (1977) *Children drawing.* Cambridge, MA: Harvard University Press.

Harris, D. (1963) *Children's drawings as measures of intellectual maturity.* New York: Harcourt Brace Jovanovich.

Hill, A. (1945) *Art versus illness: A story of art therapy.* London: George Allen and Unwin.

Jung, C.G. (1971) *The collected works.* Vol. 6. *Psychological types.* Bollingen Series 20. Princeton: Princeton University Press.

Kellog, R. (1970) *Analysing children's art.* Palo Alto: Mayfield.

Killick, K. (1993) 'Working with psychotic processes in art therapy'. *Psychoanalytic Psychotherapy,* 7 (1), pp. 25–38.

Killick, K. (1997) 'Unintegration and containment in acute psychosis', in Killick, K. and Schaverien, J. (eds.) *Art, psychotherapy and psychosis.* London: Routledge, pp. 38–51.

Killick, K. (2000) 'The art room as container in analytical art psychotherapy with patients in psychotic states', in Gilroy, A. and McNeilly, G. (eds.) *The changing shape of art therapy: New developments in theory and practice.* London: Jessica Kingsley, pp. 99–114.

Koppitz, E.M. (1968) *Psychological evaluation of children's human figure drawings.* Old Tappan: Pearson Education.

Lillitos, A. (1990) 'Control, uncontrol, order and chaos: Working with children with intestinal motility problems', in Case, C. and Dalley, T. (eds.) *Working with children in art therapy.* London: Routledge, pp. 72–88.

Lowenfeld, V. (1957) *Creative and mental growth.* New York: Macmillan.

Malchiodi, C. (1990) *Breaking the silence: Art therapy with children from violent homes.* New York: Brunner Mazel.

Matthews, J. (1986) 'Children's early representation: The construction of meaning'. *Inscape,* 2, pp. 12–17.

Matthews, J. (1989) 'How young children give meaning to drawing', in Gilroy, A. and Dalley, T. (eds.) *Pictures at an exhibition: Selected essays on art and art therapy.* London: Tavistock/Routledge, pp. 127–142.

Matthews, J. (1990) *The art of childhood and adolescence: The construction of meaning.* London: Falmer Press.

Matthews, J. (1994) *Helping children to draw and paint in early childhood.* London: Hodder and Stoughton.

Murphy, J. (1998) 'Art therapy with sexually abused children and young people'. *Inscape,* 3 (1) pp. 10–16.

Murphy, J. (ed.) (2001) *Art therapy with young survivors of sexual abuse: Lost for words.* London: Brunner-Routledge.

O'Brien, F. (2004) 'The making of mess in art therapy: Attachment, trauma and the brain'. *Inscape,* 9 (1), pp. 2–13.

Piontelli, A. (1992) *From fetus to child: An observation and psychoanalytic study.* London: Routledge.

Prokofiev, F. (2011) '"I've been longing and longing for more and more of this": Researching art therapy in the treatment of children with developmental deficits', in Gilroy, A. (ed.) *Art therapy research in practice.* Oxford: Peter Lang, pp. 19–38.

Reddick, D. (1999) 'Baby-bear monster'. *Inscape,* 4 (1), pp. 20–28.

Robbins, A. (1987) *The artist as therapist.* New York: Human Science Press.

Rubin, J.A. (1984) *Child art therapy: Understanding and helping children grow through art* (2nd edition). New York: John Wiley.

Russell, E. (2011) *Swimming against the tide: Trauma and mess in art therapy with a 3 year old girl.* Unpublished MA Theses. Goldsmiths College London.

Sagar, C. (1990) 'Working with cases of child sexual abuse', in Case, C. and Dalley, T. (eds.) *Working with children in art therapy.* London: Routledge, pp. 89–114.

Schaverien, J. (1992) *The revealing image: Analytical art psychotherapy in theory and practice.* London: Tavistock/Routledge.

Schaverien, J. (1995) *Desire and the female therapist.* London: Routledge.

Schaverien, J. (2000) 'The triangular relationship and the aesthetic countertransference in analytical art psychotherapy', in Gilroy, A. and McNeilly, G. (eds.) *The changing shape of art therapy: New developments in theory and practice.* London: Jessica Kingsley, pp. 55–83.

Schaverien, J. (2015) *Boarding school syndrome: The psychological trauma of the 'privileged' child.* London: Routledge, Taylor and Francis.

Segal, H. (1950) 'Some aspects of the analysis of a schizophrenic'. *International Journal of Psychoanalysis*, 31, pp. 268–278.

Segal, H. (1957) 'Notes on symbol formation'. *International Journal of Psychoanalysis*, 38, pp. 391–397.

Segal, H. (1978) 'On symbolism'. *International Journal of Psychoanalysis*, 59, pp. 315–319.

Smithson, R. (1965) 'Donald Judd', in Meyer, J. (ed.) *Minimalism.* London: Phaidon Press, pp. 210–211.

Sontag, S. (1964) 'Against interpretation', in Meyer, J. (ed.) *Minimalism.* London: Phaidon Press, pp. 201–202.

Stern, D.N. (1985) *The interpersonal world of the infant.* London: Karnac Books.

Wiener, J. (2009) *The therapeutic relationship: Transference countertransference and the making of meaning.* College Station: Texas A&M University Press.

Winnicott, D.W. (1967) 'Mirror role of mother and family in child development', in *Playing and reality.* London: Penguin Books, pp. 130–138.

Winnicott, D.W. (1971) *Playing and reality.* London: Penguin Books.

Wright, K. (1998) 'Deep calling unto deep: Artistic creativity and the maternal object'. *British Journal of Psychotherapy*, 4(4) pp. 453–467.

Wright, K. (2009) *Mirroring and attunement: Self-realisation in psychoanalysis and art.* London: Routledge, Taylor and Francis.

NOTES ON CONTRIBUTORS

Marcela Andrade del Corro holds a degree in psychology (ITESO, 2002, Mexico) and a master degree's in art therapy (University of Barcelona, 2007, Spain). For thirteen years she worked on projects with vulnerable populations (residential care homes, communities for women, street children and the elderly) in both Mexico and Spain. She was an invited lecturer at Queen Margaret University in Edinburgh for the master's programme in art psychotherapy, and also at the Lviv training programme in art therapy in Ukraine. In 2012 she moved to the UK, where she continues working with children and families.

Jen Bromham is an experienced art therapist. She works in an NHS child and adolescent mental health community team (CAMHS) and was the winner of the Delivering Care Award 2014–2015 from the Oxfordhealth NHS Foundation Trust. She was the co-founder and is currently the manager of the Loreto Drawn Together Parent-Infant & Under Fives Project. Jen is an associate parent-infant psychotherapist at the Anna Freud Centre and has a keen interest in psychoanalytic infant observation and its applications.

Caroline Case is an analytical art therapist and child and adolescent psychotherapist currently working in private practice with adults and children. She has had extensive experience working in the statutory services of Education, Social Services and the National Health Service in the UK. She has worked on art therapy training courses and has published widely on art therapy with children. She is based in Bristol, where she also practices as a printmaker.

Celia Conolly is a psychologist with over twenty-five years' experience in the public and private sectors. She trained as a child and adolescent psychotherapist with the Institute of Child and Adolescent Psychoanalytic Psychotherapy (ICAPP) and currently consults in private practice in Maroubra, Sydney, with children and parents. Celia has trained and supervised psychologists and counsellors for over sixteen years. She is a founding member of and manager of clinical supervision for Mandala Community Counselling Service, which offers free counselling for the disadvantaged in the community. She has taught at the University of New South Wales, the University of Western Sydney and the University of South Australia, and is currently completing her PhD, investigating intergenerational issues with parents and children in therapy.

Tessa Dalley is an experienced art therapist and child and adolescent psycho-therapist. She has worked in a variety of settings, including schools, CAMHS, an in-patient adolescent unit and the Parent Infant Project at the Anna Freud Cen-tre, London. She currently works in private practice and is clinical supervisor to practising art therapists and child psychotherapists. Tessa has published many books and articles, is a reader for the *Journal of Child Psychotherapists* and is on the edito-rial board of *ATOL: Art Therapy OnLine*. Her most recent publication, co-written with Caroline Case, is the third edition of the *Handbook of Art Therapy* (Routledge, London, 2014).

Julie Green is an art psychotherapist and lives and works in Sydney, Australia. In 1985 she completed her bachelor of arts (visual arts) at City Art Institute (now COFA) and in 2004 completed her master's in art therapy at the University of Western Sydney. Julie works in private practice and community health. She has a special interest in the non-verbal aspects of communication as expressed through mark making and its roots in the early years of development. Julie is a practising artist and regularly exhibits painting and textile work.

Anthea Hendry works as an art psychotherapist in private practice, and she is a clinical supervisor, art therapy trainer for BAAT and lecturer for the Art Therapy Northern Programme in Sheffield. She was principal art psychotherapist at Leeds Child and Adolescent Mental Health Service, where she has worked for twelve years. Prior to that she worked in social services and the voluntary sector as a social worker and manager. Her specialism over the last thirty years has been working with fostered and adopted children and their families. She trained in Sheffield as an art therapist and completed an MA in the advanced clinical practice of art psychotherapy at Goldsmiths.

Hilary Hosea has a small private practice as an art psychotherapist, working with children, young people and their families. She works from her studio, where she also paints. Prior to this she worked in a CAMHS service in Norfolk for twenty years. She graduated in art history from the University of Essex in the late 1960s and worked as a primary school teacher before training as an art therapist at St Albans School of Art and Design. As a way of extending her understanding of working with parents and infants using the medium of art therapy, she completed an MA in art psychotherapy at Goldsmiths, University of London.

Judy King has an MA in art therapy from the University of Western Sydney and a BA in fine arts from the National Art School, Sydney, and has been a registered nurse for over thirty years, working with trauma in varying capacities. Her therapeutic work has encompassed early intervention, children in foster care programmes and at-risk adolescents in the school system. Through Gunawirra she worked intensively at an urban Sydney preschool with Aboriginal children as part of a research project funded by the Healing Foundation and has run domestic violence workshops for Mudgin-Gal Aboriginal Women's Centre as part of the White Ribbon Appeal. Judy works as the art therapist at Prince of Wales hospital, Sydney, in palliative care and with clients suffering chronic pain. She also runs ongoing community-based art therapy workshops for seniors and people living with mental health issues.

Julia Meyerowitz-Katz is a Jungian analyst and art psychotherapist in private practice in Sydney, Australia. She works with adults, couples and children, offers supervision and consults to organisations. She has published several papers on working with children in art therapy, supervision of art therapy and working psychoanalytically with couples. She is a member of the editorial board of *ATOL: Art Therapy OnLine*. Julia was previously on the editorial boards of *ANZJAT* and *The International Journal of Art Therapy: Inscape*. She has taught at universities in the UK and in Australia and is an active member of ANZSJA (Australian and New Zealand Society of Jungian Analysts) and CAFPAA (Couple and Family Psychotherapy Association of Australasia).

Alice Rayment qualified as an art therapist at Goldsmiths College in 1997 after initially training in 3D design at Middlesex and practising as a glass maker. Since a training placement at Goldsmiths at an early years centre Alice has extended her clinical practice, working with the early years individually and in groups. She has worked in special educational services, family centres, and primary and secondary school settings. Her practice includes working with children and families, individually and in groups. Alice currently works in a family centre and primary schools in Cambridge and as a clinical supervisor.

Dean Reddick graduated as an art psychotherapist from Goldsmiths College in 1998. During his training Dean worked at a local authority nursery school and became interested in providing art therapy for pre-latency children. Post-qualifying he worked in a child and adolescent mental health service. For the last nine years Dean has worked as an art therapist in a nursery school and children's centre in inner London, where he has expanded his practice to work with babies and carers, art therapy groups for toddlers, individual art therapy for children under five and parent, family and dyadic art therapy. Dean has been a tutor at Goldsmiths College and lectured at the University of Hertfordshire. He works for two days a week in a large and vibrant London primary school and offers supervision to educational staff and to art therapists.

Pensri Rowe currently works as a member of an allied health team within an early childhood education and care NGO, as well as consulting as an art psychotherapist within a high school. She works individually and in groups with educators, students, children and their families, and as a supervisor. She also maintains an art practice, which is integral to sustaining her therapeutic work. Pensri's practice is informed by psychodynamic principles and is relationship-based. Pensri has experience working with clients from diverse backgrounds in a range of settings, including people experiencing difficulties associated with: grief and loss, trauma, neglect and abuse, mental and physical illness, substance abuse and disabilities.

Susan Rudnik is a state registered art psychotherapist. Susan holds a BA (Hons) in fine art and art history and an MA in art psychotherapy, both from Goldsmiths. Since qualifying in 2006 Susan has specialised in working with hospitalised children with physical and/or mental health problems on paediatric wards in London. She currently works at Chelsea & Westminster Hospital. Susan teaches on the MA art psychotherapy course at Goldsmiths.

INDEX